Raising A Daughter

Raising A Daughter

*Parents and the Awakening
of a Healthy Woman*

Jeanne Elium
Don Elium

Celestial Arts
Berkeley, California

We are extremely grateful to our clients, colleagues, friends, and families who, in our workshops, classes, parenting groups, and Don's private psychotherapy practice, shared personal accounts of their lives with us. To protect their privacy, names, anecdotes, and case histories have been changed and, in many cases, woven together. We acknowledge those whose courage to tell their stories allows us all to benefit from their tragedies and triumphs.

Celestial Arts
P.O. Box 7123
Berkeley, California 94707

Cover design by Fifth Street Design

Text design by Victor Ichioka

Library of Congress Cataloging-in-Publication Data

Elium, Jeanne, 1947–
    Raising a daughter : parents and the awakening of a healthy woman / Jeanne & Don Elium
        p.   cm.
    Includes bibliographical references.
    ISBN 0-89087-718-1 : Casebound
    ISBN 0-89087-708-4 : Paperback
    1. Girls. 2. Parenting. I. Elium, Don, 1954–   . II. Title.
HQ777.E15   1994
649' .133—dc20   94-8462
                                                            CIP

First Printing, 1994

        4   5   6 / 99 98 97 96 95

To our children Heidi and Matthew

May you walk your own paths,
with confidence and pride,
especially when it differs from ours.

Help us to be the always hopeful
Gardeners of the spirit
Who know that without darkness
Nothing comes to birth
As without light
Nothing flowers.[1]

—May Sarton
"The Invocation to Kali"

CONTENTS

ACKNOWLEDGMENTS

We gratefully thank our resourceful agent Peter Beren, for his patient, sympathetic ear and expert advice; our publisher David Hinds, for his support and leadership, managing editor Veronica Randall, for her encouragement, relentless drive, enthusiasm, and support, Neave Higgins, for her expert nit-picking and follow through, Victor Ichioka, for his beautiful text design, and the other wonderfully helpful people at Celestial Arts; Audrey Johnson, one of the fastest editors in the world; research assistant Laura Kennedy, detective extraordinaire; and our friend Bob Kliger, whose Macintosh support saved the day. We also gratefully acknowledge the people at Touchstone Counseling Services; master therapist Landry Wildwind, Wally Meerschaerdt, Audrey Silverman Foote, Bruce Silverman, Fred and Sherri Glueck; and our great neighbors on Margaret Drive.

Part I:

Girls and Women— The Challenge of Being Female

CHAPTER ONE

THE PROBLEM WITH GIRLS

*The Nature of This
Flower Is to Bloom.*[2]

—Alice Walker

"She's so moody!"

"Everything has to be pink, and she refuses to wear jeans!"

"She has whining down to a fine art."

"She's so sensitive. Everything I say upsets her."

"We decided to raise her the same as our son, but she really doesn't like playing with trucks and guns."

"She tries to please us, and especially her teachers, by being quiet, cooperative, efficient in her work, almost invisible."

"I'm afraid that I won't be a good role model for her, now that I'm at home as a mother, instead of working in my career as an attorney."

"She has two older brothers and has learned how to control all of us. She's so dramatic. You'd think the world has ended if she doesn't get her way."

"She's been dating Josh for two years, and I'm really afraid she will get herself in trouble. Kids these days. They do so many adult things without blinking an eye, and they're too young to realize the long-term consequences."

"She's such a perfectionist. We rarely see her, because of all her activities. It's band practices, flute lessons, volleyball, swimming, her job at the toy store, volunteering at the hospital, plus studying so hard."

"She wants to do everything with me. If her mother disagrees with her, she looks to me. If her mother says, 'No,' to something, she comes to me. If she's unhappy about something, she cries on my shoulder. I like the attention, but I'm not sure what a father should do when this happens. She's getting too old to cuddle and wrestle with, and I'm kind of uncomfortable when she clings to me."

"I've had it! She's so sarcastic and sullen. You'd think I was the Mother from Hell. We don't agree about anything, clothes, hair, colors, food, friends, politics, values. What I love, she hates; what she adores, I detest. Sometimes I wonder how we came to be in the same family. She was so sweet at three."

"She won't do anything until I've asked her twenty times, and she gets angry about being told to do something. Then she stomps into her room and pouts."

"She's as rowdy as her brothers. I always thought girls were shy, retiring types, who like dolls and books. You know, quiet and clean."

Do these sound familiar? Troubles with boys are different from problems with girls. To understand how, we must look at girls from a new perspective. We have to get inside the question and examine it from there; we must assume a "girl's-eye view." We have to put on a different set of spectacles, allowing us to see the world the way our daughters do. We must lay aside our limiting beliefs that girls and boys are the same, that masculine is better than feminine, or vice versa, that men are wrong, that women are wrong, that one gender is better than the other, more capable, kinder, gentler, more violent, more nurturing, smarter, more rational, inferior, easier to parent, harder to handle, and so on and so on.

When we leave behind our assumptions about girls, we begin to really see our daughters for the first time. We begin to comprehend the nature of a female, the problems she presents, the motivations behind her behavior, and what she needs from us, her parents, to awaken into a healthy womanhood. For many of us, understanding girls is like trying to fathom aliens who just got off the ship from outer space. And it is very much like that, because our culturally learned perceptions are so different from a daughter's reality. We misunderstand who girls are, because the dominant culture disregards their uniqueness by expecting females to behave like males. This assumption leaves girls and women lacking in a society that measures competence and effectiveness on the basis of how well we achieve independence; that is, the ability to act alone with power over or against others.

A girl wouldn't make a good captain. She'd have to talk about everything first, and we'd never get to play.

—Alexander, eleven

Our company policy demands we hire a certain number of women, but I'm always reluctant to choose a woman to run the staff. A manager has to stand alone, give orders, and expect them to be carried out.

—Joseph, thirty-five

Our daughters are enlivened by different goals, because they view the world in terms of relationships. Instead of striving for independence, girls seek equal give-and-take, interdependent relationships, where people actively engage with each other. Girls thrive within relationship; their self-esteem is enhanced by knowing they are part of a relationship and are able to assume care of the relationship. Girls view relationships as the basis for behavior; their actions are attempts to maintain connection with others. Girls primarily seek ways of relating that use power with others, rather than power over others. Therapists, writers, and researchers at the Stone Center for Developmental Services and Studies at Wellesley College, define this perspective as a relational way of being.[3]

Relational behavior is not a feminine creation. All humans are born with this capacity, but we begin immediately to turn little boys away from it toward the more culturally acceptable drive toward autonomy. A daughter's natural, relational abilities are nurtured and refined into the art of caretaking, of aiding the development of others through care. By understanding our daughters' relationship-oriented paradigm, or worldview, we begin to comprehend why they act the way they do.

Girls want to know four things: 1) Are we in relationship? 2) What is the nature of our relationship? 3) Who am I within the relationship? and 4) What is necessary to maintain connection within the relationship? The problem with girls becomes clearer and easier to live with when we look at their behaviors from the understanding that they need to make or maintain connection while developing an individual self; that they seek ways to care for and be cared about; and that these ways may at times be immature and counterproductive.

> *Dear Mom,*
>
> *I'm sorry I yell at you and get mad so easily lately. It's just that I love you, and I miss seeing you as much now that you have to work all the time. I don't know why I yell, but I want you to know that I love you and hope that my getting so mad doesn't affect how you love me.*
>
> *Your daughter,*
>
> *Trish*
>
> *—Trish, twelve*

The Ability To Care
Does Not Equal Weakness

We like the following Stone Center model of a healthy woman: has the capacity to be clear about her wants and feelings; acts with intention; is creative and effective; and is aware of the impact of her actions upon others.[4] These characteristics imply strength, competence, motivation, high self-esteem, empathy, care, and inner wisdom. These are qualities we parents hope to help our daughters develop—a monumental task when so many of us struggle as adults to achieve these attributes ourselves.

For girls, the struggle toward a healthy womanhood is especially difficult, because while they thrive within relationship, they can also be lost within relationship. Without understanding the essential give and take of a relational way of being, many girls learn to give to others at the expense of their own needs. They give themselves away. To avoid causing pain or inconvenience to others, they swallow their own needs and feelings. Their loss of voice turns into resentment, eating disorders, rage, depression, low self-esteem, dependency, and sexual dysfunction. They learn to be manipulative, indirect, and passive to get what they need. Other daughters reject the cultural feminine ideal, renounce relationship, and avoid the entrapment of connection. Their drive to be independent ignores their needs and feelings. They become resentful, enraged, depressed, and lonely. They learn to be overbearing, insensitive, and controlling to get what they need. Whether they overthrow or adapt to culture's gender stereotypes, many girls lose the inner connection to their own womanly strengths.

Why We Wrote This Book

DON | A client of mine was a successful corporate executive. When she first came to see me, she was depressed about the lack of romance and partnership in her personal life. She told me about herself in clipped, impersonal tones, aggressively listing the many men she had "slam-dunked" for one reason or another. Finally, I interrupted her, "You're a woman." She stared at me as though I were crazy. She looked to the left and then to the right in silence, as if I were talking to someone else in the room. Quietly she asked, "Are you talking to me?" I nodded. She began to cry, "No one has ever noticed." Through the course of her therapy, this strong, beautiful woman came to realize that she tried to win her father's love and attention by adopting a man's way. Believing her father never validated her femaleness, she rejected her feminine nature and became lost in her successes in the business world.

I was struck by the double binds facing girls and women in our culture, and I began to see the results everywhere. As a therapist, I saw men battling to understand their wives and unsure of how to be active in the lives of their daughters. I saw women enraged at their fathers and husbands, because they felt unseen, misunderstood, and devalued. I saw girls struggling to win recognition of their uniqueness, rather than simply being labeled "female." I saw daughters fighting to stay in relationship with parents who felt lost in the mixed-up "gender soup" of our times. As a husband and stepfather I worried about my ignorance of these female persons with whom I live.

I coauthored this book to help change our culture's dangerous misunderstanding of girls and women; to learn how to support my wife and stepdaughter in continuing to be the women they are, on their terms; to encourage a new psychology that no longer misses the female experience; to bring a halt to the cultural and parental messages that tell girls what they must or cannot do to be successful at home or in the world; and to open the options for girls and women to find their strengths and their softness, their intuition and their intellects, their relational ways and their individual selves.

⟨⟩ JEANNE | Writing our first book about raising sons was like falling off a log compared to writing a book about raising daughters. The reasons have very little to do with our son and my daughter. When others asked me "why?" I joked, "Girls are more complex, of course!" This may or may not be true, but after looking at the research about girls and boys, I am certain we could find results supporting either view. My reasons for finding this book so difficult to write are far more personal than cultural opinions about gender.

Being female has not been an easy experience from the inside. My happiest times were probably spent with horse and dog in a midwestern woods on the banks of a slow creek. At least, these were the most carefree times before puberty changed all that forever. Then I had to deal with "buck" teeth, boys, body image, and being popular. It wasn't until some time later that I grappled with why females were omitted from everything, from church liturgy to credit ratings. My experiences as daughter, wife, working mother, feminist, divorcée, and middle-aged woman all brought me to this place as writer.

I coauthored this book about raising daughters as a test of reality. How well have I come to understand the process of becoming and being female? Could I clearly explain to parents that process and what is needed to bring it to fruition in a healthy womanhood? My difficulty in writing certain sections of the book came as no surprise. I saw more clearly where I have more growing to do. What did surprise me was the realization that other women are confused about who they are as females and as people. No wonder my husband and other men have such a hard time understanding us! We women have been trying to voice our experiences in the words of the official culture so others would understand, but until recently, their understanding came back to us in a foreign language. I am grateful to those women researchers and writers, whose work we mention in the following chapters, for moving through cultural deafness and prejudice to hear the clear, strong voice of women's experiences. My attempt in cowriting this book has been to translate this feminine knowledge for parents in the awakening of healthy daughters, not only for my own daughter, but for all daughters *and* for all sons.

Endnotes

1. May Sarton, "The Invocation to Kali," in *Collected Poems* (New York: W. W. Norton & Co., 1993), 326.

2. Alice Walker, as quoted in *Revolution from Within*, Gloria Steinem (Boston, MA: Little, Brown & Co., 1992), 65.

3. Judith V. Jordan, Alexandra Kaplan, Jean Baker Miller, Irene P. Stiver, and Janet L. Surrey, *Women's Growth In Connection: Writings from the Stone Center* (New York: The Guilford Press, 1991), 1.

4. Jean Baker Miller, Janet L. Surrey, and Judith Jordan, "The Stone Center's Self-in-Relation Perspective On Women's Psychological Development," in an address co-sponsored by Saturday Seminars, The California School of Professional Psychology, and The Stone Center, Wellesley College, in Oakland, CA, 31 May–1 June, 1991.

CHAPTER TWO

WHAT ARE LITTLE GIRLS MADE OF?

Sugar and spice and everything nice;
That's what little girls are made of.

—Old nursery rhyme

❧ JEANNE | My daughter was sweet and nice when she was little, and she was much more than that. She was stubborn, compassionate, shy, moody, beautiful, joyful, boisterous, demanding, cooperative, hard to understand, and easy-to-please—all together in one little, but powerful person. Like all daughters, she was a mixture of sugar and spice.

How many of us, while reciting that old rhyme, have ever stopped to consider that spice does not mean "sweet?" When we "spice things up," we add more strength, more zest, a pungency or pepperiness, even a fieriness that wasn't there before. Something we are concocting now has zip, tang, "umph." It is more flavorful and more interesting. Its bite can sting our tongues, make our eyes water, and leave us feeling more alive. The unfortunate reality is that many little girls grow up being taught to be sweet and nice and that's all. They have to hide the spicy parts of themselves. If a girl is told often enough to "be nice" and "act like a lady" and is continually reprimanded for being otherwise, she is likely to bury those fiery, tangy aspects of her nature. Something essential about her will go underground.

On the other side, it is dangerous to discourage a girl from celebrating the "sugar" in her personality. If we force our daughters to be strong, independent, and aggressive in order to feel valued and "equal" to men, we set girls and women up to always feel second best.

A little girl is not only what we, her parents and society, guide her to be. She is a mixture of four compelling influences: biological, psychological, cultural, and the force of the feminine soul. By understanding the power of the biological, psychological, and soul forces, discussed in this chapter, and the influences of culture, explored in Chapter Four, we avoid the limited view of the "nature vs. nurture" controversy. Much more than heredity or environment is involved in the shaping of a human being. If we deny any of these four influences, we deny our daughters their birthright—a complete and healthy womanhood.

The Biological Influence

Our common attitudes reduce the differences between females and males to reproductive systems and rigid, sex-role stereotypes. Medical students learn anatomy, make diagnoses, and form treatment plans based on the masculine physique. Medical research and physiological development studies have until recently been conducted primarily on males, because the medical community assumes the human body is basically the same, whether male or female.[1] Similarly, most models of psychological growth are developed from a male point of view, ensuring that girls never quite live up to the standards set for achieving independence and autonomy.[2] Startling brain research findings that show differences between the female and male brains are ridiculed or buried for fear the evidence will be used against women in their struggle for equality.[3] All around us we hear the cry, "Men and women are the same!" "Girls and boys are identical."

We parents are puzzled, because what we see in our daughters and our sons, not to mention our wives, husbands, mothers, fathers, bosses, and friends, are innumerable differences between the sexes. Some writers and medical researchers can deny them, but these differences are acted out daily in our kitchens and bedrooms, classrooms and worksites. Although this book is not a comparison of gender traits, to deny the differences between girls and boys is cause for great confusion for everyone, especially for those of us who have taken on the ominous task of raising children into healthy adults.

Researcher Anne Moir, Ph.D. and journalist David Jessel, authors of *Brain Sex: The Real Differences Between Men and Women*, a readable book for laypersons about current brain studies, assert that because sex differences in behavior appear at an early age—some studies indicate a few hours after birth—females and males are programmed to experience and respond to the world in different ways. Indeed, some of us might say we live in altogether different worlds! We believe there is plenty of evidence that our uniquely masculine or feminine brains are predisposed to instinctively respond in characteristic ways. For example, where issues of love-making are concerned, men almost always want to act first and talk later. They tend to be more comfortable with actions, so their inclination is to move in this direction first. Women generally feel more connected after sharing verbally with a partner and are then ready for physical intimacy, so they often want to talk first.

Please note that we use words such as "generally," "tendency," and "instinctively" when describing biologically influenced behavior, because biology is not the only determinant of our actions. It is important not to underestimate its power to influence us, however, and understanding its impact on our daughters will help us become better guides in their journey toward a healthy adulthood.

The Feminine Plan

As awesome as the biological creation of a new life is, the making of a baby girl is fairly straightforward. Mom contributes twenty-two chromosomes plus an X chromosome, and Dad also gives twenty-two chromosomes plus an X chromosome. It is not entirely the genes, however, that determine whether we become the proud parents of a girl or a boy. From the instant of conception, the natural inclination of a fetus is to develop along female lines. It is the presence or absence of male hormones, produced around six weeks of fetal life, that fix or change the biological template.[4] If the father contributes an X chromosome, no male hormones make their presence known, so the fetus continues to follow the original plan of development into a female baby.

The feminine plan of development is activated by the female hormones, predominately estrogen and progesterone. The tiny brain is bathed in these hormones, laying down the marvelous blueprint upon which our daughters are patterned. The intricate framework of female biological tendencies is now formed and influences a baby girl's personality traits and behavior from the very beginning. Her brain is distinctly female, programmed to perform differently from a male brain.

Brain Structure and Behavior

Those experts who favor the "nurture" argument over "nature" assert that we raise our daughters and sons to conform to sex stereotypes by giving them certain toys and by allowing or disallowing stereotypic behaviors. However, it seems that before cultural conditioning has any effect, even a few hours after birth, behavioral differences are apparent. For example, infant girls react more strongly than infant boys to loud noises and the discomfort of cold or dampness. Tactile studies indicate girls are much more sensitive to touch. In fact, the most sensitive boy scored far lower in touch sensitivity than did the least sensitive girl, and this disparity continues into adulthood.[5] This perhaps explains why a man's hearty clap on the back meant in the spirit of fun can seem like a blow to a woman. It literally hurts her, whereas a fellow male buddy takes it as it was intended, a gesture of playfulness.

We are all aware of the so-called sexual stereotype that little boys are interested in things, and little girls are interested in people. Two to four days after birth, brain researchers observed infant behavior supporting these stereotypes. Girl babies remained interested in faces longer than boys, whether the person was speaking or not. At later stages, while lying in their cribs, both sexes happily jabbered away to their caretakers. Boys, however, did not require that the caretakers stayed to carry on the conversation. They were just as happy to babble at crib toys or other objects. Not so the girls. They soon lost interest in the game if the caretaker went on to other chores.[6]

> *My daughter asks just as many questions as my son does and demands just as much attention. What she asks about is quite different, however. She always wants to know what I am doing and why. My son asks, "How does this work?" I know they both want my involvement, but Elizabeth is primarily interested in the contact her questions bring, and Michael is more interested in my answers.*
>
> *—Laura, mother of three*

Psychologist Dr. June Reinisch, director of the Kinsey Institute in Ohio, observes that we are all "flavored" by the hormonal influences in utero,[7] and these flavors become more pronounced as we grow. A female's predisposition to communicate first and act later shows up early in life. Girls learn to speak earlier, show a greater interest in communicating with others, develop bigger vocabularies, and naturally prefer activities requiring interaction with others.

My son and daughter tell me where they are in very different ways. I know where my son is, because I hear him. I know where my daughter is, because she tells me.

—John, father of two

Actual differences in the organizations of the female and male brain evidently account for the differences in behavioral tendencies. Research psychologist Diane McGuinness, with fellow researchers at Stanford University found that these behavioral differences seem to be independent of culture—"as true in Ghana, Scotland and New Zealand as they are in America." In general terms, she summarizes these differences:

Women are communicators and men are takers of action.... Males are good at tasks that require visual-spatial skills, and females are good at tasks that require language ability. Males are better at maps, mazes and math; at rotating objects in their minds and locating three-dimensional objects in two-dimensional representations. They're better at perceiving and manipulating objects in space. And they're better at orienting themselves in space.... Females, on the other hand, excel in areas that males are weak in, especially in areas where language is involved. They're not as good, in general, at anything that requires object manipulation and visual sharpness—they're less sensitive to light, for one thing. But they're much better at almost all the skills that involve words.... Their verbal memory is also better. And they can sing in tune, six times more often than males can.[8]

We emphasize that research does not support the old stereotype that girls can't do math. Rather, many girls will find manipulating objects in space, map reading, and higher mathematics more difficult to do than many boys will, and girls may use different tactics to complete the tasks than boys will.

There appear to be gender differences in how information is gathered and problems are solved.[9] For example, most girls find map reading easier when they rotate the map to match the direction in which they are traveling. Most boys can more easily "see" the direction in their heads. Also, girls tend to approach abstract math problems verbally rather than through the visual means used more often by boys. Reports by the American Association of University Women show that girls learn better in groups where there is a verbal sharing of information among the leader or teacher and group members.[10]

Another example of how girls and boys approach problems and solutions differently comes from the work of Carol Gilligan on the moral development of females. She found that girls and women tend to choose moral solutions to problems based on an ethic of care and concern about how the people involved will be affected. Males more often make such decisions founded on a set of rules or laws, principles of justice, and what is logically fair.[11]

Estrogen and Female Behavior: Five Biological Influences

Between birth to seven years of age, physical development in girls and boys follows similar lines. The primary hormones at work are the growth hormones secreted by the pituitary gland. Dramatic changes in the development of daughters, when female hormone levels begin to increase, occur around age eight. The first hints that a feminine body is in the making begin to peak through. Estrogen and progesterone, the predominant sex hormones in girls, aid in the utilization of proteins, slow down growth, and promote the storage of body fat. Higher levels of these hormones make the body more rounded, swell the breasts, and prepare for the beginning of menstruation, which can occur anywhere from age nine to thirteen. With the onset of puberty, the female genetic and hormonal blueprint encoded during fetal development is manifested in obvious physical changes. Of course, not all girls follow the scientific "standard" of physical growth, and many begin their menstrual cycles earlier or later, depending upon their individual feminine plan of development.

The physical affects of estrogen and progesterone are unmistakable. Biology also prompts girls and women toward certain natural behaviors we divide into five categories: Circles, The Vessel, The Big Picture, The Word, and The Relationship.

Circles

From the beginning of time, female biology has moved women and girls in circles. The hearth—center of the community, home, and feminine dominion—was round. Women and girls of the tribe worked together in circles, grinding grain in circular motions, making round baskets, nursing the children encircled in their arms. They built their huts in circles. They danced in circles; they honored the circles of the sun, the moon, and the seasons; they were in tune with the cycling of their own bodies.

Today we sometimes say that modern women are always "running around in circles." Putting aside the criticism in this comment, we see it is literally true. The essence of feminine life is circular. Although our daughters will develop their own unique expressions, estrogen and progesterone influence females to create, to be aware of the whole, to communicate, and to be in relationship.

The Vessel

From antiquity, the feminine has been called the "Vessel of Life," "Lifegiver," "Great Mother," the "Cosmic Egg." At some point in a woman's life—no matter her race, social class, education, religious creed, marital status, career choice, political affiliation, and so on—she will face the question of whether to have a child. To be female is to carry this biological urge.

The impact of bearing children on a female's life is of such magnitude that she will forever after be changed. In the words of poet Adrienne Rich, "Whatever her choice, her body has undergone irreversible changes, her mind will never be the same, her future as a woman has been shaped by the event."[12] She can no longer think of herself as solitary "I," now held to another—no matter the distance—by an invisible bond stronger than any other force in the Universe.

> *I knew I couldn't mother my son—I was still a child myself—so I gave him up for adoption right after he was born. I never saw him again, but even now after eighteen years, on his birthday I wonder where he is and what kind of person he has become.*
>
> *—Maggie, thirty-four*

The ability to bear and nurture life from her own body has given womankind a tenuous authority throughout the history of sexual politics. As members of the early hunter-gatherer tribes, women were revered and somewhat feared for their life-bearing powers. Ancient motherhood delegated specific, well-defined roles to women of the tribe, roles that were given equal value to those of men. Without the male hunting prowess, strength, and ability to protect and the female gathering skills, community organization abilities, child-bearing, and capacity to nurture, the tribal cultures would have perished.

Gender roles began to shift with the rise of the agricultural societies. Men assumed more responsibility for community organization and spiritual life, but the most dramatic change in the reciprocal relationship between women and men occurred with the onset of the Industrial Revolution. For the first time, women were narrowly defined only by their birth-giving capacities and banished to the home. Motherhood became an institution that "ghettoized and degraded female potentialities."[13]

Late twentieth century developments, such as the Women's Movement, the economic realities of raising a family, and perhaps the psyche of Woman, herself, have contributed to women's emergence from the home, back to school, and into the world of work. Today most of our daughters almost automatically assume the incredible dual task of motherhood and career. Regardless of the shifting roles of women and men in our society, however, some sources estimate that 90 percent of American women will have a child at some point in their lives.[14] Females remain, biologically, a vessel of life.

The Big Picture

Two friends, Josh and Sarah, went to a party while a third friend, Molly, chose to see a movie. The next day Molly called Josh, and the conversation went like this:

> *Molly: Josh, how was the party?*
>
> *Josh: Rad! There was this hot bass player. Blah, blah, blah...*
>
> *Molly: Who else was there? What happened?*
>
> *Josh: Oh, nothin'.*

Later, Molly called Sarah, and their conversation went like this:

> *Molly: Did you like the party?*
>
> *Sarah: You wouldn't believe it. Ann strung the entire house with those little twinkly bulbs for lighting; Diane wore her black slink; Jamie dyed her hair purple to match her shoes; Carin was late—her dad wouldn't let her have the car so she had to call her brother at his job and wait 'til he could come get her on his break; Jon and Laura weren't speaking to each other; the food was all pink; Ann's mom tried to stay out of sight, but she was nervous about the new floors; Matt had to bring his little sister with him; Laurie has another black eye—her dad's drinking again; and Oh! there was this hunk of a bass player!*

Girls are more sensitive than boys in their very beings.[15] The female brain is wired to receive and decipher enormous amounts of sensory information. Every girl has the potential to develop a finely-tuned sense of smell, touch, taste, sight, and hearing, enabling her to pick up unspoken messages, subtle communication cues, and hidden meanings often unnoticed by others. She notices more in greater detail and remembers it longer. This may account for the intuitive under-standing of others many females have—they know more of what is really going on, because they "sense" more, and they attach more importance to personal and interpersonal facets of life. Knowing that teenage daughters feel so strongly about every little thing—because they take in more information about it—helps parents when they wonder, "Why is she so moody?" or "Why does she have to be so dramatic?" She is so dramatic, cries so easily, and seems to be on an emotional yo-yo, because she sees a bigger picture than parents—especially fathers—sometimes do.

Studies comparing the sexes in sensory sensitivity found girls and women more sensitive to sound and better able to sing in tune. They were especially adept at noticing changes in tone of voice, enabling them to more easily pick up on the nuances of emotional undercurrents felt by friends and spouses.[16]

Studies testing sight found that females see better in the dark and have a better visual memory than males do. They literally see a bigger picture: girls and women have a wider peripheral vision, because they have more receptor rods and cones in the retina of the eye.[17]

We have already mentioned the greater skin sensitivity of girls and women. They are far more sensitive than males to skin pressure on every part of their bodies. They have a lower pain threshold, but have a higher tolerance for long-term pain than boys and men.[18]

Females and males differ in their taste preferences. Females seem to be more sensitive to bitter flavors and prefer sweet tastes, whereas males more often choose salty flavors. Overall, girls and women have more perceptive taste buds.[19]

When it comes to smell, studies show females capable of more sensitivity, especially heightened just before ovulation. Before the widespread use of deodorants and scented soaps, humans were attracted to each other by smell when a female was most fertile. Studies show that women find attractive the smell of exaltolide, a synthetic, musky odor similar to a man's natural smell, hardly noticeable at all to men.[20] The nose knows!

Girls and women are culturally encouraged to practice behaviors that enhance such sensory acuity. In assuming control over matters of the hearth and heart through the mandates of culture, females are finely tuned toward the whole picture of personal interrelationships. Their biology takes them there.

The Word

My daughter learned to talk early,
and she hasn't stopped talking since!

—*Beth, mother of teenage daughter*

It's not necessarily that girls and women communicate more than men and boys do. In fact, studies indicate that in mixed conversations men interrupt and hold forth much more than women.[21] However, females put a greater and different emphasis on conversation. Feminine biology pushes our daughters to talk first and act later. They place a premium on communication, because their brains are organized for verbal mastery. The centers for language skills are concentrated in the left-hand side of the brain in females, whereas in males they are spread out in the front and back of the brain. This leads many brain scientists to conclude that women and girls favor conversation more than men and boys, because the specific brain location makes for easier access.[22]

When I want to tell my boyfriend what I'm angry
about, I have to use ten words or less. If I go on any
longer, he gets so anxious he doesn't hear anything I
say. It's different with a girlfriend. If I don't use at
least three paragraphs—one to affirm the friendship,
a second to share my feelings, and a third to assure her
I want to work this out—she is hurt and insulted, and
she thinks I don't care.

—*Cate, sixteen*

Females of all ages reveal a penchant for communication. Gender studies of preschool toy preferences showed that three- and four-year-old girls more often than boys their age choose the telephone as their favorite toy.[23] The number one problem given by most women who participated in a 1987 survey about their sexual relationships, was lack of *verbal* communication with their partners. Very few mentioned lack of sex as the problem.[24] Linguistic researcher Deborah Tannen, Ph.D., in her brilliant book, *You Just Don't Understand*, highlights the differences in "something to do" preferences of second-graders: boys choose "games to play," and girls choose sitting and talking together.[25]

Dr. Tannen goes on to explain that females use conversation to enhance intimacy, to give and receive support, and to reach consensus. Here, again, we see another difference between the sexes. While females use conversation for connection, males use conversation to solve problems, give advice, and show superiority. This clarifies a common communication difficulty between females and males. Women share feelings with their partners to receive support and understanding. They often complain that they instead get advice on how to solve the problem. This response feels very rejecting when a woman wants to be met on the level of the heart, and her loved one thrusts toward her from his intellect.

This is all further complicated by the fact that females prefer to communicate face-to-face, while males most prefer side-by-side—as in fishing or spectator sports—or back-to-back in the ancient style of fighting where a fellow tribesman protected the back.[26] A man instinctively assumes a face-to-face position to confront an adversary. It seems ironic that a woman's most comfortable pose for communication is the most threatening for a man.

The Relationship

The female brain is wired to consider the well-being of people in the circles around her—family, friends, coworkers, her community at large—above objects or tasks to be completed. Studies show that girls are more welcoming of strangers into their play-group than boys are. Girls know and remember the names of their friends. Their play involves more turn-taking and games of indirect competition, such as hopscotch and jacks. When girls quarrel or disagree, play is stopped or the game is changed to settle the conflict, whereas boys consider argument and yelling at each other as part of the game.[27] Girls are less likely to engage in confronting behavior that might alienate members of the group. Instead, they either try to incorporate a troublemaker into the play, or find subtle ways of showing disapproval for the behavior in question. For many of us, this indirectness can be maddening, but for ensuring the continuity of a group—a traditionally female responsibility—it can be quite effective.

Being held responsible for keeping the group together has a dark side. The feminine instinct for connection can turn into backstabbing, manipulation, and deviousness when no allowance is made for direct communication of negative feelings.

> *I listen to my daughter's problems with her many friends. What bothers me most is that she is dating her best friend's boyfriend on the sly. She talks to me constantly about not wanting to hurt her best friend. Then the phone rings, and she talks with the boy for hours. Afterwards, if I say something like, "It must be hard liking a boy that's your best friend's fellow," she angrily answers, "Who's side are you on anyway?" Tamara never, ever considers approaching her girlfriend about her dilemma. She sometimes weaves her circle of friends into spider webs and get caught in them over and over again. She works so hard to keep relationships together, even at the risk of hurting herself and others in the end.*

> —*Fran, mother of Tamara, sixteen*

Moving within the circles of relationship and connection is a primary source of women's self-esteem, according to Celia Halas, Ph.D., author of *Why Can't a Woman Be More Like a Man?* She says, "...the degree of a woman's happiness depends more upon the level of satisfaction between her and her loved ones than upon other achievements in her life."[28] Janet L. Surrey, Ph.D., in a collection of papers in process from the Stone Center for Developmental Services and Studies, Wellesley College, writes, "...all of us probably feel the need to feel understood or 'recognized' by others. It is equally paramount, but not yet emphasized, that women all through their lives feel the need to 'understand' the other—indeed desire this as an essential part of their own growth and development, as an essential part of self-worth and the ability to act."[29] In fact, researcher and educator Carol Gilligan, Ph.D., found in her studies that when highly successful women describe themselves, they do not mention their professional careers. Rather, they explain their connections with others—as wife, mother, coworker, adopted child, past lover, boss, and so on.[30]

The Psychological Influence

Since Dr. Freud began his investigations of the psychological development of human beings, our commonly accepted models of psychological growth and maturity have included the concepts of separation and individuation. Freud and others after him viewed psychological development as a steady progression from enmeshment with Mother toward a greater and greater separation from her into a distinct, autonomous individual, who no longer needs the dependent interaction of relationship.

Although this model somewhat follows a boy's growth—from a primary focus on Mother, towards an increased exploration of the world of home and school, to a turning to his father and other men to learn what it means to be a man in the world at large—current researchers and theorists are raising doubts that it adequately details the psychological development process in males. And certainly this model does not address the unique factors contributing to the psychological growth of females.

It has been a grave disservice to women to assume that females follow the same path of psychological development. Rather than listening to women's experiences and observing their development through lenses clear of the biases of masculine-based culture, researchers and theorists look for ways women and girls deviate from the accepted notions about growth. As a result, standard psychological theory portrays women as less separated and less individuated than men, and thus inferior in development. This assumption of "underdevelopment" can be directly linked to much of the rage, low self-esteem, feelings of powerlessness, and gender confusion among women today.

The presumption that we must each become a separate and autonomous adult implies we must learn to make decisions on our own, create a life apart from others, do not need relationship, and if necessary, can carry on throughout our lives in isolation; in other words, what some have called, "the Lone Ranger" model of psychological development.[31] This standard for human growth paints a bleak portrait of our daughters' futures, and sets goals that most females are biologically and psychologically programmed against fulfilling. In reality, girls develop within relationships.

A Tapestry: Self-in-Relation

Colorful, intricate tapestries were hand-stitched by women and men in the Middle Ages and hung on the frigid castle walls to create a sense of warmth and to record the great deeds performed by the lords who lived there. We can imagine the beginning threads, bright colors reflecting the hues of the native countryside. From the start, the threads are worked interdependently to communicate the story and to emotionally connect the viewer with each daring feat of the adventure. At first the relationship between the threads and the pattern is simple. Then it grows across the canvas in more and more complex designs, filling in the detail of an oak leaf here, the hoof of a frightened stag there.

From infancy, a growing girl creates a tapestry of ever-deepening and ever-enlarging relationships, with her self at the center. Separation and autonomy are not central to a girl's psychological development. The feminine personality comes to define itself within relationship and connection, where growth includes greater and greater complexities of interaction. Rather than learning to have a separate sense of self—as the earlier models of personality development imply for boys—our daughters develop an increasingly complex sense of self-in-relation to a growing network of others.

> Imagine yourself cooing to your babbling infant daughter while you change her diaper. She lies there, hands and legs in motion, bright eyes alert. She soaks in every nuance of your voice. You smile at her cute intensity. She responds by blowing a tiny bubble between her pudgy lips. You laugh out loud and say, "I see what you can do!" She answers with soft sounds and a vigorous kicking of her legs. She and you are pleased with the interaction between you.

Jean Baker Miller, M.D., and researchers at the Stone Center, Wellesley College, believe that from her life's beginning, a girl begins to develop an attention to and a caring for what is happening between herself and others.[32] Even in early infancy, she is affected by the feelings of mother, father, and/or other significant caregiver—and takes part in shaping their interactions by responding and watching for the effects of her responses upon them. This is the beginning of the intricate tapestry she will weave throughout her life.

Finding Her Voice: Developing a Self

Within the tapestry of relationship, a girl usually identifies most strongly with Mother. She comes from Mother; she is most like Mother; and Mother is most often the primary caregiver. The early mother-infant bond is the loom upon which a girl's tapestry of relationship is woven.

Within this primary relationship with her mother, a girl's self must form. That is, she must learn who she is, where she begins and others end, what she needs and wants, and what she thinks and feels. A girl must find her own voice and develop the courage to speak the truth about what she believes and experiences.

As stated earlier, many models of personality development stress separation from the mother as essential to the formation of a healthy self. After listening to the voices of girls and women, the researchers at the Stone Center, Wellesley College, and Dr. Carol Gilligan and colleagues at Harvard University, think otherwise. Their work indicates that relationships of mutual interaction between daughters and their mothers promote and enhance development of a sense of self in girls, rather than restricting it.[33]

> ...to feel "more related to another person" means to feel one's self enhanced, not threatened. It does not feel like a loss of part of one's self; instead it becomes a step toward more pleasure and effectiveness—because it is the way the girl and woman feel "things should be," the way she wants them to be.[34]
>
> —*Jean Baker Miller, M.D.*

Feminine Meets Masculine

To achieve a healthy womanhood, a girl must stay connected to her feminine nature, symbolized and modeled by her mother. When we speak of a girl's feminine nature, keep in mind we do not mean our culture's stereotypic dictums of how little girls should be—sweet, quiet, nice, cooperative, agreeable, nonlogical, dressed in frilly pinks, poor at math, and interested only in dolls and boys. The deep Feminine in us all is that which values caring, connection, relationship, nature, and all of life. It is also personified in Demeter, the Goddess of Grain, whom Jean Shinoda Bolen, M.D., author of the bestselling *Goddesses in Everywoman*, calls a "vulnerable goddess, she who is attuned to others." Demeter expresses women's need for affiliation and bonding.[35]

The force of cultural conditioning, discussed more thoroughly in Chapter Four, often interferes with a girl's natural inclination to remain in healthy connection with her mother. Traditionally, a mother's role as caregiver, homemaker, and part-time wage-earner is devalued in our society, so girls may turn to Father, whose world seems more powerful, inviting, interesting, and fun. Father and his world misunderstand and disregard the Feminine, so the girl becomes not only split off from her primary relationship with Mother, but from her true self as well.

> *My father was always my favorite parent. It was just more fun to be part of his projects. He told me I could do anything I set my mind to, and I did, too. Now I feel I've missed something by having a demanding career instead of a committed relationship. Somewhere along the way, I wish I had realized what was important to me. My career gives me great satisfaction, and Dad is proud of me, but when he goes, I'll be all I have.*
>
> *—Janell, fifty-five*
> *CEO of her own company*

A crucial stage in a girl's psychological development is the formation of a relationship with Father, or a significant father figure, while staying in connection with Mother. Within a father/daughter relationship, where her father values the deep Feminine qualities and supports her feminine ways, a girl remains connected to her true voice and blossoms into a healthy womanhood. Her close relationship with a father enables the young girl to develop those positive masculine traits she will need in order to be herself in the world: self-confidence, problem-solving and decision-making skills, goal setting, and a sense of inner strength and power.

Healthy psychological growth for a girl, therefore, involves the development of a tapestry of relationship in ever-increasing complexities, a lasting connection with her mother who embodies the deep Feminine, and a supportive bonding with her father who initiates her into the deep Masculine. With a balanced combination of the two principal energies from mother and father, a girl can both be in touch with her womanly strengths and be a powerful force in the world—strong and nurturing, decisive and caring, goal-oriented and aware of the needs of others. She has the courage to voice what she thinks and feels and the strength to follow her destiny.

The Soul Life

Rilke said about therapy,
"I don't want the demons taken away because
they're going to take my angels too."[36]

—James Hillman

We all live with a huge paradox in this culture. America, known as "the melting pot," where people from the world over have been welcomed, strives to make us all the same. Dominant culture treats diversity as a problem to be solved, something to be removed so things run smoothly. Immigrant children must shed their native language and learn English to function in our schools. Newcomers to any community must adopt local customs or be treated with suspicion. In our therapies we must change our symptoms, feel better, and become "the best we can be." Our daughters must conform to acceptable school behavior, wear the "in" clothes, and be good girls, or be labeled as having attention deficit disorder, being out-of-date, and a "tease," or worse.

Our striving toward conformity makes us overlook or get rid of those very parts that lead to healing and wholeness—our wrinkles, our dis-orders, our dysfunctions. Those ugly wrinkles we so relentlessly try to iron out are doorways into our longings, our starving hearts, our soul lives. It is important to understand that when our daughters do not "fit in," they may be healthfully rejecting meaningless endeavors, inappropriate expectations, or gross misunderstandings.

When Dorie was in elementary school, the teacher constantly called me in for conferences about her behavior. I often said to myself, "If she would just stop talking and sit still in class!" Looking back I realize that sitting still for long periods of time was too much to ask of any second grader. Dorie is now a college track champion on full scholarship and a top debate student. Her unlimited energy and zest for life astounds me. What got her in constant trouble in grade school are now her greatest strengths. We seem to view problem behaviors in the wrong light.

—Angelica, mother of Dorie, twenty

When we seek to smooth out their wrinkles, sand their rough edges, squash their quirks, and eliminate their obsessions, we force our daughters to reject important parts of themselves. We banish their real selves underground, where their personal "gold" lies hidden.

My sister started and ran two successful businesses by the time she turned twenty-eight. After all of this, she still thinks of herself as dumb. Recently, I reminded her that our mother always called her "pretty, but dumb." I hope she's finally beginning to realize that Mother was wrong about her; that she achieved what she has, because she is organized, intelligent, and has an astute sense for business.

—Gina, thirty

We must allow a greater vision of who we and our daughters are. In this new vision, spirituality and psychology meet. All that we are— our lovely qualities and those not so easy to live with—are parts of our individual souls. Our passions, strong emotions, thoughtful feelings, and longings of the heart move us toward our destinies.

Destiny

des-ti-ny *(des tö-ny) n., one's lot.*

—American Heritage Dictionary

A girl's destiny is her fate, her kismet, her predisposition toward her life's purpose. Some daughters know their destinies from an early age. At five, Jacqueline du Pré, one of the world's greatest cellists, heard a cello on the radio and was reported to say, "I want what sounds like that."[37] Other daughters are older before they have a feeling for or vague notion about their destinies. They blunder into them, experiment a little, or try for years before they truly find their places. We cannot know our daughters' destinies until they live them out, but we can recognize their inklings toward them; their flavor for living.

We can shift our perspective of their behaviors like Harry, a father we met in one of our parenting workshops. "Until now, I had about given up on my daughter, Judith. At sixteen, she's a hellion. But what you're saying is that instead of seeing her as a hellion, I need to see her as a leader waiting to mature. That gives me a whole new perspective of who she is. It allows me to get off her back about the messes she gets into and begin to help her find ways to use her leadership skills for things that don't get her into trouble. I can do that!"

We all approach life with a certain style or temperament. Some Native American peoples call this predilection, one's beginning place on the Medicine Wheel,[38] and a person's life task is to move around the wheel, learning to perceive in the ways of each of the four directions. Astrologers say our personalities and behaviors are influenced by the stars we are born under, and an entire cosmology of symbols and meanings predict individual dispositions.[39] Philosopher/educator Rudolf Steiner and theorist/psychologist Carl Jung defined human tendencies toward certain behaviors respectively, in terms of "temperaments"[40] and "attitude types."[41] These guides for comprehending personal identity are intriguing and provide insight into our behaviors. More understanding about why our daughters act and react the ways they do is often reassuring. "Ohhhh. Bette always sees the tiny imperfection in any beautiful creation, because that is her way, how she tends to respond first." This does not mean that we cannot change; that our stars chart our destinies in cold stone. Bette's parents will simply have to help her learn to see the beauty and perfection, as well as the flaws.

Some daughters are born with distinct styles from the beginning; others more slowly allow us glimpses of who they will become.

> *My daughter has been intense from the moment she was born. I looked down at her as the midwife pulled her up on my belly, expecting to see shock or confusion in her eyes. Not Daffney. She calmly looked into my eyes as if to say, "OK, I'm here. What's next?" Our relationship has been like that ever since. I tried to change her, but only I have changed.*
>
> —*Laurie, mother of Daffney, fourteen*

Developing the Soul

The journey of a woman's soul from girlhood through womanhood must pass through many trials, over many thresholds. This process of transformation is beautifully chronicled in the Sumerian myths of Innana, Queen of Heaven and Earth. The one that follows is called, "From the Great Above to the Great Below," and follows her descent into the underworld to meet death and to reclaim the parts of her soul that are missing.

Innana, loved by all her subjects, ruled with benevolence and fairness, responsible for the growth of plants, animals, and fertility in humans. She who was called the Golden Goddess of Abundance, was good, beautiful, and possessed the lavish gowns and jewels befitting a queen of power. Even with all of these blessings, she was unsatisfied, longing for what she could not name. She decided to visit her sister, Ereshkigal, dark Queen of the Underworld, known to the people as Lady of the Skulls. Perhaps there she would discover what was missing.

She calls Ninshubur, her faithful servant, asking her to watch for her by the door to the underworld for three days and three nights. If she does not return, Innana instructs Ninshubur to cause the women to set up a lament for her, and to go to the temples of the great gods, Enil, Nanna, and Enki, to ask them to intercede on her behalf. As Ninshubur agrees, Innana knocks loudly on the great door to the underworld.

When Ereshkigal learns of Innana's wish to enter, she ponders long and at last sees Innana's soul is ripe for the initiation of death. Ereshkigal orders the seven gates of the underworld bolted and decrees that the Queen of Heaven shall not enter the underworld as she has planned it. "At each gate, strip her of her powers," Ereshkigal orders. "I shall grind her down to the dust of death." Innana is shocked by her treatment and cries out in outrage. She is silenced by unseen hands, who take from her crown, jewels, and royal robes. In the end, Innana is stripped of her very flesh and left to rot on a meathook on the wall.

After three days and three nights, weeping Ninshubur causes the women to set up a lament for Innana. Then she hurries to the holy shrine of Enlil, mighty God of the Sky, and begs him for help. When the god refuses, she seeks out Nanna, remote God of the Moon and Innana's own father, but he also refuses. Finally, Father Enki, ancient God of Waters, has compassion on Innana and devises a plan to save her. From the dirt under his fingernails, he fashions two tiny creatures who fly to the underworld and find the mighty queen Ereshkigal in the agony of birth. As instructed by Enki, the little spirits offer her deep compassion for her suffering, and she is delivered from her pain. In reward she offers them anything. They request the corpse hanging on the wall, the corpse of Innana. They feed her the bread and waters of life. Innana arises and passes again through each of the seven gates. All that she had lost was returned to her, greater and more powerful than before. She emerges into the light, to resume her reign as She Who Has No Fear of Death, honored guide through the dark times of transformation.[42]

To develop our daughters' raw talents and passions into their mature forms is a huge task for both parents and daughters. We all go through a rite-of-passage, an initiation. The journey for our daughters is down into the underworld of soul, while we stand at the opening, ready to intercede on their behalves.

According to best-selling author and Jungian psychotherapist Clarissa Pinkola Estés, Ph.D., the feminine soul is housed in the *criatura*, or wolf-nature, of the Wild Woman archetype, a collective and universal configuration of symbols, stories, and meanings that come to us through our dreams, myths, and fairy tales.[43] The cry of the soul's wild, instinctual nature is faint to the ears of modern woman, tamed by our predominant culture's dictates to be agreeable, compliant, and helpful. We can help our daughters reclaim this essential nature, however. Dr. Estés writes, "We know the soul-spirit can be injured, even maimed, but it is very nearly impossible to kill. You can dent the soul and bend it. You can hurt it and scar it. You can leave the marks of illness upon it, and scorch marks of fear. But it does not die, for it is protected by La Loba in the underworld."[44]

How do we nurture our daughter's developing soul life? We must allow her to grow in her natural way, being open to her wildness, her quirks, her inklings toward her destiny. We must teach her to sing; tell her the old myths and stories; let her howl in the moonlight, or whatever behavior nurtures her unique nature. Our daughter's soul development requires us to defend her right to go her own way.

Children don't belong to us....
They are little strangers who arrive in
our lives and give us pleasure and duty
of caring for them—but we don't own them.
We help them become who they are.[45]

—Ruth Nuneviller Steinem

Endnotes

1. Carol Tavris, *The Mismeasure of Woman* (New York: Simon & Schuster, 1992), 97–99.

2. Carol Gilligan, *In a Different Voice: Psychological Theory and Women's Development* (Cambridge, MA: Harvard University Press, 1982), 14.

3. Anne Moir and David Jessel, *Brain Sex* (New York: Dell Publishing, 1989), 2.

4. Ibid., 23.

5. Ibid., 55.

6. Ibid., 56.

7. Ibid., 33.

8. Michael Hutchison, *The Anatomy of Sex and Power: An Investigation of Mind-Body Politics* (New York: William Morrow, 1990), 168.

9. Ibid., 170.

10. The AAUW Report: How Schools Shortchange Girls, commissioned by the American Association of University Women Educational Foundation and researched by the Wellesley College Center of Research on Women, 1992, 71–72.

11. Gilligan, *In A Different Voice*, 17.

12. Adrienne Rich, *Of Woman Born: Motherhood as Experience and Institution* (New York: W.W. Norton, 1976), 12.

13. Ibid., 13.

14. Sylvia Ann Hewlett, *The Lesser Life: The Myth of Women's Liberation in America* (New York: William Morrow, 1986), 15.

15. Moir and Jessel, *Brain Sex*, 100.

16. Ibid., 17–18.

17. Ibid., 18.

18. Ibid.

19. Ibid.

20. Ibid., 18–19.

21. Susan Brownmiller, *Femininity* (New York: Simon & Schuster, 1984), 120–121.

22. Moir and Jessel, *Brain Sex*, 45.

23. Mary Field Belenky, Blythe McVicker Clinchy, Nancy Rule Golderger, and Jill Mattuck Tarule, *Women's Ways of Knowing: The Development of Self, Voice, and Mind* (New York: Basic Books, 1986), 18.

24. Hutchison, *The Anatomy of Sex*, 135.

25. Deborah Tannen, *You Just Don't Understand: Women and Men in Conversation* (New York: William Morrow, 1990), 247–248.

26. Shepherd Bliss, "Understanding Men," a class in psychology, John F. Kennedy University, Orinda, CA, Winter Quarter, 1989.

27. Moir and Jessel, *Brain Sex*, 59–61.

28. Celia Halas, *Why Can't a Woman Be More Like a Man?* (New York: Macmillan, 1981), 17.

29. Janet L. Surrey, "The Self-in-Relation: A Theory of Women's Development," in *Women's Growth in Connection*, Judith V. Jordan, et al. (New York: The Guilford Press, 1991), 59.

30. Gilligan, *A Different Voice*, 159.

31. Jordan, et al., *Women's Growth*, 1.

32. Jean Baker Miller, "The Development of Women's Sense of Self," in *Women's Growth*, Jordan, et al., 13.

33. Ibid., 17.

34. Ibid., 15.

35. Jean Shinoda Bolen, *Goddesses in Everywoman: A New Psychology of Women* (New York: Harper Colophon Books, 1984), 17.

36. James Hillman and Michael Ventura, *We've Had a Hundred Years of Psychotherapy and the World's Getting Worse* (San Francisco: Harper San Francisco, 1992), 29.

37. Ibid., 20, 29.

38. Michael Mayer, *The Mystery of Personal Identity* (San Diego, CA: ACS Publications, 1984), 36–37.

39. Ibid., 45.

40. Gilbert Childs, *Steiner Education* (Edinburgh, UK: Floris Books, 1991), 51–63.

41. C. G. Jung, *Analytical Psychology: Its Theory and Practice* (New York: Vintage Books, 1968), 3–25.

42. An adaptation of "From the Great Above to the Great Below," Diane Wolkstein and Samuel Kramer, *Innana Queen of Heaven and Earth* (New York: Harper & Row, 1983), 52–68 and Jalaja Bonheim, "The Descent of Innana," Mill Valley, CA: Musimedia, 1993, audio recording.

43. Clarissa Pinkola Estés, *Women Who Run With the Wolves: Myths and Stories of the Wild Woman Archetype* (New York: Ballantine Books, 1992), 36.

44. Ibid., 35.

45. Gloria Steinem, *Revolution from Within: A Book of Self-Esteem* (Boston, MA: Little, Brown & Co., 1992), 65.

CHAPTER THREE

BECOMING WOMAN

Life in the desert is small but brilliant
and most of what occurs goes on underground.
This is like the lives of many women.[1]

—Clarissa Pinkola Estés, Ph.D.

I
t does not matter whether we live under the rule of a patriarchy or
a matriarchy. What matters is whether we may become who we
truly are. Throughout millennia, cultures have used female biological and psychological forces to entrap girls and women into predefined roles. Dr. Jean Baker Miller asserts in her groundbreaking
book, *Toward a New Psychology of Women*, the dominant culture defines
and shapes a growing girl's nature according to what it deems necessary
for its survival.[2] Culture achieves these ends through the parents. We
parents are the carriers of our culture's beliefs about who women and
girls must be, and we pass these beliefs on to our daughters.

Both women and men are offended by obvious sex-role stereotypes
of women in our culture. Many of us are outraged at the objectification
of women as maids in their own homes, prostitutes, low paid pink-
collar workers, and so on. But how many of us really stop to examine
the unconscious cultural beliefs that dictate our own parenting behaviors? For example, do we give the ideas of women as much weight as
men's ideas? What does the fact that we have never, in over two hundred years, had a woman as President of the United States say to our
daughters? Is the creation of a nurturing, well-run household as highly
esteemed as a lucrative, well-executed business deal?

The value a culture ascribes to the tasks performed by its members
speaks loudly and clearly to our daughters. The stories that follow

portray cultural attitudes toward girls and women in broad strokes through the ages from the partnership societies, the hunter/gatherer tribes, the fabulous Fifties, to today's technological age. Looking at the ancient mysteries of young girls' initiation into womanhood, we see how far away we have come from a connection with the earth, the continuous cycling of nature, and our own bodies. Understanding the value of feminine wisdom, strength, and power enables us as parents to question the forces that conspire to keep them underground, freeing our daughters to discover who they really want to be.

The Partnership Societies

A girl is born, and the birth attendants run rejoicing through the stone-paved streets, their high voices announcing the joyous news to the community. The new mother beams at her infant daughter. "You will be Demena, daughter of Dellia," she whispers as the midwife assists in the afterbirth. The sacred placenta is caught in the fertility bowl, a work of great beauty, carefully crafted by the expectant mother before the birth. The finely wrought piece, covered in flowers and snake designs, will be offered to the Earth Goddess in thanksgiving for a safe and healthy delivery.

The new father waits nearby, readying the offering he, too, will make to the Goddess in thankfulness for the safety of his wife and daughter. To a small bundle of sweet herbs he adds symbols of his hope for his daughter's life—the tiny replicas of a loom to symbolize craftship, a scales for stateship,[3] and a fertility bowl in recognition of his daughter's feminine nature and connection to the Goddess. He also adds a coin cut in half to symbolize abundance and the even distribution of wealth, a hank of his own hair as his support for her thoughts and ideas, and a pinch of the dark earth in honor of all things in nature.

The tiny Demena thrives, constantly nestled in the sling carried by her mother and grandmother or in the crook of her father's or grandfather's arm. She is lulled to sleep by the whirring of the looms weaving cloth, the rustling of the scythes cutting wheat, the low murmur of temple chants honoring the Goddess. Around her, Demena sees women and men of all ages together creating a life of harmony and beauty from a deep reverence for all living things. She grows up secure in her worth as a person of her household, who will one day hold an important position in her community; as a maker of the sacred ritual vessels, perhaps, or a shopkeeper, or even a breeder of the fine cattle herds her grandparents keep.

When the young girl reaches thirteen summers, she enters, with the other girls her age, the Temple-of-the-Moon Goddess to await her first blood. Here she is attended by the women of her community and taught the secrets of her approaching womanhood. She spends her waiting-time in service to the Goddess through meditation, working with her dreams, and washing the sacred vessels and ritual vestments worn by those who have been called to serve the Goddess.

On the morning of her first blood flow, special prayers of thanksgiving and rejoicing are offered by the community to welcome Demena into her new womanhood. Her body is decorated in the bright colors of nature—sea blues and greens—and she is adorned with sacred garments and flowers. Then she is presented to the throng awaiting her emergence from the Temple-of-the-Moon Goddess. A great bull has been roasting, and after a banquet in her honor, Demena assumes her place as a young woman, invested with feminine strength, life-giving powers, and the blessings of the Goddess to fulfill her destiny as a full and active member of the community.

—Composite profile of girlhood in the
Early Neolithic period, 5000 B.C.E.

A striking feature of such early civilizations is the reverence and respect given to the natural cycles of life and death, Nature, and the female form—symbolic of the Goddess, Mother of All. To experience a bodily connection to Nature, that is, to feel the cycling of the seasons and the changes of the weather in one's bones, or to work the soil with one's hands or a hoe means to intimately embrace life and death. It is what Clarissa Pinkola Estés, Ph.D., conjures up when she describes the Life/Death/Life nature.[4] It is the normal cycling of all things—of renewal, decay, and again renewal; connection, separation, connection; peaks, valleys, peaks; the building up of the uterine lining, the flow of blood, the building up of uterine lining; and on and on.

Because the natural cycles were so much a part of ancient life—both sacred and secular—a girl's first menstrual flow was cause for celebration and the initiation into womanhood. Her initiation into womanhood involved a waiting in the temple for a transformation to occur and afterward a recognition by the community that something significant had happened. She entered as a girl and emerged a woman. She was not made into a woman, she became one.

The Hunter-Gatherer Tribes

A girl is born, and the weary mother heaves a sigh of resignation. "My mate will be angry at me again for not giving him a son," she thinks. "Will I have to abandon you, too, as appeasement to the Thunder God for the safety of our warriors in battle?" she whispers to the tiny infant.

A wail goes up from the birth tent to signal to the rest of the tribe that a son was not given, and Anulak, the Huntmaster, kicks a nearby stump in frustration. "I suppose she'll beg me to keep the girl this time," he fumed. Strong sons, many sons. That's what a leader of hunters and a warrior must have to show he is worthy of his authority. Anulak decides he could ask Krane to accept this girl child as mate to his tiny son, born just two moons ago. It is settled, then. His mate may keep this one, but she must obey his decision to promise the baby to Krane's family for a good bride-price.

And so the daughter of Anulak is promised to Krale, son of Krane, for twenty hare pelts, a set of bear's claws, and a cougar's skin. The girl grows up in the shadows of the women as they work; gathering the early grasses for grain and the late grasses for baskets as the tribe moves slowly across the steppe in search of game and enemy tribes to conquer. She learns to pick the tiny berries that grow hidden among the tall grasses and woods. Her grandmothers show her how to painstakingly scrape the large animal hides her father brings back from the hunts for making their tents, heavy outer garments, and foot coverings. She is happy with the small chores she is given and is called Kwiki, for the little chirps she sings as she works. When she is older, she will learn the harder tasks of butchering the meat—saving the choicest parts for her father and grandfathers, cutting thin strips for drying, chopping fine pieces for stews, leaving large haunches for the celebration roast in honor of the animal spirits for feeding her people.

When the young girl's first moon time approaches, her mother and grandmothers build a small hut from twigs, grasses, and mud. Here she awaits her moon—alone and fearful, but somehow curious about how this strange event will change her. She sits in the prescribed manner, back straight, legs crossed, leaning back on the pole behind her only when sleeping. Daily, her mother silently brings a bitter mixture of herbal teas to drink, and then leaves her to her meditations and visions. While she awaits the Dream that will influence the rest of her life, Kwiki has time to muse about her life thus far. She faithfully learned the daily chores required to ensure survival of her tribe. She has an uncommon skill in creating the amulets used to protect the men as they hunt and war against enemy tribes. Krale will be proud to take her as mate. She is said to be graceful and pretty, and she knows her place as a female. She has learned to be small and to stay out of the way of her father's rage and the wrath of the vengeful Sky God. She hopes Krale's temper will be milder than her father's, so she will fare better treatment than her mother.

Finally, she emerges from the hut after her first moon flow. She is thankful for her totem, the hawk, given to her in the Dream and glad of its strong medicine. Her mother, who showed her how to weave the soft grasses to catch the blood, rushes to her side and leads her to Krane's hut, places her hand in Krale's, and murmurs, eyes downcast, "You are now Lela, mate of Krale. I will miss you, my Kwiki." Although she and her mother will continue to work side-by-side on the larger tasks for the tribe, Lela will now work with Krale's mother and grandmothers within his household. Lela's father, witnessing this scene, says to her grinning, as he leaves for his own tent, "So you're back. Krane will have to feed you now."

—Composite profile of girlhood in
the early Bronze Age, 3000 B.C.E.

As the invaders from the North infiltrated the Goddess-worshipping, egalitarian cultures of Old Europe, there began an erosion of fine art, architecture, and peaceful lifestyles, as well as the status of girls and women. The northern climates and gods were harsh, demanding strict adherence to the laws of men and oppressive retribution for wrong-doing. Worship of the life-giving powers of the earth goddesses was overthrown by the wrathful vengeance of the sky gods. The respect for the feminine powers of women as embodiment of the Goddess mutated into fear, hatred, and the need to suppress and control.

The roles of men and women became more defined, with tasks carrying power and authority falling to men. The tasks of child-rearing, nurturing, the making of clothing and housing, food preparation and preserving, and nursing the sick and wounded fell in value and were delegated to women. Strict rules regarding puberty initiation rites brutally launched both girls and boys into adulthood. No longer did women and men work side-by-side in labor and decision-making for the benefit of all within the tribe.

This began the long history of the enslavement and erosion of feminine power and wisdom. We can trace this process through the glory of the Greek and Roman empires, the darkness of the Middle Ages, the revival of art and society during the Renaissance, the reign of Queen Victoria, the migration of the pioneers and the settlement of the American West, and the birth of U.S. imperialism during World War I and World War II.

Women had previously labored in crude factories and sweatshops all over the world, but the First and Second World Wars provided many American women with job opportunities not previously available. Although political representation and careers in leadership and management remained closed to them, women enthusiastically entered the work force to fill slots left by the fighting men, and to do their part to help the country's cause in the war. And then the men came home, and we entered the fabulous Fifties.

The Fabulous Fifties

A girl is born, and the family rejoices. She is named Lilly Marie after her paternal and maternal grandmothers. Aunts, grandmothers, and cousins all clamor for a chance to hold the new baby and are always available for baby-sitting when Mom and Dad want to go out dancing or to the movies. Lilly's first months are spent in the blissful adoration of her family. She eats on schedule, and to her parents' delight, she sleeps through the night at an early age. She is an easy baby—sweet, quiet, and happy.

Lilly's father, a salesman often on the road, gets enough raise in salary to buy his growing family a house in the suburbs. So he moves his family out of the city away from grandmothers, aunts, and cousins and into a brand new, ranch-style home with large lawn and attached garage. The inside is stocked with every appliance imaginable to make homemaking and cooking chores a breeze. Lilly grows, surrounded by her dolls and dishes, mimicking her mother in her household chores.

Lilly's mother is proud of her new, convenient home, but she misses the support and nearness of her mother, sisters, and grandmothers. She is college-educated and spends her days cleaning, cooking, and caring for her children. Sometimes, alone at night, she thinks she might just walk out the polished front door, head west, and keep on walking.

At nine years of age, Lilly is a tomboy who loves baseball, horses, and climbing trees. She is the "apple of her father's eye," and prefers doing things with him rather than spending time with her mother. They are great pals, and she believes, with her father's encouragement, that she can do anything she aspires to. For several years, Lilly basks in her father's glowing approval, outgoing and adventurous. Then, Lilly turns thirteen, and everything changes.

One day she feels a cramping below her middle, and in the girls' bathroom, she is horrified to discover a brownish stain on her underwear. Every hour she returns to the bathroom, hoping she had been mistaken the first time. But no! The awful truth slowly sinks in. This is her Period! The Curse! Her mother had given her a horrible book last year about what would happen to her, and how she had dreaded the day. Now, what should she do? The school nurse wouldn't be so bad to talk to; her friend Peggy had gone to her last week. Lilly swallows her embarrassment and tells the nurse what has happened. The nurse kindly explains about menstruation and how to use the sanitary napkins. She gives Lilly several pamphlets to take home and sends her back to class. That night Lilly tells her mother, begging her to keep it from her father. Her mother smiles and says that she'll get used to it.

Lilly immediately notices her father is not as eager to spend time with her, no longer inviting her to ball games as often as he once did, and then usually including her mother, too. She misses the special attention he always gave her. She becomes less adventurous and sure of herself, more hesitant to volunteer answers in her classes, and less interested in her once-beloved science. She becomes more concerned about her appearance, her acceptance by friends, and her attractiveness to boys. She is dreamy, moody, and uncooperative at home, and her mother often retreats to another room, crying bitter tears of frustration, hurt, and powerlessness.

Despite her mood swings, Lilly is popular, dates often, does well in her academic work, and holds numerous major offices in school organizations. She graduates as an honor student and goes on to college, where she plans to meet the "prince charming" she always knew she would marry and rely on.

—Composite profile of girlhood in
suburban America in the 1950s

During the First and Second World Wars women shared a sense of involvement and accomplishment for the common good. Then the men returned from the European theaters of war, and women were urged to give up their jobs and go home. During the decade following World War II, much emphasis was given to home and family—Mom and apple pie. Many women were happy to take up homemaking and start a family, thankful their men had returned home safely. Story titles in popular women's magazines reflected the attitudes of the day: "How To Snare a Man," "Femininity Begins at Home," "Have Babies While You're Young," "The Doctor Talks About Breast Feeding," "Are You Training Your Daughter To Be a Wife?" "Really a Man's World, Politics," "Careers at Home," "Cooking To Me Is Poetry," "The Business of Running a Home."[5] While America settled into a time of peace and prosperity, housewives settled into new houses in the suburbs with more modern appliances than ever before and a routine of shopping, cooking, chauffeuring kids, washing, cleaning, shopping, cooking, and so on.

Daughters were caught in a bind during these years. Mom was often depressed or too involved with her children, and girls turned to Dad to escape Mom's smothering clutches. His world was exciting, holding the promise of freedom and adventure. This was great until the age of puberty, when a girl ran headlong into the *feminine mystique*[6]—culture's beliefs about who girls and women should be. In the Fifties, girls went to college to find Prince Charming, who would sweep them off their feet and carry them away to the suburbs to live happily ever after, washing and cleaning and cooking and washing and cleaning and cooking and...

The Technological Age

The sonogram reveals they are expecting a girl, and the amniocentesis indicates she is normal, so the happy parents proceed in decorating the nursery in teddy bears. Her mother resolves to treat her daughter the same as her son, avoiding the old stereotypes that limit girls to the predetermined roles of the past. She is named Molly Lynne, and after her birth, she is breastfed on demand and given the undivided attention of all family members.

Molly grows up happily amid dolls and trucks, "ninja turtles" and "Legos for girls." At home she learns to tag along with her older brother and boys in the neighborhood, and at preschool she prefers to play "house," dress-up, and paint with the other girls.

Her mother is satisfied Molly has the best of both the feminine and masculine worlds. She, herself, works full time in a demanding and challenging career for an international corporation. Although a full-time housekeeper alleviates the need for much cleaning, and Molly's father does the grocery shopping for the family, Molly's mother feels exhausted from her job, the cooking, and other details that keep a household running smoothly. She often feels guilty that she has so little time to spend with her children during the week. She drops them off at preschool at 7:00 A.M., and her husband picks them up after work at 6:00 P.M. Her night meetings sometimes prevent her from getting home before Molly and her brother are asleep. Although weekends are spent catching up on household chores to get ready for the next busy week, she tries to spend alone time with each child to learn what and how they are doing at preschool.

As she matures, both parents encourage Molly to try everything, although she often looks to her father for help when things get difficult. She does well in school, is popular with her friends, and participates in ballet, gymnastics, science club, drama, archery, and flute lessons. Expected to succeed, Molly pushes herself towards perfection.

When her period starts at eleven, her world comes crashing down. Her mother wants to throw a family dinner party to celebrate Molly's puberty, but Molly is horrified and embarrassed at the thought. It seems her body is against her. She suffers severe cramping before and during menstruation, loss of appetite, inability to sleep, and a general malaise that makes her feel worthless, ugly, and unlovable. At thirteen, Molly decides she is too fat and begins a restricted diet that leaves her exhausted and emaciated. All of the mother's efforts to reach her daughter are rebuffed in angry, reproachful blame and defiance. Her father, once supportive and fun, now seems aloof and demanding. She feels abandoned by the one person she thought she could always count on. To hide the pain, she artfully manipulates her dad into buying her expensive presents, clothes, and activities.

Once confident and outspoken, Molly learns to hide her true feelings to fit in at home and at school. She becomes silent about the reality she sees around her. She learns that to be in relationship with her parents and friends, she cannot always tell the truth about how she feels or what she sees, so she learns to keep a part of herself out of relationships in order to be in them. A part of her goes underground.

Now seventeen, Molly decides to study for an engineering degree at a prestigious university across the country. She leaves home confused but determined to do her best. She makes friends, finds a house, gets a job to help her parents cover expenses, and pursues her studies. Although Molly dates often, she puts off thinking about marriage, planning to finish her degree and establish herself as an engineer first. Still tortured by food and her weight, Molly gains thirty pounds during her second year.

Burdened by her weight, the rigorous study regime she has carved out for herself, and her perfectionistic need to succeed, Molly begins using pills to help her stay awake during the long hours of study and then to sleep after she finally gets to bed. Realizing she is headed toward an emotional and physical collapse, Molly calls home for help. Her father, always quick to leap in and fix everything, lectures her about the load she's been carrying and tells her to get on the first plane home. Her mother, sensing her daughter's despair, says quietly, "I'll be there tonight." Showing confidence in her, Molly's mother listens to her problems and helps her find therapeutic help. Molly joins a campus twelve-step program and slowly gains understanding of her weight battle, her need to please, and her overuse of drugs.

—Growing up in the
Technological Age, The 1990s

Never before has such a smorgasbord of life choices been available to girls and women. There have always been working mothers—single moms who had to work to support their families and mothers who chose to work for themselves and to help out with family finances. Commonly, their jobs were service-oriented, such as secretarial, nursing, and teaching, with little room for advancement into the higher paid positions of management. The struggle for equal opportunity in the workplace, fought for during the Women's Movement of the late 1960's and 1970's, still goes on, but many of today's young women take their choice to have both a family and a career for granted. With the cultural creation of "Supermom," there is still a lot to be won.

We cheer as loudly as anyone the opportunity for women to develop their potential as human beings in the world community. Our planet can no longer afford to waste the gifts, talents, and resources of over half its inhabitants. Women are needed on every level of the public and private sectors of career life.

JEANNE | Unfortunately, the cultural stereotypes still dictate, both overtly and covertly, how women should achieve success in the career world, what kind of leaders we must be, and that we still carry the burden of arranging for child care and doing home upkeep. The two biggest errors we made during the early years of the Women's Movement were to disregard the needs of working mothers and to lead women to believe that we must enter the work world under the rules of the male standard. We are only just beginning to know what feminine leadership really looks like, that it can be as powerful and as effective as man's leadership, that we don't have to be male clones to be successful in the workplace.

Many feminists in this country were outraged by the title of economist and writer Sylvia Ann Hewlett's provoking book, *A Lesser Life: The Myth of Women's Liberation in America*. Dr. Hewlett wisely explains, however, why the European Women's Movement is such a positive force for working women, fashioned on what some American feminists of the nineteenth century considered the basic cause of women's inequality: housework and child care.

Most women's lives are touched by children in some way, if not through natural birth, then through adoption, stepfamilies, nieces, nephews, and so on. European feminists went right to the heart of what women need—the support services necessary to enable women to be a creative force in the workplace without having to sacrifice their roles as mothers and homemakers. Rather than pursuing equal rights, as in America, the social feminists of Europe felt equal rights were a small part of the struggle. They asserted that women deserve compensation in the labor market to help ease their dual role of work both inside and outside the home. Here are the sad facts that continue to handicap American working women:

- The United States is the only industrialized nation in the world that does not have a mandatory maternity leave policy.

- The United States is one of the few industrialized nations in the world that does not pay for up to five months' maternity leave.

- The United States is behind most other industrialized countries in providing affordable, beneficial, safe, healthy child care for children whose parents work.

- The United States has the widest wage discrepancy between male and female workers compared with other industrialized nations, and if a woman takes time off to have children, the gap gets wider.

- The United States gives little or no support to the care of children, whereas the right to free and extensive postnatal care, adequate maternity and/or paternity leave, and flex time for breastfeeding and caring for children when they become ill are part of the fabric of European life.[7]

The mother of the Women's Movement, feminist and writer Betty Friedan, muses that until now the choices have been either a full-time commitment to being a wife and mother, or to a lifelong career in the male pattern. She asserts, "...from all we know of human psychology and history,...neither woman nor man lives by work or love, alone.... The human self defines itself and grows through love and work."[8]

The choices facing our daughters in the technological age are a mixed blessing. Most women continue to want the ties and responsibilities of having and raising families. Most women want creative and challenging work that allows them a sense of giving and belonging to the larger world community and that financially rewards them for their efforts. To try to do both in this culture is to flirt with the impossible. The term "Supermom" wasn't coined out of nothing. Working women today are trying to achieve in the work world what men have achieved all along—but men have always had the help of a woman at home who took care of all the other details of living! Today, the working woman is also that woman at home, and without support services in the workplace and a respect for the work women do within and outside the home, the attempt to do both is taking its toll—on women, on men, and on our children.

❧ *JEANNE* If I could give my daughter one thing, I would give her a world that valued the personhood of women, understanding that creative work in the community is as necessary to her feminine soul as nurturing children and/or creating a home. In my world the question to the working mothers would not be, "How are *you* going to find child care for *your* children while you work?" The world I would give my daughter would ask, "How can we *together* find solutions to enable women the freedom to work while raising healthy children, because they are our collective future?"

Endnotes

1. Clarissa Pinkola Estés, *Women Who Run With the Wolves: Myths and Stories of the Wild Woman Archetype* (New York: Ballantine Books, 1992), 37.

2. Jean Baker Miller, *Toward a New Psychology of Women* (Boston, MA: Beacon Press, 1986), 118.

3. To promote an equitable language that includes both males and females, we use craftship, rather than craftsmanship and stateship, rather than statesmanship.

4. Estés, *Women Who Run*, 130–131.

5. Betty Friedan, *The Feminine Mystique* (New York: W. W. Norton, 1963), 38.

6. Ibid., 7.

7. Sylvia Ann Hewlett, *A Lesser Life: The Myth of Women's Liberation in America* (New York: William Morrow, 1986), 164.

8. Betty Friedan, *The Second Stage* (New York: Summit Books, 1981), 95.

CHAPTER FOUR

THE CULTURAL FORCE—
A QUESTION OF COMPETENCE

I realized Papa was strict and hard on me
because a boy had to amount to something,
whereas Mary Toy didn't, being a girl.[1]

—Will Tweedy, *Cold Sassy Tree*, Olive Ann Burns

◁▷ *JEANNE* | "...whereas Mary Toy didn't, being a girl." This almost throw-away line by Will Tweedy, the lively young narrator of Olive Ann Burns's funny account of life in a small southern town, jolted me awake. The reasoning of a fourteen-year-old boy speaks reams about the cultural heritage our daughters take on as they grow to adulthood. "I thought we had grown beyond those old-fashioned attitudes as citizens of the 90's," we might say. But in the minds of many, daughters do not have to "amount to something," because they just grow up, get married, have babies, and depend upon a man to do the hard stuff for them.

As we stressed earlier in this book, who our daughters are at birth and who they become in adulthood depends upon the influence of four powerful forces—the biological, the psychological, the cultural, and the deep well of the feminine soul. There's not much we can do about the biological force; as we have seen, those influences were laid down with the genetic code before birth. We discussed how a healthy psychological development is dependent upon the formation of a healthy sense of self within the context of relationships of ever increasing complexity. And, we outlined how parental attitudes and circumstances can do much to either squash or set free the tiny, fluttering spark of a girl's soul—the essence of who she is—into the flame of her true womanhood.

It is the cultural force that truly tests the mettle of parents. Thus far, culture has suppressed feminine power by using the characteristics of female biology to limit what girls and women can be and do. Our culture has traditionally defined the traits of assertiveness, independence, and decisiveness as masculine, and cooperation, nurturing, and communication as feminine, while devaluing the latter—losing sight of the fact that all these human qualities are equally vital for the continuation of life as we know it.

In her Harvard studies of women and girls, psychologist and author Emily Hancock, Ph.D., found that girls lose their true identities as they grow up. She writes, "At the buried core of women's identity is a distinct and vital self first articulated in childhood, a root identity that gets cut off in the process of growing up female."[2] A girl loses her "root identity" in the predefined roles our society prescribes for her: good little girl, teenage vamp, busty cheerleader, virgin beauty queen, tough young career woman, contented wife, devoted mother, raging bitch, middle-aged frump, little old lady. The tragedy in being channeled into these cultural stereotypes is that girls become separated from their own sense of self early in life and either forget or never find out who they really are.

> *Until I turned thirteen, I was pretty much allowed to do what I loved—climb trees, ride horses, play baseball, roam the creek beds on our land. Then, it wasn't "ladylike" to be so rowdy, so I had to wear dresses to school, pay attention to my hair, and keep my fingernails clean. Once life was so free, so open. Then I became confined, out-of-sync, bored. Now I go from one job to the next, one man to another.*
>
> *—Jennie, forty-five*

The long arm of culture reaches into every home in America, through television, books, newspapers, magazines, and our educational system, dictating our parenting practices and attitudes and telling our daughters who they should be. Without conscious consideration, we parent the way we ourselves were parented—raising our daughters to conform to the cultural standards without even realizing it. We discipline according to the "experts" and yield to what our children believe they want, because of what they see on TV, on a billboard, or in a friend's closet.

Competence: A Parenting Guide

Our greatest challenge in raising healthy daughters is to consciously consider whether the current cultural lens is the best way through which to view them. We have to ask ourselves each step of the way whether a particular attitude or cultural "rule" nurtures a healthy self-esteem, giving a girl the competence to become who she truly wants to be.

We borrow the idea of competence from therapists and researchers Carly Rivers, Rosalind Barnett, and Grace Baruch.[3] They write, ". . . the acquisition of competence involves looking at society and figuring out what skills will enable you to survive—and thrive—in that society."[4] How well our daughters survive and thrive in this culture will depend upon how well we teach them to be competent in living life. We may not think so, but parents wield the most power over culture to influence our daughters' growth. Let us examine together how cultural attitudes and practices limit the competence of girls and women and what parents can do to enhance the growth of capable daughters.

Dissociation

To begin to use cultural forces for the good of our daughters we must first shake ourselves awake from the cultural trance we all live in. This is no small matter, to untangle our true beliefs from what we have been taught to believe about who and what girls and women are. The experience of growing up female in western culture has at times been so painful that we cope by dissociating from awareness of injustices or hurtful feelings. This psychological term, *dissociation*, describes the process of burying painful memories and feelings and denying the reality of what we see, enabling us to go on living our everyday lives as if everything were fine. Both women and men dissociate from the reality of their experiences.

...psychology in its research practice had somehow not noticed that there were no women in the samples. You know, you have to ask yourself: Where were they working? No women in the samples of adults or adolescents, and women were involved in doing this research. So that is why we have to talk about dissociation. We have to talk about dissociation, because women were co-authoring books, such as The Psychological World of the Teenager, *a study of 175 boys! No, seriously. You have to think about that; you can't answer that in a logical way. You have to think about what is the process that allows a woman to author that book. Or to co-author Levinsen's book,* Seasons of a Man's Life: Stages of Adult Development.[5]

—*Carol Gilligan, Ph.D., Director*
The Harvard Project on Women's
Psychology and Girls' Development

Because the blinders of dissociation are so effective, we risk being overly obvious by explaining Dr. Gilligan's concern. The titles of these two studies are so disturbing because they imply that boys and men are who we investigate to find out all we need to know about the psychology of teenagers and adult development. Somehow we have been taught to believe that the experiences of girls and women are not important in the study and understanding of human behavior. If we know men, then we know all of humankind. These prevalent cultural attitudes totally deny the uniqueness of the female experience, limiting the development of girls and women and depriving a needy world of the gifts, talents, and resources our daughters have to offer. Now is the time for us as parents to confront our dissociations and begin to recognize the cultural attitudes and behaviors that entrap and stunt our daughters' growth.

It's a Girl!

Before my daughter was born, I decided I would treat her the same as I had treated my son. No frilly, pink dresses, no Little Mermaid room decor, no limits on

*toys to dolls and dishes. I would encourage her to be-
come anything she aspired to—rocket scientist, doctor,
pilot. Now at four, she loves frilly, pink anything,
prefers dolls and dishes to anything, and loves the
Little Mermaid! When she grows up she wants to be a
cheerleader and a mommy! Have I done something
wrong?*

—*Carol, mother of Shawn, eight, and Molly, four*

Whether we mean to or not, most people treat girls and boys differently. A pink room decor and a pink bow in her hair signal to the
world, "I am a girl. I think differently, act differently, and communicate
differently from a boy." And she will—regardless of what color she is
dressed in! Unfortunately, the pink paraphernalia also activates our
cultural attitudes and preconceptions about girls, which dictate how we
treat her. And we don't even know her yet! She's just arrived!

However we decide to treat them beforehand, our daughters have
their own unique preferences and behaviors. Our attitudes and beliefs
learned from culture about how girls should be determine whether we
help our daughters broaden and deepen those preferences and behaviors, or whether we assist in narrowing and limiting their options
for growth and development into healthy women.

Studies of child rearing practices for girls and boys indicate that we
parents, perhaps unconsciously, train our daughters and sons for much
different paths in life. Like Will Tweedy in Olive Ann Burns's *Cold
Sassy Tree*, little boys are more often "made to tow the line" and to
accept responsibility for their actions much earlier than little girls.
Girls, expected to be sweet and compliant, "get off the hook" more
often than not through their charm and wit. By working through the
consequences of their behaviors, boys learn to deal with authority, to
solve problems, and to have confidence in their abilities to handle
whatever confronts them in life. Because we tend to see girls as fragile
and in need of protection, we—especially dads—rush in too soon to
help our daughters complete a task or solve a dilemma. Too often girls
grow into womanhood without the self-reliance to know what they
want and the competence to know how to get it. Therapist Celia Halas,
Ph.D., writes in her informative book, *Why Can't a Woman Be More*

Like a Man? "Little girl qualities of helplessness turn into womanly habits of indecision and irresponsibility."[6]

> *As I grew up, my father did everything for me. He balanced my checkbook, got me my first job, bought my first car, had the car regularly serviced, and on and on. After I was married, my husband did the same things. Now we are divorcing, and I'm terrified. So much of the world is foreign to me, and I feel incompetent to deal with these basic life needs.*
>
> *—Maureen, forty-six*

No matter how sweet, compliant, pretty, and dainty, or loud, demanding, moody, and unpredictable our daughters may be, they need experiences that enhance their feminine strengths and balance their feminine weaknesses. What do we mean by *feminine?*

For our definition of feminine we go back in time before the separation of the spiritual life from daily living to the Goddess cultures. In these cultures the Goddess was considered the "guardian of the innermost things."[7] She was entrusted with what was considered the holiest of human activities—fire-keeping, food preparation, and holding the sacred center of tribal life. She was feared and venerated for her life-giving and death-dealing powers. She was Healer, Keeper of the Animals, Midwife, Weaver and Spinner of Tales, Protectress of Travelers and Warriors, and Patroness of the Arts. Sophia, the Goddess of Wisdom, integrates the seven branches of learning, considered by modern thinkers the exclusive domain of man—Arithmetic, Geometry, Astronomy, Grammar, Rhetoric, Dialectic, and Music.[8] Plato lectured on the *anima mundi*, the Feminine Principle, as being within all of nature, and the Stoic school of philosophy credited her as the only vital force in the universe.[9]

From these early beliefs a deeper, more encompassing meaning of The Feminine emerges. Life-giver, Guardian of the Inner Life, Keeper of Sacred Space, maternal, vital, wise, spiritual, protective, strong, powerful, compassionate, and connecting begin to define the awesome potential our daughters carry within them. Important to include in this new understanding of The Feminine are the fiercer aspects, such as aggressiveness, anger, destruction, and defiance. Demeter, Goddess of Grain, is also the mythic mother whose rage and grief over losing her daughter, Persephone, to Hades, God of the Underworld, is so powerful that she causes all of life to wither and die for half of each year.[10]

How we describe our daughters in our hearts and minds is translated into our beliefs about who they are and can become. In turn, our beliefs dictate our parenting practices that determine whether we guide them into roles that deny their true natures or into experiences that empower them to fulfill their destinies.

Toys and Play

"I have some good news and some bad news," a young mother told her friend. "Our daughter, Lisa, loves the workbench we gave her for her birthday, but she uses it as a stove!"

Children learn gender roles by modeling what they see their parents do. Not surprisingly, a girl's early play includes the activities she sees around her. Perhaps Lisa saw her mother (or both parents) cooking more often than she saw one or both of them using a workbench and tools.

⟷ JEANNE | In my family, my dad worked with tools and wood, and he saw to it that my brother learned how to use and care for his tools. I regret he didn't do the same for me. I have a natural skill for woodworking, but the tools feel so clumsy, and I often don't know the proper tool to use for a particular job.

Marian Burros, writer for the *New York Times* reports, "In a year when more women than ever took seats in Congress and were appointed to important government posts, and when the First Lady was given the responsibility for health care reform, very little has changed at home for women who work, even at the highest levels." [11] Although gender roles for women and men are shifting to a more equal footing, daughters still see their mothers performing most of the household tasks. Women, even if they work outside the home, are still most often the cook, primary parent, laundress, housecleaner, and organizer of family activities, and men are most often in charge of lawn upkeep, car maintenance, and home repair.

It is natural for children to use whatever objects or toys will suit their games; for example, the workbench for a stove, leaves for plates, pine cones for cookies, and so on. All children benefit from encouragement to use their imaginations to re-create the real world around them in their play. Here they work out the difficulties that naturally occur in daily family life—their frustrations in not getting their way, having to share, not being able to do something beyond their capabilities—dealing with the limits and boundaries of learning to be a human being.

A child's play teaches the life lessons needed for competency in adult life. We suggest a tour of a child's room, checking the toys and room environment for gender role messages, opportunities for creativity, and capacity for encouraging the development of competence. An old study cited in the work of Rivers, Barnett, and Baruch, mentioned earlier, found that boys' rooms were equipped with more of a variety of toys that prepared them for action out in the world and that girls' rooms contained toys that required more quiet, house-oriented activities.[12] We suspect this difference is still true today.

⟨⟨ ⟨⟨ *Don* | OK! I am now entering my eight-year-old son's room. One can tell right away this is a boy's room, because of the big shoes in the basket by the door. Here are other clues further in—the dinosaur mural across one wall, a bright bin containing thousands (I am exaggerating, a little) of Legos, a barrel of Lincoln Logs, a large drawer of assorted wooden building blocks, a cubby with a motley collection of ninja turtles, a box of tools and nails, a drawer of various "weapons"—slingshot, sword, water pistol, rubber band gun, a basket of spiders, reptiles and dinosaurs, a baseball glove, a large container of balls, and a tall stack of large cardboard blocks in primary colors. I also see a large, wooden doll house equipped with family and furniture, baskets of rocks, feathers, and pine cones, a collection of wooden animals, knights, and gnomes, a bin of musical instruments, a basket of marbles, a cache of magnets, a box of dishes, food, and cooking utensils, a china tea set, a cardboard castle, a puppet theatre and puppets, shelves of games, puzzles, and magic tricks, and thousands (again, I slightly exaggerate) of books of all flavors. And that's

> it, except for his trucks and cars out in his backyard fort, roller blades and bike in the garage, chess set in the living room, and art supplies in the kitchen.

Most of these toys enhance mastery and competency through development of large and small muscle and eye-hand coordination, as well as visual-spatial acuity. Many are action-oriented and require creativity and originality to be fully enjoyed.

The following is a composite of how clients and friends described the contents of their eight-year-old daughters' rooms:

> A glass animal collection of dogs and horses, a shelf full of stuffed animals, two American Girls dolls and accessories, a doll cradle, boxes of board games, a large assortment of books, a tall pile of jigsaw puzzles, four books of the American Girls paper dolls, a drawer of costume jewelry, animal calendars, an assortment of animal posters, a walkman, a collection of Barbies with accessories, a GameBoy, the Slovenian family dollhouse and schoolhouse with accessories, a cooking set, an iron and board, a baseball mitt, a table and chairs, a tea set, modeling clay, crayons, drawing and construction paper, paints, stamps, and ink pads. In the garage are a bicycle, a scooter, pogo stick, roller blades, two-square ball, skateboard, and a tetherball. There is a treehouse in the backyard.

We notice that most of the toys mentioned are oriented toward domestic and care-giving activities that do encourage creativity and imaginative thinking, but there is little emphasis on toys that enhance active play, visual-spatial, or large/small motor development. We acknowledge that girls may prefer certain toys over others—a doll over a ninja turtle, for example—but we suggest offering a wider variety of toys and activities (described in detail in Chapters Nine and Ten) that develop competence and self-confidence through the mastery of challenging toys which require action, problem-solving, and creative thinking.

"I'm So Fat!"

How many of us actually know anyone whose body really looks like Barbie's? Nevertheless, studies show that girls as young as five already understand a woman's body is supposed to be a perfect 36"-24"-36". By age nine they begin to look critically at their own bodies, judging to see how they measure up.[13] Wellesley College psychologists Elissa Koff's and Jill Rierdan's 1991 study of Boston sixth-grade girls found an alarming concern with counting calories, avoiding fat, exercising to lose weight, and guilt about eating.[14] The natural rounding of the body during adolescence from normal hormonal changes signaling maturation becomes disgusting, hated, ugly FAT! Where do our daughters learn these attitudes about their bodies?

⇛ *JEANNE* My family used me for weight when I was little. I was the one to sit on top of the ice cream freezer at Granny and Granddad's, because the crank turned easier. My older cousin was too big, my brother and other girl cousin were too small; I was just right. As my dad graded our gravel country lane, I sat on the road grader, so it didn't skip over the hills of gravel, making a nice, even path. Dad also made stirrups from rope for me to stand in, so the posthole digger could cut through the thick clay on our land. I got the idea that I was big, that is to say—fat. When I was in my early thirties, I asked my mother to send my childhood photographs taken yearly until I was grown. When the thick package came, I opened it expecting to see a chubby little girl with buck teeth. I was shocked to see that I was never fat!

Most of us grow up with messages from our families about how we will look or act. "Oh my! You're shaped just like your Auntie Jo," or "She's going to be tall, just like my mother." "Be careful, lest you end up like Cousin Mae, with no husband and having to work all your life!" Those remembered words either horrified us, challenged us to become something totally different, or became self-fulfilling prophesies. The subtle and insidious messages girls and women receive about their bodies—this is too big, that's too little, too many wrinkles here, need a tuck there—cripple self-esteem and inhibit the ability to truly feel pleasure and enjoy life to its fullest.

We are speaking not only of sexual pleasure, but also the pleasure of experiencing the world through senses that are totally awake. How often do we allow ourselves to sit down to a meal, the food beautifully presented, enjoying the variety of colors, textures, smells, and tastes, and truly savor each mouthful with no thought of whether we should eat it or not, because it is high in fat, sugar, or cholesterol? Can we truly feel the caress of a cool breeze on our hot skin, or be aware of that inner surge of feeling when we meet someone we are wildly attracted to?

Sixth-grade girls who count every calorie they eat for fear of gaining an ounce, are destined to view their body as an enemy. Constantly comparing, constantly checking, constantly fearful that her body betrays her imperfections, a girl's viewpoint becomes constricted, her senses grow confined, her feelings shut down. She loses her source of intuition, her inner guidance system that tells her the truth about how she feels about what happens to her and around her. The psychological costs of these losses in girlhood become dissatisfaction, indecision, vulnerability, a feeling of isolation, loneliness, and a lack of spontaneity and joy in adulthood.

The messages from culture about body image are projected almost anywhere a girl looks. The lady on the Black Velvet billboards lounges larger than life above the freeways. Television commercials—louder, more colorful, and faster-paced to catch the eye—are especially persistent in their appeal to young girls to be more popular by using this soap, wearing these jeans, choosing that lipstick. Movies and children's programs feature hip kids with trendy fashions, and a girl whose figure is average or large is portrayed as either funny, unpopular, or neurotic.

Magazines for women and teens carry more ads for cosmetics and beauty fashion than articles, and according to a survey cited by writer Carol Tavris in her provocative book *The Mismeasure of Women*, women's magazines put more emphasis on weight and body image than do men's magazines. An analysis of forty-eight issues of popular women's magazines revealed sixty-three ads for diet foods; there was one ad in the same number of men's magazines. Articles in women's magazines discussing body shape or size numbered ninety-six; for men, there were eight such articles.[15]

> *My dad commented constantly on every woman's body. We'd be driving in the car, see a woman walking down the street, and he'd say, "Look at those watermelons fighting it out. She could stand to lose some weight." Right in front of my mom he'd say, "Wow! Look at that beauty. Now there's a fine specimen!" I could die,*

especially if a friend of mine was in the car with us. My mom never said a word, but she was really rigid about what she ate.

—Jane, twenty-two

Early in life females get the message that the body's natural shape, smell, coloring, and size is never quite right unless they use certain products, maintain the right weight, and wear the "in" clothes. The tyranny of the fashion and cosmetics industries and the popular media campaigns to sell products contribute to the rise in eating disorders among girls and young women, to the increase in cosmetic surgery, and the burgeoning number of breast implants, despite the well-documented dangers and side-effects. The extreme loss of connection with the body, as manifested in anorexia, splits families apart in their quest for what went wrong with their daughters and how to live with the terrible guilt they carry.

Our daughter was always high-strung. She cried continuously her first five months of life. I've never really known how to be close to her, but her teen years were the worst. Her mother and I nearly lost her after she stopped eating, and we didn't really understand her problem. All we could think was, "What did we do wrong?" She was always a beautiful child, and we told her often enough, but she just couldn't see it after she turned fourteen. We were shocked when the doctor told us she was slowly starving herself to death. Thank God we found out in time to find someone to help her.

—Leo, father of Justine, twenty

There is probably no way to shield a daughter completely from society's messages about the perfect female body, short of putting her to sleep and surrounding the castle with a forest of thorns as in the Sleeping Beauty. Rather than rigidly protecting her until she can be delivered up to some handsome Prince Charming, we can teach her to think for herself about what is a healthy weight and body shape, help her develop good eating habits, and provide opportunities to find exercise that's fun and builds competence. She learns these attitudes and habits most easily if parents and older siblings model these behaviors for her. We will discuss specific ways to help daughters develop a healthy body image in Chapters Nine through Twelve, when we explore what girls need from birth through seventeen. Family attitudes, choice of toys, media programming, and children's literature are discussed to provide practical ideas to allow daughters to be confident and in touch with their growing bodies.

Menstrual Taboos

The saddest result of culture's "be perfect" body image is that girls learn to reject their bodies' natural beauty, function, and purpose. The early philosophers spoke of the body as a house or temple for the soul, and ancient cultures worshipped the feminine form because of its spiritual, life-giving powers. Our culture's body-worship has evolved into the quest for the young, tanned, smooth, large-breasted, small waisted, difficult-to-achieve form, which never sweats, develops blemishes, wrinkles, or menstruates.

Past cultures recognized the occurrence of the menarche as a rite-of-passage in the life of a girl. Menstruation rituals—the blood mysteries—were an intricate part of village life. It is likely that women's menstrual cycles correlated with the cycles of the seasons and the moon, and were occasions for celebration and worship.[16] Menstruation was recognized and either feared or honored, but not denied. Family therapist Linda Riley, writes, "In these societies, women were not afraid of themselves or of each other. There were no good and bad images of the feminine; monthly cycles were not looked upon as evil; women did not experience themselves as being devalued members of their society...all aspects of themselves were honored."[17]

Few of the attitudes and practices are left from the cultures which respected the cyclical waxing and waning of a girl's energies. Today in our culture the subject of the menstrual cycle is taboo—among women, girls, and within families. This contributes to the widespread symptoms associated with premenstrual tension or syndrome (PMS) and menstruation itself.

According to Susan M. Lark, M.D., more than 150 PMS symptoms have been documented. The following is a list of some of the more common ones:

irritability	acne	anxiety
boils	mood swings	allergies
depression	hives	hostility
cystitis	migraine headaches	urethritis
backaches	less frequent urination	dizziness
asthma	abdominal bloating	fainting
sore throat	tremulousness	rhinitis
hoarseness	joint pain and swelling	constipation
weight gain	breast tenderness and swelling	
sugar craving	cramps[18]	

My period came when I was only eleven, and I was devastated. My mother seemed nervous and didn't really want to talk about it, and my father totally ignored me. My brothers snickered and made faces of disgust at me when they found out. I felt dirty and angry at my body for betraying me. Before that "curse," I had been like the boys—riding horses, swimming, climbing trees. Always at "that time of the month," I got depressed, and I still do. I feel really low, as though I lost something precious back then; maybe my freedom, or self-respect.

—May, forty-five

When young girls learn to see their bodies as an enemy, a monthly battle is waged inside. Jungian theorist Ann Ulanov suggests that the degree with which a female is in tune with her monthly cycles affects her experiences, moods, and capabilities. She writes:

At ovulation, a woman's body is receptive and fertile. She may then feel an emotional expansiveness, an abundance of sexual energy, a new potency in her creative ideas and insights. If her ego is not in touch with this phase of her cycle, she often squanders her energy in increased busyness or talkativeness, or perhaps in nervous flirtations. If she is related to what is happening in her body and psyche, this time of the month can give her increased confidence and new certainty in her own capacities. . . . At menstruation . . . a woman often feels an in-gathering of her energy and feelings to a deeper center below the threshold of consciousness. If estranged from that center, a woman experiences this phase as a 'curse,' as moodiness, as oversensitivity and pain and irritability. If she is in accord with herself, this phase can be a time of developing fertile insights, new relationships, or creative possibilities suddenly opened to her during ovulation.[19]

And in *A Circle of Stones*, Judith Duerk asks us to consider how our lives would be enhanced if we had been encouraged to embrace this physical change.

How might your life have been different, if, as a young woman, there had been a place for you, a place where you could go to be with women? A place where you could be received as you strove to order your moments and your days.

A place where you could learn a quiet centeredness . . . to help you ground yourself in daily patterns that would nurture you through their gentle rhythms . . . a place where, in the stillness at the ending of a task, you could feel an ancient presence flowing out to sustain you . . . and you learned how to receive and to sustain it in return.

How might your life be different?[20]

Clearing away the menstrual taboos means seeing our daughters fully. It is especially difficult for us to see them as sexual beings, but the waxing and waning of the menstrual cycle throughout a woman's life is part of the fundamental nature of her being. Not to recognize that such a powerful, cyclical force wields tremendous impact on a female and all those around her is to stand in the middle of a cyclone and not notice the wind is blowing. In the four chapters dealing with age-specific issues, we explore practical ways to support daughters as they deal with the onset of menstruation and how to accept it as a powerful part of family life.

Living in an Unsafe World

Aware of the real dangers our daughters face in a violent culture, we parents begin early to clip away at those parts of a girl we fear will get her in trouble. By the time she enters the transition into sexual maturity, we hope she knows how to keep from getting hurt.

> *I want my daughter to be safe, to avoid the hurt and shame I felt as a teenager growing up in my neighborhood, so I taught her to be nice, to smile, be agreeable, and helpful. My husband always says he doesn't like "mouthy women," and I figure he's like most men, so I don't interfere when he punishes her for being angry or talking back.*
>
> —*Janie, mother of Trish, sixteen*

The truth is we set up girls to be victims by expecting them to be nice, compliant, and helpful, rather than confident, competent, and assertive. Knowing what she wants and being able to say "No!" can be a girl's best defense. Chiori Santiago, an award-winning column writer for a family magazine, defines the usual process of trying to make girls safe. "As teenagers, boys earn more freedom and privileges, girls become more cloistered. Boys cruise around at night; girls must stay home. Boys take the bus alone; girls must not. Boys are taught to face the world with courage; girls are taught to view it with fear."[21]

We are not advocating "throwing all caution to the wind." The threat of physical harm is real for girls and women. Accurate statistics on sexual crimes are difficult to obtain, but all findings indicate an alarming and growing problem in our culture. Various studies estimate that 3.5 to 15 percent of all women will be raped,[22] and the East Bay Rape Crisis Center in Oakland, California, reports that the chances of being sexually assaulted before a girl reaches her eighteenth birthday are one in four.[23] Other studies predict that one in four women will be sexually assaulted on university campuses during their college years.[24]

Sexual harassment begins early for girls. Fifty-four percent of Berkeley High School's female students reported being sexually harassed while at school.[25] This was from a small sample—1,246 students—but we suspect this high school is typical of other urban schools across the country. That our daughters must endure pinching, grabbing, persistent requests for dates, and suggestive comments in a place where they are required by law to be and where they spend a great amount of their time, seems degrading if not criminal. Just hearing these statistics could make even the most stouthearted of us want to hide out at home. Imagine what this information says to girls about how the world views females; as objects to be used and manipulated through the use of threat, fear, and violence.

How do we begin to make the world a safer place for our daughters to grow and thrive? Let's go back to our working definition of competence: "...the acquisition of competence involves looking at society and figuring out what skills will enable you to survive—and thrive—in that society."[26] OK. We have looked at our society and found it violent against girls and women. How do we help daughters develop the competence to deal with this fact? We begin with the girl and work outward.

Girls must develop a sense of strength and power. Remember the feeling of confidence that floods your body after struggling with a problem and suddenly solving it? A small girl exudes a new confidence when she can do something by herself for the first time. A political leader can instill loyalty in her constituents simply through a persona of authority and confidence. Studies reveal that people can either invite or discourage a mugging just by their manner of walking down the street.[27] Walking along with one's "head in the clouds," a certain timidness, or appearing apologetic about taking up sidewalk space are open invitations to an assault. We do not at all mean to imply that a victim is to blame for her assault. However, a woman who walks along the street exuding an awareness of her own strength and of the world around her discourages potential attackers.

Two cultural beliefs cripple our daughters' sense of strength and power: girls are helpless and, therefore, need our protection, and girls are fragile and must be handled with care. If we believe girls need our protection, we fail to teach them to rely on their own inner resources in times of trouble. If we believe they are fragile, we will not challenge them to do their best.

The idea of protection concerning girls is a tricky thing. There's protection and there's Protection. All girls need their parents' protection in different amounts at various ages. As infants and toddlers we protect them from harsh lights, from loud noises, from swallowing small objects, from falling, from cold, from hunger, from learning about the hard realities of life too soon, and so on. As they grow older we do our best to protect them from traffic by teaching them safety rules about crossing the street; from being kidnapped and molested by cautioning them about suspicious strangers, unsafe areas, and insisting they travel in a group. We educate them about the dangers of alcohol and drug addiction and unsafe sexual practices. This parental protection enables our daughters to thrive in relative safety, enhancing their chances of growing into a healthy adulthood.

Protection with a capital *P*, or what some have labeled *overprotection*, separates girls from themselves and limits the development of self-reliance—the knowledge that if all else fails, they can depend upon their own inner resources to do what is necessary. Girls learn self-reliance through thinking, planning, and acting on their own initiative. Too often this process is thwarted by premature assistance and advice from parents and teachers. We foster the development of self-reliance by supporting our daughters' efforts and showing confidence in their abilities. The biggest mistake a father can make is to jump in too quickly, criticize how his daughter is doing a project, and take over to finish it. Girls may approach a problem differently than boys but end up with the same result. Realizing there is no right or wrong way to do something, rather effective and ineffective ways, allows us to step back and give daughters room to experiment a little, to find their own way without the pressure of doing something just right. A wise father watches how his daughter is progressing, gives encouragement, and offers assistance for her to accept or decline as she goes along.

According to research completed by psychologists Mary Field Belenky, Blythe McVicker Clinchy, Nancy Rule Goldberger, and Jill Mattuck Tarule, boys are rewarded for exploring and risk-taking and girls are rewarded for being quiet, predictable, unimaginative, obedient, and conforming.[28] Although these behaviors make a little girl easy to be around, they do not prepare her for living life. Faced with inevitable life choices, such as what peer group to join, when to become sexually active and with whom, what career directions to embark upon, and how to commit to a life mate, girls are handicapped if they have not tested their strength of will on the small stuff. Being allowed to risk making mistakes enables girls to learn they can handle the consequences. They realize the world won't end, and they won't lose our love. With this confidence and sense of their own power, they will be able to say "No" to drugs, "No" to the wrong crowd, and "No" to sex before they are ready. And just as importantly, they can say "Yes!" to what they want in life.

Girls must develop physical competence. The unconscious belief that girls are fragile motivates us to be overly cautious about our daughters' physical abilities. We may have mixed feelings about encouraging them to excel in areas that until recently have characeristically been a boy's domain. The episode in the classic story, *Anne of Green Gables*, when Anne takes a dare to walk across the gable of her house and falls,[29] either gives us the shudders, or secretly reminds us of the thrill of our own childhood feats of daring. Either way, we need to monitor our instinctual urge to caution our daughters to be careful.

> *My brother was always into things—climbing on tables to reach the pretties on high shelves. Upon discovering him, my mother would throw up her arms, shrug, and bring him back to earth with a sigh that said she had resigned herself to a boy's nature. However, when my love of heights took me to the top of the jungle gym or the backyard tree, she stood beneath me with arms outstretched as though to catch me, or hands over her mouth as if to stifle a scream. All the while she gave a running, cautionary commentary— "watch your step, not so high, don't look down"—until I lost the excitement of my adventure.*
>
> *—Maryanne, twenty-nine*

Most boys are encouraged and expected to participate in team sports and other physical activities. Girls need and deserve these experiences, too. Physical strength and ability give girls confidence in themselves, and the mastery of new skills enhances self-esteem.

Because some girls are not naturally as physically active as boys tend to be, they may need our encouragement in finding a sport they love. Some girls relish the competition of team sports and others may not, so following our daughter's lead is important. She may be inclined toward the more individual sports of swimming, golf, tennis, the martial arts, track, or gymnastics, rather than baseball, soccer, or basketball.

Self-confidence and physical fitness are powerful talismans against abuse. Also paramount is some kind of self-defense class for every girl at the appropriate age. This training will not ensure our daughters' safety, but it will give them an advantage they would not otherwise have. Graduates of BAMM, Bay Area Model Mugging, an organization that teaches self-defense classes to women, assert they feel safer in the world and more empowered.

> *I had to push my own limits in BAMM and discover where my strengths are. I learned to set boundaries with people in new ways, and learning to say "No" carried over into other areas of my life. I can tell my boss when he's taking advantage of my time, and I don't feel I have to be on call to do everything my mother wants like I used to. I'm more in charge of my life now.*
>
> *—Donna, twenty-two*

Most boys learn how to fight and how to fall as they grow up. Erika Bunin, BAMM graduate, asserts that how to fight is "taught out of girls. We're told not to fight, because we're weak and fragile so we're more likely to get hurt if we fight an attacker. Contrary to that belief, statistics show that any determined effort to fight back, like screaming and kicking, is a deterrent to being assaulted. Most people don't stop to realize that women have more strength in their legs than most men do in their upper bodies. BAMM teaches us how to take advantage of that strength against an opponent."[30]

Girls must learn to deal with anger. Behind anger constantly lurks the possibility of violence. For this reason, women and girls often fear anger—their own and others—and they have learned to become either helpless in the face of it or depressed.

> *No one was ever angry in my family. You just didn't show it. If I cried I usually got sympathy, but if I yelled I got the cold shoulder. Now, I fall to pieces if anyone gets angry at me. I spend lots of time making sure it never happens. I can't bear to be ignored or left alone.*
>
> *—Sharon, thirty-one*

Anger is a powerful indicator that something is wrong. Without its helpful warning signal, a girl is powerless to understand what happened, to voice her feelings about it, to ask for help, or to muster the courage to do something to change it. Our culture's stereotypes of the angry woman as witch, hag, shrew, bitch, or nag go far to stifle full expression of women's fury. Allowing our daughters to feel and express their anger enables them to have access to more of their feeling life. When we are out-of-touch with any deep emotion, we often eat rather than yell, drink alcohol rather than cry, shop on "maxed out" credit cards rather than feel our anxiety, and become involved in unhealthy sexual relationships rather than acknowledge our loneliness.

Anger is a strong emotion, an important ally in a girl's inner guidance system. Chapter Seven explores the mobilizing power of anger, and how we parents can help our daughters use and handle its energy as a positive, empowering force.

Girls must develop a voice. We hear a lot these days from the psychological circles studying the development of women and girls about listening to girls' voices and helping women recover their true voices. The silencing of women by patriarchal culture over thousands of years has inflicted a wound so deep that we are just now beginning to recover from its impact. Women's voices were silenced in the home when they became the property of Man, the "Householder." Women's voices were silenced in the community when they were prohibited from owning land or shops and from speaking or writing publicly. Their voices were silenced in the Church where only male priests were anointed. During the Middle Ages, women were burned as witches because of their healing powers and herbal wisdom. To live and survive in a modern patriarchal culture, women have continued to silence themselves to please others, to keep the peace, and to meet the all-consuming needs of family, friends, and community. The loss of women's voices has led to the sacrifice of women's selves.

Through the valuable work of Jean Baker Miller, M.D., others at the Stone Center, Wellsley College, and Carol Gilligan, Ph.D., Director of The Harvard Project on Women's Psychology and Girls' Development, we are finally empowering women and girls to take off culture's patriarchal muzzle and speak the truth about the reality of their experiences. Dr. Gilligan, in her groundbreaking research of adolescent girls, speaks of the point in adolescence when girls must go underground, must silence their voices, must take parts of themselves out of relationship to stay in relationship.[31] In Chapter Eleven we discuss how parents can support teenage girls through this process.

Is this loss of voice inevitable for girls, or can we parent in ways that enable them to talk about how they feel, about what they experience, about what is important to them in their lives? Because relationships are a primary source of self-esteem for girls and women, daughters need to know they will not lose our love if they speak up for what they want or tell us how they feel about things. This trust develops from the day they are born. Teaching girls to make specific requests, rather than being indirect and agreeable, will help them avoid the pitfalls of having to be manipulative and calculating to get what they want.

> *My husband complains I can't tell him straight out what is bothering me or what I want. He's right. I'm just like my mom. Whenever she wants something, she's totally indirect. She'll say, "Is it hot in here?" rather than, "Please turn down the furnace. I'm too warm." Instead of telling my husband what I want to do on a Friday night, I'll ask him what he wants, say "Oh, all right," and then feel resentful that I didn't get to do what I really wanted.*
>
> *—Wilma, thirty-five*

We may have to stretch ourselves to be more open to hearing the truth of our daughters' realities. Children are often brutally truthful. We are not suggesting girls be allowed to vent their feelings upon others with no consideration of the effects. Rather, we are talking about the things girls see that our culture deems invisible. A wonderful example of this is quoted by Dr. Carol Gilligan from a paper written by one of her research participants. Anna, a fourteen-year-old girl writes, "Wouldn't there have been a lot of animal stuff on Noah's Ark after forty days?" [32]

Girls Can't Do Math

In the early 1880's, the widespread belief that higher education was detrimental to a girl's health, prevented many aspiring students from attending college. Those whose parents were of a more liberal mind studied at home or attended a school for young ladies, such as Sarah Pierce's Litchfield Female Academy, where they learned how to be virtuous young wives or perhaps teachers. A proper education of the times included watercolor painting and fine needlework, and a rare schoolmistress like Sarah Pierce also required her students to study ancient history, Latin, and Greek.[33]

The times and educational practices have changed, of course, but an extensive report, compiled by the American Association of University Women (AAUW), concludes that girls are still at a dis-advantage in today's educational system.[34] According to this report, the belief that girls and boys have identical experiences in school is entirely erroneous. Several key practices and situations promote gender inequity.

Teachers give girls less attention in the classroom. Various research shows that classroom teachers not only call on boys more often than girls, but they listen when boys call out the answers. When girls call out the answers, they are typically told to raise their hands or to wait until they are called upon. African-American girls are recog-nized even less than white girls, despite their more frequent attempts to initiate interactions.[35] Because teachers assume girls will be conscientious students, they tend to encourage boys more often by commenting on their work, offering suggestions, and giving praise.

When girls need help, some teachers either complete the project for them or tell a girl to ask another student for help. This can be especially discouraging for girls, who thrive educationally on relational interactions with teachers.

> *Boys get more attention from the teacher, because they get in trouble more. Sometimes they're talking to another person; sometimes they shout out the answers; and they're always pushing, shoving, and cutting in line.*
>
> —*Kristen, nine*

Education becomes a spectator sport for girls.[36] Too often girls form a quiet background for the activity of the classroom and are encouraged to assume the supporting roles of listeners, supporters, and helpers. Experience and practice in being leaders, committee chairs, and solo performers give girls the self-esteem and confidence to actively participate in their education and in directing their own lives. Sadly, the research indicates that girls are too often left out of the action in too many classrooms.

Two distinct curriculums are taught in school. We are all aware of the academic curriculum—reading, writing, and arithmetic—taught in our daughters' schools. There is a second, hidden, and often biased curriculum taught as well.[37] This second curriculum teaches children traditional, sex-role behavior. These behaviors are subtly reinforced and go unnoticed by most of us.

Comments such as, "The girls may go first, because they've been very quiet," keep girls in confined, expected roles, limiting their choices of response. The casual treatment by school personnel of the sexual harassment of girls in schools, such as "Boys will be boys," sends a harmful message to both girls and boys: "Girls are not worthy of respect," and "It's OK for boys to wield aggressive power over girls." The encouragement of rough, competitive games between girls and boys leave many girls on the sidelines for several reasons. Teachers often fail to teach girls the fundamentals of sports that enhance confidence, build competence, and increase the desire to play. Because many girls lack the early training that makes them "at home" in their bodies, they feel overwhelmed by games that go too fast and are dominated by players with greater skill. Too often, teachers fail to equalize play opportunities and team memberships in order to make the girls' experience more positive and successful.

Girls are left out of or isolated from the curriculum material. According to Alicia Hetman, AAUW California Division Educational Equity Task Force Chair and classroom teacher, there is an imbalance in the selection of topics that interest girls. For example, standard history texts feature wars and weapons, often of great interest to boys but arousing little enthusiasm in girls.[38] Girls and women, themselves, are visibly absent from the chronicle of historical events, and the relational details of the lives of people who made history—of great interest to girls—are neglected.

The portrayal of girls and women in many school texts perpetuate the stereotypes that limit and inhibit the full human development of females in our culture. First readers continue to depict boys as the adventurers, heroes, and leaders, and girls as care-givers, followers, and homebodies. In addition, studies reveal that the use of nonsexist and multicultural materials enhance learning for all students.[39] Sadly, a 1989 study of the books most frequently assigned in public high school English classes found that only one in ten was written by a woman and none was written by a writer from a minority group.[40]

Different expectations for girls affect their performance in math and science. The gaps previously seen between boys and girls in math achievement have declined and continue to do so. In high school, however, boys continue to outnumber girls in advanced math classes and in top-scoring math groups. In science the differences in achievement between boys and girls are wide and show no signs of narrowing. Some researchers attribute the gender gap in science to different learning styles; boys are encouraged to explore, to take risks, and to learn from experience, all traits that enhance achievement in science education.[41]

Glimpses into the psyches of girls and boys reveal astonishing differences in their responses to achievement. When boys do well in math, for example, they attribute their success to talent, whereas girls credit their high marks to hard work and good study habits. Surprisingly, research shows parents believe the same thing. Many teachers, also, seem to think boys are naturally talented in math and science, and girls are naturally talented in reading, indicated by the extra attention given to boys during math and science classes and to girls during reading classes.[42]

We find it interesting that the differences in math and science achievement between girls and boys do not hold up cross-culturally. It seems math achievement is not considered unfeminine in the Japanese-American, native Hawaiian, and Filipino-American cultures, where girls experience less negative peer pressure and are encouraged by parents to pursue math and science careers.[43] In Asian-American cultures it is assumed that both girls and boys have the capacity to do well in math and science, and achievement is attributed to effort more than talent.

Girls from minority families are especially at risk in school. Minority girls confront racism as well as sexism, and girls from low-income families must also face schools in dangerous neighborhoods, low expectations from teachers, poor health care, and inadequate nutrition. Study after study reveal that more than any other variable, a girl's socioeconomic level predicts her educational success.[44]

Some studies of minority families suggest that black and Hispanic families especially value cooperation and group interaction, whereas the American educational system stresses competition and individualism, thus putting girls from these cultures at an even greater disadvantage.[45] Multicultural representation within the school curriculum is limited, and most girls from minority groups fail to find their lives reflected in educational materials, lesson plans, or learning activities. Additional studies of classroom treatment reveal that teachers give minority students of both sexes less attention, thus decreasing self-esteem and the desire to be part of classroom activities.[46]

Low self-esteem contributes to other factors affecting the academic success of minority girls. Some studies link the incidence of early pregnancy with low self-esteem,[47] and since 1988 there has been a rise in teen pregnancy, almost entirely among Hispanic and black girls between fifteen and seventeen.[48] Dorotha Hogue, an award-winning teacher from Denver, Colorado, describes the fate of some of her students, "Pregnancy is only one of the things our students have to deal with. Most have been victims all their lives—victims of poverty, of physical, sexual, and emotional abuse."[49]

Accurate school dropout statistics are difficult to acquire, and minority girls who do drop out give various reasons. Female dropouts among all ethnic groups have much higher poverty rates than male dropouts, and girls more often than boys give "family-related problems" as the reason for dropping out. One study revealed that having a large number of siblings and a mother with a low level of education are reasons why girls leave school.[50] Yet, the most common reasons given by girls who drop out are school-related.[51] Poor grades, lack of teacher interest or support, and feeling left out of school culture, including peer groups as well as school curricula, all contribute to failure in school and low incentive to continue.

Parents, teachers, and other respected adults have more influence on girls than peer groups. We know that once our daughters reach adolescence, a dramatic shift occurs, from wanting to achieve academically to a focus on appearance, friendships, and boys. This change can affect crucial educational and career choices our daughters are likely to make. Without our interest, involvement, and guidance they may be influenced to choose nonchallenging or ill-fitting classes and careers by well-meaning but biased peers, teachers, or career counselors.

> *Susan's father encouraged her to be an engineer like he was. She was good in math and science, and engineering would be a solid, exciting career for a bright, ambitious young woman like his daughter. She listened carefully to him but never really considered becoming an engineer. "Girls didn't do that, and I didn't want to be one of the girls who did . . . engineering isn't for women." At least this was the message she received from her numerous teachers throughout her schooling: You're a girl; don't worry about math and science. Girls don't need those things; let the boys master those subjects.[52]*

> *—Susan Bailey, Director*
> *Wellesley College Center for Research on Women*

The best way to help girls in math and science is to have an open mind about their abilities and to be encouraging from the beginning. Natural scientists, young children literally soak up how the world works. When we allow ourselves to see the world through their eyes, we awaken again to the power of wonder and curiosity. Sharon Jadrnak Luck, director of the Women in Engineering Program at Penn State University, asserts that girls learn best from hands-on activities and experiences with bird feeders, aquariums, ant farms, gardens, cameras, telescopes, magnets, and magnifying glasses.[53] Allowing girls to get dirty, ask questions, take risks, and experiment on their own builds a sense of mastery that will carry them through the toughest chemistry lab test or calculus course.

A good mathematics foundation involves learning how to think about a problem and plotting the steps for solving it. Schools and parents are often guilty of forgetting that the "how" of doing something is really more important than the answer. It's the same principle as the practice of teaching a hungry person how to fish, rather than giving her a fish. With fishing skills she can always get herself something to eat. To enhance math ability, girls need games and toys that develop spatial abilities, such as blocks, puzzles, dominoes, Legos, checkers, chess, model kits, origami materials, and hand tools. Parents can bring math and science home by showing daughters how they are used in daily life, such as balancing a checkbook or cooking a meal.

When asked why he thought girls' math scores plummet around age twelve and thirteen, Fred, father of Sarah, thirteen, and Elaine, eleven, said definitely, "The answer is simple: They don't want to put the effort into it! There are so many other distractions—boys, girlfriends, MTV. They don't think that it's important. I tell them it is important. You've got to learn it. Whether you use it or not, is not important at this point, but you learn it, so you have the ability to use it as a tool. Don't put yourself a step below Johnny over here, because Johnny has to grow up to be a rocket scientist, and you're just going to go home and make babies. Baloney! That's not the way it's going to be."

Here again it becomes a question of competence. What does our daughter—who is like no other daughter—need to live a happy, satisfying life? Will being competent in math or science help her fulfill her dreams and contribute her share to an ailing world? Trying to make her excel in a subject she isn't interested in is different from requiring competence. Forcing her to be something she is not, will only foster resentment and rebellion. If a daughter hates math and her natural talents seem to lie in other directions, let us teach her how to get the math job accomplished. Maybe she will have to hire someone to do her taxes, or ask her "significant other" to be responsible for balancing the checkbook each month. Either way, she is taking care of business. We have taught her how to get things done.

> *I want my girls to get by on their smarts. If they need to use their charm, if they need to use their wit, in the appropriate location, fine. I've used my charm to get by in certain situations. But, I don't want my girls to use it as a means of survival. Sometime that charm's going to wear off. It's like a football player who's the best on the field for ten years, and afterwards, since he flunked out of college because he never went to class, runs a liquor store or sells used cars the rest of his life. I don't want my girls to have to do that or rely on some guy to take care of them.*

> *—Fred, father of two girls*

We celebrate the diversity of choices our daughters have to create full and interesting lives that reflect the true nature of their beings. Our sometimes challenging, always fascinating job is to help them discover who they are. In times past, parents relied on cultural norms and values to guide them in raising their children to be active and responsible members of society. Today, cultural norms and values change so rapidly that modern parents often feel adrift in a very large sea without a chart to guide them safely through the unpredictable waters of our daughters' lives. Parenting in these modern times demands deep introspection to clarify what we value.

What do we want in our own lives?

Are we living our dreams?

Do we feel creative, productive, of service, fulfilled, truly alive?

Can we model a life we are proud of living for our daughters?

Children are naturally drawn to the current values and fads of the day, and they demand to participate in them with their friends. When our values conflict with the cultural norms, we are called upon to take bold and audacious steps to hold tight to what we truly believe is right for our families, making the necessary changes for our living to be more in alignment with our dreaming. Reaching out to other parents for support can be just the life preserver we need during family-daughter storms. A supportive relationship between Mom and Dad and a clear understanding of these unique, individual roles in a daughter's development foster a safe journey toward adulthood.

Endnotes

1. Olive Ann Burns, *Cold Sassy Tree* (New York: Dell Publishing, 1984), 249.

2. Emily Hancock, *The Girl Within* (New York: Fawcett Columbine, 1989), 3.

3. Caryl Rivers, Rosalind Barnett, and Grace Baruch, *Beyond Sugar and Spice: How Women Grow, Learn, and Thrive* (New York: Ballantine, 1979), 1–13.

4. Ibid., 3.

5. Carol Gilligan, "Joining the Resistance: Moments of Resilience in Women's Psychological Development," in an address to the Spring Foundation for Research on Women in Contemporary Society Conference, "The Resilient Woman: Struggle in the Face of Adversity," Stanford University, Palo Alto, CA, 25 Jan. 1992.

6. Celia Halas, *Why Can't a Woman Be More Like a Man?* (New York: Macmillan, 1981), 32.

7. Barbara G. Walker, *The Woman's Dictionary of Symbols and Sacred Objects* (San Francisco: Harper & Row, 1988), 226.

8. Ibid., 234.

9. Ibid.

10. Jean Shinoda Bolen, *Goddesses in Everywoman: A New Psychology of Women* (New York: Harper & Row, 1984), 174–175.

11. Marian Burros, "Women Still on Double Duty," San Jose Mercury News, 9 June 1993, sec. E.

12. Rivers, et al., *Beyond Sugar*, 90.

13. Jennifer Kintzing Cadoff, "How to Raise a Strong Daughter in a Man's World," McCalls, Feb. 1992, 60.

14. Elissa Koff and Jill Rierdan, "Perceptions of Weight and Attitudes Toward Eating in Early Adolescent Girls," Journal of Adolescent Health, June 1991, 307–312.

15. Carol Tavris, *The Mismeasure of Woman* (New York: Simon & Schuster, 1992), 32.

16. Penelope Shuttle and Peter Redgrove, *The Wise Wound: Myths, Realities, and Meanings of Menstruation* (New York: Bantam Books, 1990), 62.

17. Linda Riley, "Women's Developmental Stages by Way of the Blood Mysteries," Master's thesis, John F. Kennedy University, Orinda, CA, 1992.

18. Susan M. Lark, *PMS: Premenstrual Syndrome Self-Help Book* (Berkeley, CA: Celestial Arts, 1984), 19–20.

19. Ann Ulanov, *The Feminine in Jungian Psychology and in Christian Theology* (Evanston, IL: Northwestern University Press, 1971).

20. Judith Duerk, *A Circle of Stones* (San Diego, CA: Lura Media, 1989), 55.

21. Chiori Santiago, "Girl Power," Diablo Magazine, May 1993, 37.

22. Katherine Seligman, "Sex, Justice on Trial at Santa Cruz," San Francisco Examiner, 25 Jul. 1993, sec. A8.

23. East Bay Rape Crisis Center phone conversation with Jeanne Elium, Oakland, CA, 30 Jul. 1993.

24. Seligman, "Sex, Justice on Trial," A8.

25. Christine Whalen, "Harassing Starts Early," San Francisco Chronicle, 8 Mar. 1993, sec. B3.

26. Rivers, et al., *Beyond Sugar*, 3.

27. David Surrenda, Ph.D., in a Filipino martial arts class, John F. Kennedy University, Orinda, CA, Spring Quarter, 1983.

28. Mary Field Belenky, et al., *Women's Ways of Knowing: The Development of Self, Voice, and Mind* (New York: Basic Books, 1986), 65.

29. L. M. Montgomery, *Anne of Green Gables* (Toronto: Bantam Books, 1984).

30. Erika Bunin, Bay Area Model Mugging (BAMM) graduate, phone conversation with Jeanne Elium, Berkeley, CA, 10 Aug. 1993. To locate a self-defense class for women in your area, call Director Sharon Doran. BAMM (415) 592-7300.

31. Carol Gilligan, "Joining the Resistance."

32. Ibid.

33. Carole Owens, "To Ornament Their Minds," *Victoria Magazine*, Sept. 1993, 14.

34. The AAUW Report, *How Schools Shortchange Girls*, commissioned by the American Association of University Women Educational Foundation and researched by the Wellesley College Center of Research on Women, 1992, 2. To order, call (800)225-9998, ext. 91, or write the AAUW Sales Office, P.O. Box 251, Annapolis Junction, MD 20701-0251.

35. Ibid.

36. Alicia Hetman, "Taking the Initiative Towards Education Equity," an address to the second annual "Bridging the Gender Equity Gap" conference, Diablo Valley College, Pleasant Hill, CA, 6 Mar. 1993.

37. Raphaela Best, *We've All Got Scars: What Boys and Girls Learn in Elementary School* (Bloomington, IL: Indiana University Press, 1989).

38. Hetman, "Taking the Initiative."

39. AAUW, *How Schools Shortchange Girls*, 62.

40. Ibid.

41. Myra Sadker and David Sadker, *Failing at Fairness: How America's Schools Cheat Girls* (New York: Charles Scribner's Sons, 1994), 122–23.

42. Ibid.

43. The American Association of University Women, "Equitable Treatment of Girls and Boys in the Classroom," June 1989, 2. A brief included in the Initiative for Educational Equity packet. Order from the AAUW Sales Office, P.O. Box 251, Annapolis Junction, MD 20701-0251, (800)225-9998, ext. 91.

44. Ibid., 54.

45. Ibid., 3.

46. Ibid.

47. Ibid., 38.

48. Ibid., 37.

49. Ibid.

50. Ibid., 48.

51. Ibid., 49.

52. Renee Graham, "Carefully Taught," San Jose Mercury News, 1 Mar. 1992, sec. 1L.

53. Dianne Hales, "Future Female Scientists," *Working Mother*, Mar. 1991, 79.

Part II:

Parenting a
Daughter

CHAPTER FIVE

THE PARENTING PARTNERSHIP: MOTHERS & FATHERS WORKING TOGETHER

*...when I'm at the beginning of something
I am a fool.*[1]

—James Hillman

She says: You never do *anything* around the house!

He says: What do you mean?! I do the dishes; I pick up the kids; I mow the lawn!!!!

She says: There you go again, wanting medals and applause for helping out.

He says: I don't want medals! I'm just responding to your accusations about my not doing anything around the house.

She says: (Sigh) This isn't about *things*.

He says: (Looking a bit wild-eyed) If it isn't about *things*, why did you say I don't do *anything* around the house?

She says: You never listen to me. You're never here.

He says: What do you mean, never here??? I took off an extra day's work for a three-day weekend. I've been working on all these projects that have been sitting around because of how busy we are (He looks up in the middle of his sentence, and she is gone.)

She walks away feeling angry, hurt, and hopeless. He walks away feeling crazy, caught in a maze, his brain working overtime to figure out this mysterious *thing* that he isn't doing. If he wasn't here all weekend, where did she think he was?

Women and Men: Big Difference

The previous interaction holds a secret of why mothers and fathers, married or divorced, constantly fight. There are many variations, but the themes are the same: Women and men enter any situation with different expectations. Both assume they think alike. These big differences keep men from belonging in their families, feeling isolated and confused. These big differences keep women locked into being in charge of the home life, feeling isolated and angry. These interactions are played out generation after generation, perpetually passed down to daughter and to son.

Because of these big differences, both genders miss out on that satisfying feeling of teamwork, where each partner is aware of and responsible for doing what is needed to make the home life run smoothly, healthfully, and happily. Sons miss out on this training, and daughters grow up with low expectations of men, because their fathers lived on the fringes of family life. They watch their mothers run the show, their fathers helping when asked but rarely understanding how to assume partnership. As we discuss what a daughter needs from each of her parents, we must consider how these big differences affect the mother/daughter and the father/daughter relationships.

Same Situation, Different Thinking Styles

Men and women enter situations with different thinking modes, behavioral styles, and motivations. Men think in terms of *goals*, *objects*, and *tasks* to be done. The purpose of relationships and the reason for interaction is defined by the *goal*. When a man enters a room of people, he is there for a particular purpose. Whether it is social, personal, or career-oriented, he looks around, evaluates who might get in his way, who could help him reach his goal, and the best strategy to follow. He is in strategic-thinking mode.

Strategic

1- Of or relating to strategy

2- Important or essential in relation to a plan of action

3- Essential to the effective conduct of war

4- Highly important to an intended objective

5- Intended to destroy the military potential of an enemy

—The New American Heritage Dictionary

Women generally enter situations thinking about the group and the potential relationships. The group and these relationships are the focus out of which tasks and goals emerge and are achieved. When a woman enters a room of people, she notices the group, how she fits in, how the group relates, and the needs of individual members in relation to the group. Out of these concerns, goals are met. Strategic thinking occurs within the relationships in the group.

Relation

1- A logical or natural association between two or more things; relevance of one to another; connection

2- The connection of people by blood or marriage; kinship; a relative

3- The way in which one person or thing is connected with another

—The New American Heritage Dictionary

When women struggle to get things done, problems may arise, because their focus on group dynamics can override the strategic thinking and action necessary to reach a goal. When men struggle to get things done, their tendency to lead with strategic thinking can override relational thinking, the necessary attention people need in order to bond and to be motivated to move together toward goals.

This fundamental difference in how men and women tend to enter situations—goal/strategic/object focus vs. group/relational focus—is the misunderstood cause of most ongoing conflicts at home. Both genders believe they have the same priorities. It takes only a few sentences for communication to break down, leaving woman and man shocked, hurt, and feeling that the other is simply refusing to cooperate. They rarely really resolve the issues confronting them, leaving both in uneasy resignation. Usually, however, both woman and man, mother and father, are doing their best to cooperate from their own point of view.

DON | Early in our marriage, Jeanne complained I didn't do anything around the house, and she was right. Living as a single guy for twelve years is not good training ground for the routine of family life. My laundry rules—when the towel stands by itself, it's time to wash it—worked well when I was single. I always had plenty of time to walk on the beach, read a book, play tennis, or go out on a date. But, I was learning that family life required a different set of guidelines.

Being the liberated man I was, I decided to try to solve my wife's complaint by learning to do *things* around the house. After ten years, I knew how to clean kitchens, wax floors, fix stuck doors, wipe the counters down leaving no water standing, fold laundry, and clean the bathroom. Something was still missing, because occasionally, I still heard that I didn't do any*thing* around the house. I felt angry and defeated. What did she really want? I knew what I wanted—for her to be pleased with the *things* I did, to be more affectionate, and to be open to more sexual intimacy. I did care about the household stuff, but those *things* were connected to powerful drives, and these powerful drives could sometimes make interactions explosive.

JEANNE | Early in our marriage, I sometimes felt so overwhelmed I just wanted to live alone again. I was so tired of having to think for everyone. This is often the most frustrating aspect of family life. Don made these frantic, Herculean attempts to do things around the house. I appreciated his efforts, but he did them without considering what needed doing first, how it changed our routines, how our children's health was affected, and how special projects and events fit into the daily grind of home maintenance. I still felt responsible for the "shit work" and resigned to the probable fact that Don would never "get it."

DON I gave up. I feared this dilemma was a man-woman difference so huge that I was incapable of ever understanding or changing it. No heroic antics could save this situation, I thought.

JEANNE I, too, felt hopeless. Why did we repeat these predictable interactions? Was I just being too compulsive, needing everything to be just so? But, I didn't think it was just me, because I often heard other women complain about this very thing. I summoned my courage to talk with my women's circle for some clarity. "My husband acts like a teenager at home," I blurted out and burst into tears. I was shocked when the compassionate women in my group began to laugh. "Our husbands act like teenagers at home, too," they all agreed. Our discussion topic was set for the evening. I left for home feeling supported, understood, and hopeful, because of a statement from Kathy. "My husband and I have code words I use when he gets off track and into single focus. 'Group mind, remember group mind!'" she said. That phrase stuck with me.

DON When I heard the "all men are teenagers at home" story, I felt pretty angry and chagrined at the same time. Deep down, I wondered if maybe the women were right. I was determined to figure this out. Knowing that most men focus on things first and people second, I decided to consciously switch my thinking to group-mind mode for a day and see if it made any difference in how I felt within our family. I was astounded at the results. What follows is a comparison of how I operated before and after I understood group-mind thinking.

Feeding the Cat Before Group-Mind Thinking

On my way to the garage, I stumble over a basket of wet laundry, leaving it where it sits waiting to be taken out to the dryer. Once in the garage, I focus on the cat's dish, dump cat food in the dirty dish, ignore the empty water dish, throw empty cat food can near the recycling bin, and return to house. Perfect execution. My mission accomplished. Wife mad.

Feeding the Cat After Group-Mind Thinking

On my way to the garage, I notice the laundry is ready to be taken to the dryer, so I pick it up on my way out. Once in the garage, I put laundry in dryer, clean out vent, and turn dryer to appropriate setting. I clean out cat's food dish, dump in cat food, fill water dish, rinse can, put in recycling bin, and on my way out pick up some junk that had fallen off a shelf. Jeanne and I are partners in running our family.

I was just getting ready to take credit for this great discovery when I realized what we were dealing with. Jeanne was talking about *things* in a context of what the greater group needs. I was thinking about *things* in relation to individual goals and the tasks to be done—how men are taught to be in the world and at home. The solution wasn't where I thought it was—in more and better *things*. The solution was in a new way of thinking. Rather than coming home asking myself, "What task needs doing?", I now came home asking myself this crucial question: "What does our group need now?" Jeanne constantly thought about the needs of our whole family. The single grocery list in my hand was a product of her planning a week's worth of menus, choosing healthy food products, finding alternatives to nonrecyclable food containers, being cost-conscious, and keeping up with everyone's changeable likes and dislikes. My shift from task-focus to group-focus was the key.

JEANNE	Don was pretty elated after this discovery. I was hopeful, but skeptical. Many women function from group-mind thinking so naturally that it isn't an event. It is a way of being. I told Don to be careful. I knew the next thing he would probably do was to act as if he had discovered it for all humankind. That would anger me and a lot of other women. And I told him to warn his male friends and clients that their wives and girlfriends will also be skeptical at first.
DON	I was beginning to realize what Jeanne meant by wanting us to work together as leaders of our family. She automatically approached *things* from relational thinking—group mind— what did the whole family need day by day? And she wanted me to share that responsibility with her. My single focused, strategic-thinking mode left her to be on top of what we all needed to thrive, be happy, and function as a family. And until now, I had seen it as a "woman thing." No wonder she got angry, and no wonder I felt left out. It's not only a woman thing. It's my responsibility, too.

Belonging: Hearth vs. Hunt

The old line "A man's home is his castle," and the underlying message that he should be treated like a king in it, still lingers on in our culture. Ancient men were men of a tribe first and members of a family second. There was not the worry of where one belonged.

We do not advocate a return to the "good ol' days," but ancient gender roles were well-defined to meet the survival needs of the tribe, and members were valued for their contributions. Men knew their place as hunters and protectors, skillfully and proudly fulfilling their responsibilities. Women ingeniously tended the hearth, clothed the tribe, and nurtured the young, secure in the knowledge of their vital functions. Although we do not know for certain, we suspect there was little quibble over the fact that men did not help out around the hearth. They were not allowed to, just as it was taboo in many cultures for the women to hunt.

Hunt

1- to pursue (game) for food or sport

2- to search through (an area) for prey

3- to make use of (hounds, for example) in pursuing game

4- to pursue intensively so as to capture or kill

5- to seek out; search for

6- to drive out forcibly, especially by harassing; chase away

—The New American Heritage Dictionary

Like ancient man, men today are still programmed to function in goal-oriented groups at work, but it all breaks down once they arrive home. Although most modern men are endlessly busy at home, many feel like outsiders, and research shows it is still women who do most of the hearth-tending. [2]

hearth *('härth) n., home: a vital or creative center*

—Webster's Ninth New Collegiate Dictionary

Many mothers have built-in radar that tells them where their children are. Human life would have ceased to exist long ago without this innate capacity of relational thinking—the ability to consider the whole while doing many tasks at the same time. Men are predisposed to focus on the task, and each does so in varying degrees. Women are inclined to focus on the rhythm and interaction of the group and its environment, and some of us are better at this than others. Within this rhythm all sorts of *things* are accomplished. We are, of course, each well-adapted to the roles culture has assigned us, but we must expand our view of the big picture and extend beyond our defined roles, to develop group-mind thinking in whatever context we may find ourselves.

"Stirring the oatmeal" is an humble act—not exciting or thrilling. But it symbolizes a relatedness that brings love down to earth. It represents a willingness to share ordinary human life, to find meaning in the simple,

unromantic tasks: earning a living, living within a budget, putting out the garbage, feeding the baby in the middle of the night.[3]

—Robert Johnson, *We*

We no longer need to live within the tribal group to survive. Modern women and men are brought together into marriage and family out of a desire to belong, to be an active part of something bigger than themselves. We belong by finding the courage to learn new ways of relating to our families, by learning to "stir the oatmeal."

I'm amazed at the changes at our house, since my husband came home talking about "group mind." Jim's the same Jim, but we talk more about things, and he's joined me in the thinking about home and the kids. Actually, the kids noticed it first. Our teenager, Laurie, said to me, "What's with Dad? He seems more here or something." I told her to go ask him.

—*Anna, thirty-three*

The Role of Father in a Daughter's Life

Whatever you can do,
or dream you can do,
do it.
Boldness has genius,
power, and magic in it.
Begin it now.[4]

—Goethe

From the moment of birth, daughters need their fathers to recognize and embrace their dreams and ambitions. The world is open to them like never before, and fathers provide models of assurance and competence girls need to follow their hearts' desires. Fathers walk a fine line between valuing their daughters' feminine ways of being and drawing out their masculine qualities and abilities. Without both sides, daughters grow up with something essential missing. Fathers and daughters have important tasks ahead of them. From their fathers, girls learn about authority and power, competence, anger, the world of work, balance of relationships, money, risk-taking, follow-through, and self-esteem.

Breaking the Dangerous Arrangement

Not so long ago in our cultural history, daughters were presented to their fathers only after they were bathed, diapered, and dressed, adored objects to be admired and kissed on rosy cheeks before being sent off to Nanny in the nursery. Father was feared and revered, the head of the household, disciplinarian of the children and staff, and financial provider. He was protected from the children, because he was so tired when he returned home from work. This old arrangement distanced Daddy from the family, making him mysterious, powerful, and bigger than life. Time with him became special, because he was not part of the daily routine.

Today, fathers are emerging from this exiled place in family life. One study reported that sixty percent of fathers polled under the age of thirty-five, shape their career plans around family concerns.[5] More men realize that when fathers live on the fringes of family life, their daughters miss the masculine nurturing, guidance, and protection that only fathers can provide. Relating to a man who is aloof and uninformed about daily concerns sets up a dangerous pattern between not only fathers and daughters, but also with every other man a girl meets. Girls learn not to expect much more from their fathers than doing chores and projects around the home. As they grow, this expectation extends into their relationships with other men. This dangerous arrangement fosters disappointment, loneliness, and anger in daughters and feelings of inadequacy, frustration, and isolation in fathers. Many fathers are on the outside of their families and unable to be truly present in their daughters' lives. Daughters, trying to win the attention and affection they crave from this first, important man, learn to be coy, manipulative, and indirect.

> *I had often played on the beach with my daughter.*
> *We'd find a place where the waves weren't too big, and*

she'd dig in the sand while I read the newspaper. I always thought we were having a great time, but when I think of it now, I realize Lissel pestered me constantly, "Look at this, Daddy! Watch me dig this hole!" I'd nod, "Ummmm," and go back to my reading. Her voice would get more insistent, more whiny, until I'd say, "Okay! Time to pack up and go home." When Don told me about this group-mind thing, I decided to try it at the beach. I got down on my hands and knees and tried to look at my daughter's sand castle through her eyes. We built on it together for a few moments, and I felt great. Really connected to her in a new way. We were sharing something important to her. No whining. We were a team. Then I got sidetracked into digging a hole on my own, just enjoying the feel of the sand in my hands. I forgot Lissel was even there. Her whiny voice brought me out of it, and I tried to get back that shared feeling we had. We worked on that sand castle for an hour, and it seemed like only minutes. Lissel's eyes were shining when we stopped. I'm sure mine were, too!

—Bernard, father of Lissel, five

Bernard, the father in the previous story, initially related to his daughter from a single-focus mode. Single-focus thinking enables us to accomplish individual tasks and realize personal goals. Through it we are carried away into flights of fantasy, creative inspiration, spiritual insight, emotional clarity, and psychological renewal. We could not live without it. When we allow single-focus thinking to predominate, however, we distance ourselves from others. This dangerous arrangement creates chaos when fathers spend time with their daughters in the guise of "playing." Girls get tricked into thinking they will have their father's attention. When they discover they only have their physical presences, daughters feel deceived, incompetent, angry, unlovable, and somehow guilty. What did I do to lose my father's interest? How can I win it back? What do I need to change about myself to be more appealing, more interesting, more desirable?

We easily see where this questioning leads girls. Somehow they are at fault for their father's distance. They must not be good enough, smart enough, pretty enough, pleasing enough. Low self-esteem is one of the most predominant female experiences. It begins early in life, and it is directly linked to the quality of the father/daughter relationship.

A Father's Role from Birth to Age Seven

Men are more active than ever before in the lives of their families. We notice the numbers of fathers in our parenting workshops continually increase; Child Development Instructor Bob Zavala reveals that fathers fill a larger percentage of the educational classes at Los Medanos College, Pittsburg, California;[6] and booksellers note more men buy books on child-rearing than previously. This happy trend confirms that men view active fathering as a positive life-time goal. Learning to live within the core of family using the principles of group-mind thinking not only enriches the lives of fathers, but mothers and daughters, as well.

Between the ages from birth to seven, girls need infinite time, attention, and custodial care. Fathers who learn the art of diapering, holding, burping, rocking, looking deeply into baby's eyes, encouraging and applauding her first attempts to control her world, and playing "toss the baby in the air" with their full attention, reap huge rewards, and so do their daughters. Fathers, whether or not they feel confident in caring for their tiny girls in the beginning, give mothers a necessary relief by simply spending time with their babies.

I thought my wife was silly at first, always looking at the baby, smiling at her, responding to her every coo and grunt. Then I noticed that Carrie started smiling and kicking her feet whenever my wife walked in her room. She really responded to her. I didn't get the same reaction, so I started talking to Carrie, letting her grab my finger, rocking her. It wasn't long before she knew when I was around, putting up her little arms to be picked up. It felt wonderful!

—Jeff, father of Carrie, eighteen months

This early bonding adds new threads to a girl's growing tapestry of relationships. When fathers take part with mothers in their daughters' lives from the beginning, girls can bask in a balance of both the masculine and feminine ways of being. A girl's beginning years are spent absorbing the relationships around her, and her patterns of interacting with others reflect what she sees in her own family, between Mom and Dad. Her early sense of who holds the power and authority within the home and family determines how a girl feels about her own self-worth. Daughters thrive when parents have equal input into important family-life decisions. Fathers must consider and become involved in decisions about:

Child care—Who will be primary caretaker? Can one or both of us work at home? If we must use day care, how do we choose the best one? How are family needs and career demands reconciled?

Discipline—Do both parents share similar child-rearing philosophies? What do we do when we disagree? Do we fight in front of our daughter?

Toys—What is the purpose of play in a girl's life? What toys are okay for girls? What values do toys teach her? When do we buy her toys? How do we choose positive image books? Who reads to her?

Television—What are family rules regarding TV viewing? How do we feel about the effects of television on young children? What cultural values does TV teach our daughter, and are they okay with us?

Education—How do we want our daughter to be educated? Do we strongly endorse the "three R's" or do we believe in an integrated system including the fine arts, music, dance, and languages? Do we believe in public or private schooling?

Family health—What medical approaches do we endorse for our daughter? Do we believe in vaccinations and the widespread use of antibiotics? Who takes her to the doctor? Who stays home when she is ill?

Spirituality—What religious principles should we teach our daughter? How do we answer her questions about God? How do we celebrate our spiritual beliefs?

Family holidays—How do we observe Christmas? Hanukkah? Halloween? Easter? Passover? What family traditions are important? How are birthdays celebrated?

Family routines and rhythms—What bedtime rituals shall we share with our daughter—a bedtime story, prayers, lighting a candle, sharing memories from the day? How shall we help her greet each new day—a prayer, special breakfast, cuddling in bed?

Family meals—Who cooks? Do we sing or say a grace together? How do we choose a healthy diet? How can we teach her to have a good body image? How do family members use food?

Family chores—How is the division of labor divided? What chores are appropriate for a girl and when should she start? Should an allowance be connected with family chores?

We all have our own family issues to consider and negotiate. Rather than assuming that mothers are the ones to stay home with a sick girl, or that fathers should choose their daughters' form of schooling, parents must find what works best for their families, no matter the prevailing cultural attitudes. Parental agreement on the issues of family life requires time, openness, flexibility, the willingness to let go of old family patterns, and the courage to challenge cultural stereotypes and expectations.

Although great changes occurring in the last several decades allow girls and women greater freedom to be more themselves, fathers must question their own gender-bias issues. Do we believe our daughters should aspire to become whatever they choose? Or do we really feel a "woman's place is in the home?" Do we believe in equal opportunities in education? Or do we shudder when we think of a girl on the boys' baseball team? Do we value our daughter's brains and competence? Or do we think she'll just go to college to find a husband? Do we applaud our daughter's attempts to learn a new skill? Or do we rush in before she hurts herself?

What daughters from birth to seven need most from their fathers is their time and attention. Unfortunately, most men become fathers at the same time their careers need their greatest efforts. In the past, most of men's time and energies were given to providing for the financial security of their families. This left little for taking part in daily family life, and fathers were in the uncomfortable position of weekend father and occasional baby-sitter to give Mom a needed night out. Happily, changes are happening on both the home front and in the world of work. Men, realizing they have missed out on the emotional closeness family life offers, are shifting their priorities. In a 1990 *Men's Life* survey in *USA Today*, sixty-three percent of those polled asserted that they plan to give more time and attention to their families, even if it requires they pass up some advancement in their careers.[7]

As the 1990s began, U.S. Department of Labor statistics indicated that at least 257,000 fathers from age twenty-five to fifty-four were raising their children, while mothers worked outside the home.[8] It is encouraging that more fathers are staying home, but girls need both their parents. Men and women must work together to maintain close relationships with our children and not fall into the current cultural trend of finding others to care for them so that we can concentrate on our careers and other adult pursuits. We must find alternative work schedules that are supportive of family needs. Especially during the early years, daughters need time—lots of time—from both parents, to assure them a healthy womanhood. A few minutes of "quality time" a few days a week is not sufficient.

A Father's Role from Ages Eight to Twelve

As we discuss in more depth in Chapter Ten, girls in the middle years are active, confident, and assertive. Their emotions are in full bloom, and everything is either wonderful or awful, with not much falling in between. How fathers involve themselves in their daughters' lives during these years profoundly affects how girls manage their transition into adolescence.

As daughters develop their ever-increasing tapestries of relationship, always attuned to how people relate to each other and to them, Dad ranks high on their popularity lists. They crave his undivided attention and listening ears. They especially want their feelings heard, understood, and respected. Daughters feel diminished when fathers are critical, overly-rational, withholding, or impatient around the expression of emotion. The feeling life—messages from the heart or soul—

comes through strongly now, and daughters bloom when fathers are open and available to sharing on this deep level.

> *When Nikki's puppy died, we just sat and held each other. We both cried and cried. I remembered when my own special dog died and understood her grief. My own seemed just as sharp and poignant.*
>
> *Nikki's not shy to bring up a memory about her dog, now that she knows I cared, too. It's something that hurt us both and brought us very close, because I was able to be there with her.*
>
> *—Jon, father of Nikki, ten*

Anger is a powerful feeling often not allowed in girls. Many of us learn to fear anger, our own and others'. We learn early in life that anger is not allowed, that anger can lead to violence, and we substitute another emotion more acceptable to our families. Often this more acceptable emotion is sadness; therefore, many women cry when they are angry. Tears become a substitute for the expression of anger. Being cut off from anger deprives girls and women of a powerful ally. Anger indicates a violation, an injustice, or that something is wrong. Some of us hear another's expression of anger as a personal affront, that we are bad or somehow to blame. Some of us use anger to "get things off our chest," to get our way, to make an impact. For some, anger is a bold act; for others, it is frightening.

Some of us *were* allowed to express our anger as children. A recent study reported by *USA Today* showed that women, thirty-four and younger, were more able to express their anger than women over fifty-five. Interestingly, most who were able to express their anger could not do so to the person they were angry with. A wife tells her husband about being angry at a coworker; a girl tells her mother she is angry with a friend.[9] Being indirect or talking to another person about our anger is a natural outcome of feeling vulnerable, powerless, and weak. When daughters must relate to fathers who remain distant and aloof, they resort to inappropriate expressions of anger or cut off this valuable connection to their inner guidance systems.

I always felt I had to be very sweet and nice around my dad. He wasn't one to really talk in a personal way about anything, especially with a girl, so I never really knew him. You know, what he thought about himself, his work, his childhood, stuff like that. He controlled my sisters and me with money. So, whenever we wanted something, we'd be on our best behavior, before we asked. I never knew whether he'd give me what I wanted, blow up at me, or just plain ignore me. I'd worry about asking him for days before I'd get up the courage to do it. I've been timid around men, because of my dad, and I hate it when someone yells at me. I just go along with whatever they want rather than make a fuss about it.

—Jennifer, twenty-nine

Measuring up to Dad's expectations is extremely important for girls between eight and twelve. Quick to see through token approval, daughters seek their father's genuine praise, and they need clear and reasonable expectations. Like boys of this age, girls want to know the rules and whether they will be enforced. They want to know whether Dad will back them up when they need it; they ask, "Will he really be there for me?" One place girls especially need their fathers' support is in school, where many teachers still have low scholastic expectations for girls, give girls less attention than boys, and fail to protect girls against sexual harassment.

Maeve wanted to play baseball, and she complained that the girls didn't get good equipment, had less practice time on the school field, and got little support from staff. Because of all this, she wanted to play on the boys' team. I have to admit, she's pretty good, and I thought she deserved a chance to try out. The boys' coach and some of the boys were pretty mad that I pushed the issue with the Title IX office of our district. I didn't really push this thing because of inequality. I just wanted to stand behind my girl; help her achieve what she wanted.

She had a good year on the team. Taking a lot of stuff off some of the guys on the team wasn't easy for her, but she stuck it out, and I'm proud of her.

She doesn't give up easily, and neither do I!

—*Gerald, father of Maeve, twelve*

Girls in the middle years want to be included in Dad's world—they may or may not be interested in the same things, but they want to feel accepted by this special man in their lives. Being asked to a ball game, to the movies, to join Dad for a day at his work, out to dinner, to run an errand, to play a game of football in the backyard, to help with a woodworking project, to work together in the garden, and so on—whether or not she wants to—helps a girl feel valued, competent, and confident in herself.

We often hear it said that team sports teach boys valuable life lessons—responsibility, assertiveness, competence, physical fitness and strength, good sportsmanship, conflict resolution, confidence, and how to be a team player. As more athletic opportunities open for girls, fathers play an important supportive role. Many girls relish the risk, adventure, and competition of active team sports. Others show no interest, fearing the competition or being hurt. Some prefer individual sports, where they compete against themselves and practice in their own timing. Whichever category describes our daughters, they need encouragement to try, and fathers must use patience, understanding, and a good ear.

I was really glad to hear that Tess's school started including girls in soccer, but she came home very upset about it. Said she hated it, and hated boys. Never wanted to play soccer again. I was raised playing soccer, loved to play, and still do. I let her rant on a little, and then tried to find out what happened that day. Come to find out, there was no real supervision, and the boys hogged the ball; wouldn't let the girls have a chance.

Besides that, no one taught them the rules or any fundamentals. Tess felt lost and frustrated out there on that field. Well, I marched in to the principal's office next day, and told her it was a good thing they had girls playing soccer, but they were going about it all wrong. She asked for my help right off. Now, after a few practices at home, and making the game more even between the girls and the boys at school, Tess likes playing and so do lots of her friends. They're pretty good, too! She's really proud of herself for sticking to it.

—Mike, father of Tess, eleven

Another area where dads can be active in a daughter's life is in money matters. Money—how to make it, and how to manage it—is a sign of power in this culture. Between the years of eight and twelve is a good time to begin offering practical opportunities for girls to learn about finances. Daughters younger than eight learn about saving in their piggy banks and how to identify the coins. Eight- to twelve-year-olds benefit from having their own savings and checking accounts, learning to keep financial records, and saving for something special. Through this practice they learn about short-term and long-term goals. Older daughters—ten, eleven, and twelve—can also manage money for bus fares, school lunches, and special outings. Around the matter of money, it is important to be clear about what is expected, how money is earned, what happens if it is lost or spent recklessly, and so on.

We do not mean to imply that mothers are not competent to teach their daughters about money. In fact most financial lessons probably come from Mom, while she and daughter shop for clothes, groceries, and so on. We are suggesting that money is another area where fathers can become more involved in their daughters' lives, especially since more partners seem to be handling the finances together these days.

A Father's Role from Ages Thirteen to Seventeen

The onset of puberty can make or break the father/daughter relationship. While girls in the middle years studied others and the world around them with a critical eye, this severe scrutiny is turned inward during the teen years. Why is my body changing? What will others think? Will I be attractive enough? How do I act now? Will I fit in? Adolescent girls often feel at sea and measure their self-worth on the ebb and flow of their relationships. If their best friend suddenly abandons them for someone more popular, which is not uncommon, girls inwardly wonder how they were to blame. Perhaps if I were thinner, nicer, smiled more,...? As we discussed in Chapter Two, girls in early adolescence are at greatest risk to develop psychological problems because of their perceived need to hide or change themselves in order to maintain relationships and to be loved.

Fathers are just as nonplused as their daughters are about a new intellectual maturity and the physical changes that come with the onset of menstruation. The worst mistake for a father to make at this time in his daughter's life is to withdraw himself from her, because he does not know how to deal with his own response to her developing sexuality. Daughters need reassurance from the first man in their lives that these changes they are undergoing are okay, that their father still loves them. Fathers provide a safe harbor where daughters can pause, take a deep breath, say, "I'm okay, Dad thinks I'm great," and return to the confusing seas of adolescence.

When fathers and daughters fail to maintain their connection through the transition into the teen years, many fall into the cultural trap of "dipping into Dad's pocket." Daughters, looking for any kind of sign their father still cares, begin asking for money. Dad, feeling guilty because he abandoned his daughter, "shells out," hoping to make up for it. Gordon Clay, creator of "Father and Teenage Daughter Rite of Passage" weekends, constantly sees this dynamic. "Fathers get scared when their daughters begin to mature, so they retreat behind their ability to buy things. Fathers look back on their daughters' adolescence as a time of their asking for money, tantrums, and brooding if they didn't give it. The women I see are enraged, because Dad withdrew just at the time when they needed his closeness the most."[10] Between thirteen and seventeen, fathers must find a way to say to their daughters, "You are now a young woman of whom I am proud. I enjoy our closeness, and I support you in finding your way in this world. I am here for you."

One key to staying connected with their daughters is for fathers to broaden their understanding of their own sexuality. Traditionally, the focus of male sexuality has been event-oriented—intercourse and climax. A man's full sexuality is his *being* and his way of relating to the world. Sexual energy has many forms, some of which are care, affection, closeness, and creativity. For men this understanding must be learned. "I tell fathers," continues Gordon Clay, "When you hug your daughter, if it feels uncomfortable, continue. If it feels wrong, stop! Most men know exactly what I am saying and what I mean."[11]

When my daughter started her period, I felt awkward and tongue-tied. I withdrew and hid behind my sarcasm. One day, Teddy was in one of her moods, and I teased her about it. She erupted and really let me have it. "I hate it when you make fun of me and my friends. You just sit back and judge me. I hate it!" Then she ran to her room and slammed the door. I was shocked and thought, "What have I done?" I joined a fathers' group not long after that, and I'm learning about the mistakes I made and how to get closer to my daughter. I'm glad I'm not missing out on her last years at home by hiding behind my fears about her growing up.

—Nick, father of Teddy, fifteen

When fathers remain in close relationship with their daughters, the other trials of adolescence do not seem so ominous and traumatic. Keeping communication open enhances the setting of clear limits and fair consequences. When fathers and daughters know where they stand with each other, it becomes easier for fathers to accept boyfriends, elaborate or weird clothes, and obnoxious language patterns without the need to be overprotective, harshly critical, or lay down the rules with an overbearing hand. Fathers can allow growing daughters more responsibility and trust their judgments to make reasonable choices.

Affection and connection assure a teenage daughter that Dad approves of her approaching womanhood. Through his healthy emotional and physical caring she learns that the male force can be good, loving, direct, kind, caring, and strong. She learns to tell the difference between a man who respects and cares for her and one who wishes to manipulate and take from her. What better gift could a father offer to his daughter?

A Father's Role from Ages Eighteen to Twenty-Nine

As daughters enter early adulthood, they continue to look to their fathers for advice, approval, and support as they deal with the challenges of college, career choices, and/or married life. Young contemporary women often put off decisions about relationship and motherhood, while giving their time and energies to completing advanced degrees and developing their careers. They ask fathers about finances—negotiating a salary, developing a budget, tax breaks, investment opportunities, buying a new car, a down-payment on a house, and so on. They may want to know the more practical details of a father's career, how he got started, why he chose his field, how he advanced, what his career goals were, how satisfied is he now, and what would he do differently. Through his candor, a father offers the wisdom of hindsight and experience to his daughter in the early adult years. If their relationship has been open and honest, she benefits greatly from her father's counsel.

Adult daughters need their fathers to have dreams of their success in whatever they choose to undertake, whether a career of family and hearth-tending, of service in the world, or both. Most fathers hold visions of their sons following in their footsteps or of going beyond what they have achieved. It is important that fathers do the same for their daughters.

If the father/daughter relationship has been a rocky one during her growing up, a daughter will often be drawn to resolve their difficulties as she nears thirty. Her attempts may be awkward, angry, or disguised, and fathers may be afraid to risk the pain of opening old wounds.

> *Victoria was always critical of me, even early on. After I divorced her mom, I never seemed to please her. When she was around ten, we did some things together, because she liked to go to the races with me, but when she turned fourteen, she became a stranger,*

and I became a pariah. I never recovered any standing with her. Lately—she's twenty-eight now—she's called a couple of times to see how I'm doing. Asked me some questions about my childhood, what my home life was like. Kind of like she's trying to sort things out between her and me.

—*Jeb, father of Victoria, twenty-eight*

When friction is really high, and fathers and daughters are stalled in communication, both may have to swallow some pride to seek help in resolving their conflicts. At any age, in any stage of development, fathers are vitally important in their daughters' lives. And children are our greatest teachers. Fathers and daughters need each other for assistance on their personal, spiritual journeys toward their futures.

The Role of Mother in a Daughter's Life

Don and Jeanne,

It's really funny how my opinion of my mother has changed so much over the years. Growing up I thought she was wonder woman and could do no wrong and knew all the answers to everything. Then I fell in love with a guy she wasn't sure of and for years I thought she really let me down and fooled me and I have felt really betrayed. (I'm happily married to that guy.) Recently, (an event) really shocked and humiliated my family. It really made me realize what an outstanding, strong, special woman my mother is. Now that I'm older I have a realistic view of her and I am feeling at peace with myself because I feel better about my mom.

The point of this whole story is the impact a mother has on a daughter...and I hope I can be a good mother to my children having learned this now.[12]

Thanks,

Jennifer Cross

Good Mother/Bad Mother Myths

"Like mother, like daughter." "You're just like your mother!" "Oh, no! I sounded just like my mother!" For many women, their biggest fear is they will become just like their mothers. Many mothers offer their daughters mixed messages: "Be like me. Don't be like me." What are daughters and mothers to do? There is no doubt about the importance of Mom in the life of a daughter. To many she is either a cherished mentor or a feared specter whose impression lasts a lifetime. Since Dr. Freud, psychological literature has blamed mothers for causing everything in their children's behavior from bedwetting to murder. Mothers are either too attached or unable to bond well with their children. They have been labeled among other things, as engulfing, inattentive, hysterical, controlling, enmeshed, overbearing, neglectful, clinging, and symbiotic. Janna Malamud Smith, a clinical social worker, writes, "As part of my work I have made many home visits to very poor women in housing projects. I witness the obstacles these mothers must overcome to arrange a day's worth of juice and Pampers for their toddlers. They have no money, bad housing, no day care, no way to earn a living, no physical safety, few reliable relationships and no social support. But when their children are evaluated at mental-health clinics the all-too-common requiem for the mother's effort is simply 'neglectful and unmotivated.'"[13]

In her insightful book, *Toward A New Psychology of Women*, Jean Baker Miller, M.D. asserts that the Good Mother/Bad Mother myths are perpetuated by a culture that finds "it is easier to blame mothers than to comprehend the entire system that has restricted women."[14] This cultural injustice creates a tragic double-bind for both mothers and daughters. Mothers unwittingly betray their daughters by trying to protect them from the dangers of a gender-restrictive culture. Daughters learn from the media, self-help books, their therapists, their fathers, and even from Mom, herself, to blame her for their troubles, thereby losing a most valuable ally. We find it interesting that more mother-blaming occurs among middle-class white women than among women of color and those raised in poverty. Rather than blame their mothers for being weak and unmotivated, minority and working-class women recognize their mothers' courage as victims in the face of violence and oppression.[15] The more we understand mothers as truly human, both heroic and victimized, the more able daughters and mothers will be to realize their unique and solid connection.

Revisioning Motherhood

We think it is time to take Mother off the hook and look realistically at who she is in her daughter's life. Although modern daughters are more aware of women's issues and seek positive and affirming ways to connect with their mothers, traditional psychological theories continue to conspire to keep mothers and daughters apart. Most of us still adhere to the idea that to develop a separate self, daughters must sever their ties with Mother and turn to Father to achieve the adult status of independence and autonomy. Many parenting books acclaim the important role of fathers in creating daughters who are happy and successful in the world outside the family. Very few women, having achieved power in their careers, credit their mothers.

Recently, researchers and theorists, adopting a voice-centered relational approach to the theory of women's psychological development,[16] are revisioning psychological development in girls. It is also within the mother/daughter relationship that we find the harmful effects of assuming that girls' psychological development follows the same path as boys'. When we evaluate, or re-value, a mother's role in her daughter's life, we reclaim the mother/daughter relationship as holding the potential for great closeness, sensitivity, support, and friendship.

Viewing girls' psychological development in the new light of a *self-in-relation*,[17] we no longer hold to the idea that girls must sever their ties with their mothers. Girls must achieve a separate selfhood, but it is a selfhood that develops within the ever-increasing complexity of relationship, especially in relationship with their mothers, with whom they share a commonality that goes beyond the conflicts, entanglements, and misunderstandings so inevitable to family life.

Who Is Who?

Foremost for mothers in maintaining a healthy mother/daughter connection, is to be clear about who they are. Who are we in relation to our own mothers? Our husbands or life-mates? Our lovers? Our sons? Our ex-husbands? Our bosses? Our coworkers? Our friends? Our daughters? What roles do we play in the many lives that intertwine our own? Some mothers are the family peacemakers, always smoothing prickly feelings between members. Others are "chief cook and bottle washer," constantly waiting on and anticipating everyone's needs. Some mothers demand power, assigning and overseeing household chores with an iron hand. Others demand alliance, pitting family members against one another to maintain control. Some mothers adhere to the Good Mother myth, vigilantly presenting a loving and cheerful front, therefore, denying anyone's negative feelings. Others are caught in the role of the Bad Mother, constantly blaming, angry, tired, and guilty. Most mothers are all of these and much more.

Knowing what roles they hold in their relationships allows mothers clear distinctions between themselves and their daughters. We must also clarify our values, goals, dreams, frustrations, and disappointments. Accepting the fundamental truths that mothers and daughters are connected, will always be connected in some unnamable way whether together or miles apart, and because of this connection will get confused about who is who, takes the burden off mothers to be perfectly good, or perfectly bad. When the inevitable entanglement with her daughter comes, a mother who knows herself can remember her own uniqueness and see her daughter's as well.

> *My mother and I had a real blowout over how I encouraged my Rena to speak out about what she thought. Mother raised me to defer to the men in a group, not to cause uncomfortable disagreements. She thinks Rena goes too far when she voices what she sees. Mother's afraid Rena will get herself in trouble. While I have compassion for her generation, I had felt cut off from what I thought and felt, and I don't want that to happen to Rena. On the other hand, Mother has a point about teaching Rena how and when to say something.*
>
> *— Dale, mother of Rena, thirteen*

Mothers as Mentors

Whether or not they want to admit it, most daughters pattern themselves after their mothers. Simply by their daily presence, mothers influence their daughters in countless ways. When that influence is conscious, both mothers and daughters benefit from the support and encouragement to be all they can be.

Look for unconscious ways we mothers influence our daughters. There are innumerable ways daughters pick up messages from their mothers about themselves, women, men, and life in general. The balance of power between wife and husband speaks volumes to our daughters about how women and men are valued and respected. Are important family decisions jointly made? Do both parents set limits and consequences for their children? Do family careers—hearth-tending and money-making—receive equal consideration? Do parents spend time together? Do we allow ourselves to do things we enjoy doing? Do we nurture our spiritual natures?

> *I was appalled to hear my daughter say she hated her looks. When I told her how beautiful she is, she said, "Oh, Mom. Nobody really likes how they look. I watch you look in the mirror all the time, and you always make a face, like you're disgusted or something." I made a point to notice how I felt the next time I looked in a mirror, and she was right. I grimaced when I saw my bland hair color, rumpled blouse, and double chin.*
>
> *—Angie, mother of Carlie, eleven*

Find more realistic images for women. Mothers have always worked both inside and outside the home. Never before, however, have we expected women to shoulder the tremendous burdens of the "Supermom" label, "doing it all," being the perfect mother, the perfect wife, and the perfectly successful career woman. The working mother is on a dangerous treadmill with no end in sight, unless fathers, society, and women themselves, ease the pressure and create more realistic options and goals for women. As more and more women assume the responsibilities of single mothers and heads of their households, the images of the working mother doing it on her own become enslaving, rather than empowering. The State of California is proud of a new program that gets single mothers out of the home and into the work force. But weren't they already working, working in one of society's most important jobs, raising the next generation? What happens to these children? Poverty rates are highest in households headed by single mothers—forty-seven percent among whites and seventy-two percent among black households.[18] With one low income, single mothers find good child care hard to procure, and this extra worry stresses an already overburdened familial structure.

Patricia Aburdene and John Naisbitt, authors of *Megatrends for Women*, have good news, however. They predict more support for families from the work world and society in general that will create more realistic roles for women.[19] Different family configurations will be considered normal and acceptable. Married couples with children will be outnumbered by stepfamilies, single-parent families, lesbian-couple families, never-married mothers, gay-couple families, families with adopted children, families with househusbands, living-together families, grandparent families, and so on. The revaluing of the family from all corners of society will create more realistic choices for mothers and their daughters.

Teach daughters to speak out. Betrayal begins early as a mother teaches her daughter to be sweet, compliant, and silent. There are many reasons for doing this. We fear for our daughters' safety if they are too outspoken, too different, too visible. Feminism aside, parents do not always find it easy to hear their daughters' opinions, feelings, complaints, disagreements, and thoughts. Honestly, most of us find it more pleasant to live around others who are agreeable and accommodating, and many women are taught to believe that if they were just less demanding, their relationships would work better.

When daughters grow up deprived of their "voices," something essential is missing. Giving voice to one's thoughts and opinions, fears and triumphs builds self-esteem and courage. Mothers can pass on the lineage of silence and female bondage, or they can empower their daughters to say "No!" to constraints, to argue for their rights, to speak out against injustices, to voice their anger toward violation.

> *Stephanie and a friend just started at a new school. They immediately ran into trouble from a boy that started rumors about them. Vicky asked Stephanie to just ignore him. After a few days, some of the other girls accused Vicky of saying bad things about them. They confronted her and Stephanie in the hallway, saying this boy told them that Vicky was spreading lies in the school and that they didn't like it. Stephanie tried to defend Vicky, and things got worse. Stephanie came home in tears, upset that Vicky refused to say anything to school authorities and that they were being unjustly accused. Knowing there was a grievance procedure for the kids at school, I asked Stephanie if she would like my help in working it out. It was her decision, and the grievance committee brought all sides together. I was very proud of Stephanie for standing her ground and speaking the truth about what had happened. The girls learned something about sticking up for each other and how believing something before they check it out with the person concerned leads to unnecessary separation and conflict.*

> *—Barbara, mother of Stephanie, twelve*

Speak up for our daughters. When daughters see their mothers speaking out, voicing their opinions, and fighting for their daughters' rights to equal opportunities, they learn that taking a stand demonstrates inner strength and competence. We are not presuming that every mother must take up placards and march in front of City Hall. Women speak out in many different ways, and we each must find our own style. Some of us write letters to our congresswomen and men. Others of us start support groups and share our quiet struggles with others. Many of us work to improve the communication of power in our own relationships at home. Some of us form committees and work for change in our public schools. Others of us teach our sons to respect the equal rights of all persons. From our actions, our daughters will discover their own unique styles. At least they will know they can speak out by our examples.

Come to terms with our own mothers. Many of us live in the shadows of poor relationships with our own mothers. We vow to do things differently with our daughters, only to find we repeat the mother/daughter lineage and treat our daughters in the ways our mothers treated us. If we did some matrilineal genealogy, we would probably find the same interactions between our mothers and their mothers, and on and on. Family patterns do tend to repeat themselves, unless we bring them out of the family closet into the light of conscious scrutiny, understanding, letting go, and forgiving. Each of these steps is an intricate process, not to be hurried or overlooked. Sometimes childhood traumas between mothers and daughters are too painful, buried, or forgotten to heal without help. We need the support and guidance of a professional counselor to assist us through the closet's accumulation of old childhood junk. Cleaning out the clutter of relationship with our own mothers makes room for clear relationships with our daughters.

Motherhood Transitions: The Years from Birth to Seven

Women who become mothers undergo tremendous changes throughout the course of their daughters' development. The birth of a daughter signals for a mother the beginning of a lifelong relationship, full of the promise of understanding, connection, and support, as well as the fears of betrayal, hurt, and abandonment.

Contrary to common opinion, many mothers do not automatically know how to raise daughters, how to develop a close relationship while allowing a girl to develop her own sense of self and purpose.

A mother's feelings in the early years of her daughter's life are often mixed, especially if she has been working in a career outside the home before her daughter was born. Turning from the larger world of work to the smaller, softer-focused world of Baby can be quite shocking for those of us who had no idea that infants required so much attention. During the early months, mothers and infant daughters both need the support of fathers or other significant people to surrender to the essential bonding process occurring between them. A mother benefits from allowing the outside world to fade for a time, to nurture her body's change from pregnant, expectant vessel to nurser and provider. With the demands of a new routine focused around a baby, it is easy to forget what a tremendous transformation the body undergoes. Time is needed, also, to adjust to the changes—both within a mother's self and within the family—this tiny creature brings; changes we could only imagine before the birth.

As daughters begin to explore the world around them, mothers struggle to find the balance between protection and restriction, encouragement and perfectionism, applause and overindulgence. Allowing herself to look again at the world with new eyes and calling forth her own childhood wonder-of-it-all enables a mother to enjoy and be enriched by her daughter's delight and exploration. It can be a time for looking with a fresh eye at family routines, division of household chores, values, lifestyles, and future dreams. It is a time for honest discussion with a parenting partner about those critical issues discussed in the father's section concerning work, discipline, television, family health, child care, toys, spirituality, and so on.

These early years are also the most vital in developing ways a mother nurtures herself. If from the beginning of her daughter's life a mother models that she, too, is important and worthy of care in the family relationship, a daughter will grow up with a healthy self-esteem, able to fully care for herself and others.

The Years from Eight to Twelve

In the middle years, mothers are inspired by their daughters' abilities to navigate the world, to organize, and to assume leadership. Mothers may momentarily worry about tendencies to be adventurous and outspoken, but an eight- to twelve-year-old's confidence is catching. This is a time when many daughters naturally gravitate to masculine-oriented activities, constantly choosing action over housework, outdoors over indoors, Dad over Mom. It is a time when the mother/daughter relationship undergoes a shift in priorities. A mother may feel abandoned or slightly jealous about her daughter's attachment to her father; especially if the mother's relationship with Dad is not as close as she would like it to be, or there is no relationship at all, in the case of divorce. During this time, mothers must remember that their daughters are not trying to separate from them but to come to terms with their masculine sides. In the middle years, daughters need to spend time with fathers, or other important men, to develop their masculine abilities and to learn how to relate to males. Daughters learn these all-important lessons best while staying in firm connection with their mothers.

Between the ages of eight and twelve, a daughter needs her mother's understanding and support to discover the world on her own terms. When disappointments occur and the world is not the oyster she thought it was, a girl counts on her mother to listen to her woes, cheer her on, and advocate for her when she meets an obstacle too large to understand. A daughter's primary focus during these years may be on her father, but she continually relies on the important relationship with her mother for a grounding to her essential, feminine self.

The Years Between Thirteen and Seventeen

Early adolescence can be awful and wonderful for both mothers and daughters. Some mothers find their relationship takes on new closeness, as daughters confide their bewildering experiences of growing up. Vital to a young girl's life is a mother or other older woman who listens carefully to and acknowledges her experiences, thoughts, and feelings. Colby College professor Lyn Mikel Brown, Ph.D., coauthor of an important book about girls and women, *Meeting at the Crossroads*, feels that saying, "Yes, this does seem unfair. I understand what you're seeing. I don't know what to do about it, but let's think about it together," confirms the reality of young adolescent girls' experiences and provides a meaningful alignment with their mothers and other women.[20] These relationships form the touchstones that empower girls through adolescence towards a healthy womanhood.

Many adult daughters look back on their adolescence as a time when their mothers provided reassurance and information that helped them over the rough places in their journey toward womanhood. Others feel betrayed and abandoned, because their mothers were unable to differentiate their own unhappy teen years from their daughters' experiences. It is especially important and perhaps especially difficult for mothers of teenage daughters to be clear about who is who. On such issues as sexuality, mothers walk a fine line between informing their daughters about the dangers—early pregnancy, sexually transmitted diseases (STDs), bad reputations, being hurt or sexually used, and so on—and teaching their daughters about sexual intimacy—connection, giving, receiving, feeling good, and so on. Whether daughters are open to their mothers' advice often depends upon where a mother stands in her own sexuality, or how honest she is in communicating the dichotomies. Not an easy task for any of us.

In the late teens, mothers recover some of their intelligence, influence, and chic they may have lost in their daughters' early adolescence. While the peer group remains paramount, daughters take a greater interest in their mothers' sphere of work and activities in the outside world. Who is this person separate from her role as my mother? What power does she hold in circles outside my family? What does she have to teach me about the responsibility of women? What positions do women have in the wider scheme of things? What can I achieve as a woman in the world? Mothers mentor their daughters into their futures by inviting them into their social, service, and career worlds. Being included in their mother's work activities, gives girls a realistic picture of the workplace and what happens there. If a mother gives service as a volunteer, a daughter can gain empathy and understanding for those less fortunate. As an older teen spends time with her mother, their relationship begins the transformation from parent/child into one of friendship and support for the adult years.

The Young Adult Years: From Eighteen to Twenty-nine

As daughters join their mothers in the ranks of womanhood, the mother/daughter relationship graduates into a friendship on more equitable footing. Many women complain that this never happened with their mothers. "She always saw me as a daughter. Always had to tell me what I should do." "She could never learn anything from me. Thought it was an insult if I tried to teach her something I knew from my own experience." "She still can't see me as a person separate from her!" Perhaps the hardest transition of all is for mothers to trust themselves and their daughters enough to give their relationship room to grow. Despite the fears, doubts, and perceived failures, we made it through, and now our daughters will blossom into their own lives, confident of our support, availability, and connection.

> *Around eighteen, I began to see my mom in a new light. The things she did when I was younger sort of bored me, but now I find myself interested in similar things—books, political causes, women's issues. Our relationship has shifted to one of mutual respect. I mean, we both feel we have a lot to teach each other. And she's there when I have a problem about managing on my own; she's easy to talk to, and she's a big fan of mine. All that helps!*
>
> —Heidi, *twenty-one*

Divorce and Stepparents

> *Whether he is widowed, divorced, or never married, the single father inexplicably finds himself fighting intense, bitter emotions and attitudes he never knew existed. And all that comes on top of trying to be a halfway decent dad—or feeling guilt because he is not.*[21]
>
> —Drs. Frank Minirth, Brian Newman,
> and Paul Warren, *The Father Book*

> *The thought of the three of us on welfare, living in a crime infested neighborhood, dressing in Salvation Army clothes and worrying about our next meal sickened me.*[22]
>
> —Doreen Virtue, *My Kids Don't Live With Me Anymore*

The traditional dangerous arrangement that fathers and daughters inherit from our culture—distant and special—is more difficult to change when divorce occurs. Divorce brings more distance, less time together, and more variables in the family stew. Mothers and daughters may become rivals, competing for allegiance and time. Divorce drives a wedge between all family members, starting with Mom and Dad and spreading to the children. Daughters, pulled between their love and loyalty to each parent, get caught in the middle.

Both parents suffer from cultural stereotypes—divorced mothers can only raise their children in poverty, and divorced fathers disappear. Fathers and mothers feel attacked on all sides. Men often react by becoming angry. Looking for ways to solve the problems facing them, they try to force solutions through combative, blaming, or strategical means.

> *I finally went to a therapist after a raging episode with my ex. We fought over a stupid five minutes! I was supposed to pick up the kids on Christmas Day, and I got stuck in traffic. After she spit in my face, I pushed her, and the neighbors called the cops. In therapy, I remembered the same pattern between my folks. My dad would take as much as he could, and then he'd blow up at my mom and us kids. I'm learning to find ways to let off steam, before I blow. It's made a big difference in how my ex and I settle issues over the kids. Lets them off the hook, too.*
>
> *—Darrell, father of Jerome, eight and Delia, five*

A divorce in a man's life may be his first experience of being unable to solve a problem by applying his commitment, will power, and masculine force. His anger often overlays deep feelings of grief and loss. A father's relationship with his daughter suddenly becomes something out of his direct control and influence, and he is faced with a new relationship born out of his process with grief.

Men come in hurt, angry, and wanting revenge. As we talk about the stages of grief, they have more understanding about their urge to deal with things in the old ways. The breakup of a family often brings a man in contact with feelings he never had to face before. He has to open his soul.[23]

—Bobbie Frey, M.A., family therapist
Divorce Recovery Support Groups

When fathers deal with their feelings of anger, loss, and grief, they can be more open to their daughters' feelings. Divorced fathers must give their daughters time and attention, hold them to family rules, make expectations clear, and be open about their own feelings. While Dad deals with his personal issues about the divorce in therapy or support groups, he and his daughter may find counseling helpful to share deep-seated anger and grief and to work out the perimeters of their new relationship.

Divorcing mothers, too, experience anger, grief, loss, and fear. How will this break affect my children? How will I support us? How do I raise my kids and take care of all the intricate details of keeping the family going? Can I make it on my own?

It's so hard! He's still making a hundred thousand dollars a year, and I'm making twenty thousand, if I'm lucky. And I'm losing my daughter to him for half of her life each week. He has a new sweetie and a new apartment, and I have our family dog, a huge house, and all the bills. My friends tell me that I'll be glad it happened in six months; that I'll have my self-esteem back, and a life of my own. Right now, it's really hard to imagine.

—Dorothy, mother of Chelsea, seven

Sharing fear and anger about a divorce with daughters is risky for mothers, especially if they are the custodial parent. Daughters from birth to fourteen need to feel secure and unburdened by the worries of family finances—food-on-the-table, rent or mortgage, other bills, and so on—and are not capable of being sounding boards for deep feelings of fear, rage, and grief. Mothers are best supported by adult friends, support groups, and counselors, there to hear feelings and sort out practical plans of action. Daughters are best supported when mothers are clear about their own feelings and can keep them separate from their daughters' experiences.

Daughters commonly blame their mothers for the break up, or they side with them against their fathers. Neither position is desirable for a healthy adjustment to divorce. Depending upon their ages, daughters feel betrayed, lost, depressed, abandoned, angry, indifferent, frightened, and sad. They may deny their feelings, push Mom or Dad away, and pretend nothing is wrong. Girls in early adolescence, already psychologically at risk, may take their parent's divorce especially hard. Where most boys act out their feelings, many girls turn inward, becoming more self-critical and self-abusive. Those who do turn their feelings outward, may abuse drugs and alcohol, act out sexually, challenge family rules, skip school, and become sullen and uncooperative at home. Both parents must be particularly careful to avoid putting daughters in the middle by blaming each other to their daughters. Reassuring girls that they are loved, that they are not the cause of their parents' troubles, and that both parents will be there for them, no matter what, provides the continuous connection daughters of divorcing parents fear they will lose.

Although some statistics reflect the disadvantages of divorce on families, and we do not trivialize the trauma and deep feelings all experience, most family members recover quite well.[24] When new routines become secure, both parents may now find that, with the difficulties of their marital relationship behind them, they have more time and energy to be more involved with their daughters. With their marriage problems no longer looming over the household, parents can see their girls more clearly. It is important that fathers insist upon time with their daughters, taking time off from their work, bringing their daughters to their work, offering to pick them up for music lessons, doctor's appointments, and shopping, doing fun things together, staying with them when they are home sick from school, and so on.

When mothers spend special time with their daughters doing things they both enjoy, their relationship and connection are strengthened. A daughter needs the reassurance that her mother, despite the new job, or new apartment, or new single status, is the same person, still willing to listen to thoughts and feelings, still keeping the family rules firm, still the loving mom she counts on.

Stepmothers/Stepfathers

The polite way to talk about stepparenting is to call it a challenge. Some days many of us would call it "Mission Impossible." The individual roles of mother and father in girls' lives holds true for stepparents and stepdaughters with one large difference. Most parents begin at the beginning, and stepparents step in at any time along a girl's journey toward womanhood. And, on the average, it takes three to five years before a daughter gives the stepparent any authority in their relationship. Of course, the time varies with each family, some adjusting sooner, some never able to accept what seems to them an interloper. Here are some points we found helpful:

Never presume to take the place of the natural parent. However much daughters love their stepparents, they remain loyal to their natural parents. This is usually as it should be. Having to choose only creates more separation between daughters and new family members. Most helpful for all concerned, especially daughters, is for the partners to present a united front. Back each other up, discuss differences in private, and the number one rule: stepparent yields to natural parent in differences concerning their daughters. In private, both parents must feel they can express their feelings, opinions, and needs about child-rearing without fear of ridicule, rejection, or criticism. When it comes to final decisions and follow through, the natural parent has final authority. Presenting the decision together, however, further establishes a stepparent's authority in the parental role.

Take time to grow into the stepparenting role. The development of trust is a slow process, especially so with older daughters. They will test to see whether or not the new parent will stick around, how much acting out they can take, how dependable they are. Ask stepdaughters for information about family routines and rhythms and join them, rather than changing them immediately. Create fun times, and do not promise more than can be done.

Strengthen the marriage relationship. Couples must spend time together in play, work, and defining each other's parenting roles. In difficult stepfamily relationships, daughters easily detect any little crack in marital alliance and go for the jugular. Speaking up for each other and being willing to work things out, provide the security daughters need—to know they will not have to go through another loss and separation; that they can get on with the business of growing up without having to put energy into their parents' relationships.

Respect a daughter's need for privacy. There will be areas of stepdaughters' lives that are off-limits to stepparents. Keeping track of two families is often frustrating, and stepdaughters may feel conflicted about what to tell and how. Give them room, respect their private feelings, and be available if they should want to talk. Sometimes a somewhat removed, third party is easier to talk to than a natural parent, so stepparents may be sought out for clarity and perspective on the natural parent relationship. In such cases, of course, it is best to remain a neutral listener, rather than blaming or siding with one or the other parent.

In issues of sexuality and nudity around the house, family discussions and agreements make individual comfort levels clear to everyone. It may be helpful to consider how these issues are treated in a daughter's other family, how they were handled in the past, and what works well for all concerned. Traditionally, daughters talk to their mothers about sexuality, if any talking occurs. When stepmothers are open and available, being able to talk about important and confusing issues helps stepdaughters let down their barriers and begin to develop closer connections with them. Most important is to respect a daughter's needs for privacy in these matters.

There are no limits to love between stepparents and stepdaughters. Whatever limitations arise, as they do in all relationships, learning the boundaries slowly and keeping open hearts soften even the toughest situations.

In traditional family configurations, as well as single parent households and stepfamilies, the raising of daughters into healthy women requires the cooperation of a parenting team. The job is much bigger than one parent, or even two parents, can do alone. We encourage us all to step out of our familial isolationism and reach out to other like-minded parents, friends, relatives, teachers, and senior citizens for their support, time, wisdom, and reassurance in helping our daughters awaken into healthy women.

Endnotes

1. James Hillman and Michael Ventura, *We've Had a Hundred Years of Psychotherapy and the World's Getting Worse* (San Francisco: Harper San Francisco, 1992), 24.

2. Arlie Hochschild, *Second Shift* (New York: Viking Press, 1989).

3. Robert Johnson, *WE* (San Francisco: Harper & Row, 1983), 195.

4. Goethe, as quoted in *The Scottish Himalayan Expedition*, W.H. Murray (London: Dent & Son, 1951).

5. Shirley Sloan Fader, "Are Men Changing?" *Working Mother*, Feb. 1993, 49.

6. Bob Zavala, M.A., phone conversation with Don Elium, Los Medanos College, Pittsburg, CA, 22 Dec. 1993.

7. Fader, "Are Men Changing?", 50.

8. Ibid., 51.

9. Karen S. Peterson, "More Women Vent Anger, But Not at the Source," USA Today, 15 Nov. 1993, 1D.

10. Gordon Clay, phone interview with Don Elium, San Anselmo, CA, 13 Jul. 1993.

11. Ibid.

12. Jennifer Cross, a letter to the authors, 14 Oct. 1992.

13. Janna Malamud Smith, "Tired of Taking the Rap," *This World*, San Francisco Examiner, Sunday, 1 Jul. 1990, 13.

14. Jean Baker Miller, *Toward a New Psychology of Women* (Boston, MA: Beacon Press, 1976), 139.

15. Ibid.

16. Carol Gilligan, "Joining the Resistance: Moments of Resilience in Women's Psychological Development," an address to The Spring Foundation for Research on Women in Contemporary Society conference, "The Resilient Woman: Struggle in the Face of Diversity, Stanford University, Palo Alto, CA, 25 Jan. 1992.

17. Janet L. Surrey, "The Self-in-Relation: A Theory of Women's Development," in *Women's Growth in Connection*, Jordan, et al. (New York: The Guilford Press, 1991), 51–66.

18. US. Congress, House Committee on Ways and Means, *Overview of Entitlement Programs: 1990 Green Book* (Washington, DC: US. Government Printing Office, 1990), 956, Table 56.

19. Patricia Aburdene and John Naisbitt, *Megatrends for Women* (New York: Villard Books, 1992), 217.

20. Patricia Holt, "Shocking Story About Harassment of Young Girls," San Francisco Chronicle, 21 Jan. 1994, C9.

21. Frank Minirth, Brian Newman, and Paul Warren, *The Father Book: An Instruction Manual* (Nashville, TN: Thomas Nelson, 1992), 213.

22. Doreen Virtue, *My Kids Don't Live with Me Anymore* (Minneapolis, MN: CompCare, 1988), introduction.

23. Bobbie Frey, M.A., an interview with Don Elium, Touchstone Counseling Services, Pleasant Hill, CA, 17 Jul. 1993.

24. Susan Faludi, *Backlash: The Undeclared War Against Women* (New York: Crown, 1991), 26.

CHAPTER SIX

FENCES: DEVELOPING HEALTHY PERSONAL BOUNDARIES

Good fences make good neighbors.

— Old saying

I n our first book, *Raising a Son: Parents and the Making of a Healthy Man*, we wrote boys need to know three things: 1) Who's the boss? 2) What are the rules? and 3) Are you going to enforce them?[1] Keeping these three questions in mind when setting fences and choosing consequences helps a lot in the parenting of boys. Girls, however, are motivated by a different set of questions: 1) Are we in relationship? 2) What is the nature of our relationship? 3) Who am I within the relationship? and 4) What is necessary to maintain connection within the relationship? Viewing the purpose of our daughters' behaviors as *making connections* enables us to set limits and choose consequences that help them thrive. Although girls also need to know the rules, they are more focused on the flavor of the relationship with the "boss," than what the rules are.

Clear Personal Boundaries

Your personal boundaries protect the inner
core of your identity and your right to choices.[2]

—Gerard Manley Hopkins

"How can I teach my daughter about clear, personal boundaries," many mothers cry, "when I'm in five different recovery groups, owe my therapist for three months of therapy, let my boss walk all over me, and don't really have clear, personal boundaries myself?" Fathers, also, are confused about the changing male roles and wonder who they are supposed to be in relation to family, work, friends, and community. As we as a culture recover from our myriad dysfunctions, mother, father, and daughter must learn about personal boundaries together.

We read a lot these days about codependency, over-involvement, and under-involvement. These conditions develop from lack of clear, personal boundaries—knowing where one begins and ends. All of us have our moments of taking on too much responsibility for other people's feelings, pain, good or bad behavior, and so on. Parents are especially vulnerable to blaming ourselves for our children's every misdeed. Most experts assert that women are more likely than men to participate in codependent behavior. Their early training and perhaps their biology as well, certainly make them predisposed to be over-involved in the lives of others. Then they are criticized for it, or they become resentful and angry for the constant demands made upon them. This situation sets up quite a paradox for girls and women. Culture assigns the roles of nurturing, caretaking, and mothering to women, while at the same time devaluing these vital tasks. Jean Baker Miller, M.D., clinical professor of psychiatry at Boston University School of Medicine and Director of Education at the Stone Center, Wellesley College, writes in her groundbreaking book, *Toward a New Psychology of Women*, "There is no question that the dominant society has said, men will do the important work; women will tend to the 'lesser task' of helping other human beings to develop."[3] Had women not succeeded so well at their designated "lesser task," modern society might be in even worse shape than it is!

As women realize how important their work is, both at home and in the workplace, they are more able to allow men to assume their share of nurturing responsibilities. Developing relationships that nurture others as well as ourselves requires clear, personal boundaries. To help our daughters develop personal boundaries, we need to have a clear understanding of our own. Take the following quiz[4] to discover the health of your own personal boundaries.

How Healthy Are Your Personal Boundaries?

Answer each question with a number between 1 and 5. 1 indicates always, 5 indicates never.

	1 Always	2 Often	3 Sometimes	4 Seldom	5 Never
1. I have trouble deciding what I want.					
2. Rather than feeling unhappy about something, I make the best of it.					
3. I change my plans, behavior, or opinions to match those around me.					
4. I find myself doing more and more for others and getting less and less satisfaction.					
5. I believe the opinions of others over my own.					
6. I live hopefully, while waiting for something good to happen.					
7. I believe I have no right to secrets.					
8. I think constantly about the behavior of others.					
9. I get into relationships with people who are unable to care about me.					
10. I make excuses for other people's behavior when they hurt me.					
11. I am easily manipulated by flattery.					
12. I rely on others to create my excitement.					
13. I do favors when I really don't want to.					
14. I allow others to abuse me and my friends.					
15. I feel hurt and victimized.					
16. I do not feel anger.					

	1 Always	2 Often	3 Sometimes	4 Seldom	5 Never
17. I help others, because I think I should.	___	___	___	___	___
18. I feel afraid and confused.	___	___	___	___	___
19. I mostly feel that things are beyond my control.	___	___	___	___	___
20. I think I am living a life that is not my own.	___	___	___	___	___

Now, total your answers. If your score is 50 or lower, it may be helpful to take a class, do some reading, work with a counselor, or talk with a person you know who has strong, personal boundaries, so you will be a better model for your daughter.

Having an internalized sense of where her responsibility to herself and others begins and ends gives a girl the power of self to be in the world with assurance and confidence. When others take advantage of her generosity, she can say "No! Enough!", knowing what is best for her without the feelings of guilt that keep many of us locked into abusive relationships with our children, spouses, lovers, bosses, friends. A girl with a clear understanding of who she is knows what she likes, what she wants, and how to act on it, or at least isn't afraid to ask for help in getting what she wants. Clear, personal boundaries enable girls to defy sexual stereotypes in the face of strong opposition.

> *I have very wide shoulders and strong arms for a girl. I always have. I used to hate it, and kids teased me a lot. Then my brother taught me to throw the javelin. My mom had a fit when I demanded to be part of the track team in that event. She said girls just didn't do that. The track coach was pretty skeptical, too, until I threw the javelin for him. Now I'm part of the team, and I love it. Mom's come around, too, but it really doesn't matter what others think. The thrill of the throw is enough.*
>
> *—Janet, sixteen*

A girl in touch with her inner feelings, recognizes whether she is happy or unhappy. She doesn't let herself be swayed by the feelings of others around her, although she takes them into account. She is willing to do more when the task demands it, if the payoff is worth it. She has high personal standards that apply to everyone, and although she is flexible, she expects others to be accountable for their actions. She does not allow herself to be used and hurt by others. She is able to choose relationships with a mutual give-and-take of care and affection. She has varied interests, pursues hobbies she likes, and knows that others stimulate her excitement but are not responsible for it. She is not afraid of expressing anger and views it as a signal that something is wrong. She is able to say "No" to favors asked when she knows she will feel resentful afterwards. Mostly, she feels secure and confident, always aware she has choices in any circumstance. She protects her privacy and insists that others maintain their own personal boundaries. The life she lives is close to her vision of how she wants it to be.

People with healthy personal boundaries are self-directed and able to maintain relationships with others. Helping our daughters develop a strong sense of self will assure them the freedom to follow their destinies happily and purposefully. Sherry Glueck, writer and parent educator, says of her two daughters, "They are both extremely verbal in standing up for themselves and have good negotiation skills. Sometimes they're not easy to live with, but I'm happy about how they have turned out. As a girl, I was expected to go along with whatever was decided. I've had to learn to speak up for myself as an adult. I'm glad our girls are learning it now. They're hard to live with sometimes, because they push me to the limit, but I think they will use these skills all their lives. I know that if they ever got in a bad situation, they'd be able to get out of it, because they have confidence and are good at articulating how they feel."[5]

Punishment Doesn't Work

A pet owner brought his dog into the vet for a checkup and complained that the dog soiled the carpet. "Oh that's easy to stop," the vet said. "When she soils the carpet, rub her nose in it and throw her out the window." The pet owner returned home and administered this treatment for thirty days. The vet became curious and called the pet owner to see how the punishment was working. "Not so good" said the pet owner, "Now when my dog soils the carpet, she rubs her nose in it and jumps out the window."

Punishment infers the use of force, and as an act of deterrence, only breeds anger, resentment, and the desire for revenge. Because punishment usually involves shame, ridicule, threat, violence, and isolation, its use often reinforces the exact behavior we want to extinguish.

> *My daughter's preschool teacher called with the concern that Karen was hitting other children when she became frustrated during play. After that call, I became so frustrated, myself, that I almost swatted Karen on the spot. Then I realized where she had learned to hit when she was frustrated—from me! I began to see that I swat her all the time. I feel so inadequate.*
>
> *—Betty, frustrated mother of Karen, four*

The old adage, "The punishment should fit the crime," is inappropriate in the arena of parenting. If we consider our daughters' misbehaviors as crimes, we're off on the wrong foot from the beginning. The truth about punishment is it rarely relates to the misbehavior. The only lesson learned from being yelled at or humiliated for spilling one's milk at dinner is Daddy yells loudly, and it's frightening and embarrassing. Punishing our daughters may make us feel better by relieving our frustration, but it does little to teach them to be more careful or to use better table manners. Spanking, swatting, yelling, grounding, and time-outs may temporarily stop whatever misbehavior our daughters are guilty of, but most of the time, the annoying, nasty, irresponsible, or dangerous behavior will re-emerge someplace else, because punishment does not teach how to regulate one's behavior.

◁▷ ◁▷ DON | When you press down a part of yourself you don't like, you will eventually meet it on the other side of town. Or marry someone just like it! Punishment is an act of pressing down and denial. What we deny, we become slave to, because it doesn't go away. It just pops up someplace else. When our young daughters express anger, for example, and we say, "Little girls don't get angry," the anger goes underground, and we meet it in another part of town, namely in adolescence.

Parents we see have tried so many odd things. They try taking stuff away, giving kids stuff, and regulating stuff. It never works more than a short while. It's not about stuff at all. It's about what lies between a girl's ears—her brain and how she learns to use it. She has to be able to decide how her choices will affect her now and later. Her choices need to come from the courage to be herself; to face isolation from friends who may not agree with her; and to think things through to their logical conclusions. We can't wait until a girl becomes a teenager to teach her this, because there's too much going on by that time, too many things pulling her this way and that. We have to begin when she is young to teach her how to recognize that deep feeling in her gut that knows what is best for her to do in spite of what anyone else might think. Most kids know that feeling, but they have to learn to follow it. Don't we all?

—James, a family stress counselor

Fences and Consequences Defined

Fences, unlike punishments, clearly mark out the perimeters of any specified territory. Young children learn where it is permissible to play, because their backyard fence plainly outlines the safe area. They learn about the invisible fence that surrounds the stove, and that Grandma has an invisible barrier around her cabinet of antique teacups. Humans instinctively erect boundaries around themselves, and we all learn to respect comfortable distances for communication.

Initially, fences are for safety. These fences require much reinforcement, because the consequences are life-threatening. Don't play in the street; you'll be hit by a car. Don't touch the stove; you will get burned. Don't get into a stranger's car; we may lose you. Don't leave your dolls on the stairs; Mommy will trip and fall. Don't eat the pretty red berries; they might be poisonous. These fences we call BRICK WALLS. Because the natural consequences of disregarding these fences are so dangerous, parents must find outcomes that prevent repeated fence-crossing and prepare the way for development of self-regulating behavior. BRICK WALLS are set firmly with no room for negotiation, and the consequences are tough, so that girls know parents mean business. A logical outcome for continuing to leave toys on the stairs is that they go into the "hide-away" box to rest for awhile. They will reappear tomorrow, but their loss is enough to help a young child begin to consider that her toys have a specific home, and the stairway is not it. In the case of pretty, poisonous berries, a most effective approach is to say firmly but kindly "No" and to offer something safe to explore orally in exchange for the unsafe one. Patience and diligence is the key here for parents, because it is an unusual child who learns something after the first lesson.

> *Our first daughter needed only a certain look, and she knew we meant business. It's a different story for our second daughter. A look or a certain tone of voice have no impact on her urge to explore everything in her world. When she might endanger herself, we have to be right there, take her by the hand, try to distract her, and give her something else that's safe to do. And we have to do it over and over and over again! I just hope she makes it to adulthood.*

> *—Beth, mother of Emily, six and Christie, two*

As our daughters grow, fences and consequences become more than red flags demarcating the boundaries around dangerous people, events, or things. They become the internal boundaries that enable our girls to act wisely. Dr. Harriet Lerner, Ph.D., psychotherapist and best-selling author of *The Dance of Anger* writes, "Women in particular have been discouraged from taking responsibility for solving our own problems, determining our own choices, and taking control of the quality and direction of our own lives."[6] Sadly, women become dependent upon others to make them happy, which leads to blaming, nagging, anger, guilt, feelings of helplessness, and depression. This pattern begins in early childhood, when girls are taught to rely on others for guidance, are let off the hook for their misbehaviors, and learn to care for others at the expense of their own needs.

BRICK WALLS are a girl's first lessons in learning to face the consequences of her behavior. Consistency in following through with consequences allow these fences to become internal, self-regulated behaviors. When our daughters are older, these internal boundaries are kept in place by the fences we call SPOKEN VERBAL AGREE-MENTS. With these fences, our daughters act responsibly when agreements are broken. They apologize and make amends for their behavior. Action is taken out of a sense of commitment to their relationship, rather than from a fear of punishment. This behavior cannot be expected of girls until they have developed a sense of responsibility and understand cause and effect, usually between eight to ten years of age.

> *We had a big adjustment to make when Ann started driving. I can't sleep until I know she is safely home again. She promised to call if she was ever going to be late for any reason. She recently forgot to call, and I was a wreck before she got home an hour late. She had a good reason for being late, but she didn't make the extra effort it took to call. I explained how nervous I get; she understood, and her apology reassured me. I know I can trust her to follow through on her commitment.*
>
> *—Pat, mother of Ann, sixteen*

Like the old saying, "Good fences make good neighbors," appropriate fences and consequences enable daughters to grow into healthy women. Learning how to set good boundaries for themselves enables girls to recognize where their responsibilities toward others begin and end. Secure internal boundaries help girls know the difference between wise and unwise choices. Parents as fence builders need to move away from approving or disapproving of our daughters' behavior, to the more empowering position of determining what fences and consequences are needed to help them learn who they are, what their responsibilities toward themselves and others are, and how to act wisely while making their own decisions.

PICKET FENCES and RUBBER WALLS help families run smoothly and efficiently. PICKET FENCES outline what is the expected behavior of personal hygiene, neatness, assigned chores around the house, and so on. They are clear—we brush our teeth and wash our faces—and are usually regular, repetitive, and cyclical—we brush our teeth after every meal and wash our faces before going to school in the morning and before bed at night. Another example relates to household chores—your job is to empty the wastebaskets on Monday, Wednesday, and Friday mornings before school. A seven- or eight-year-old child occasionally hops over a picket fence, because she forgets, is tired, or bored. A reminder is often enough, if she is motivated to fulfill her family job. If she fails to follow through repeatedly, minor consequences or negotiation may be necessary. The designated job may be too hard for a young child, or she may really detest doing it. We know a young girl who gets queasy at the sight of anything disgusting, so emptying the wastebaskets may be too much to ask. She excels, however, at organizing, so a perfect task for her is dusting and putting the living room in order. She does this task with much care and pride.

Good fences nurture the awakening of a healthy sense of self. Fences must be spacious enough to allow girls to take risks and sometimes fail. The impact of learning from one's mistakes is far greater than being rescued by Mom or Dad and robbed of the chance to test one's strengths and find one's limits. RUBBER WALLS are fences big enough to allow freedom of movement and small enough to bounce them back to safety and reassurance. Girls feel lost and abandoned without clear limits to outline the acceptable parameters of their behavior, and they feel smothered if fences allow no room for taking risks, making mistakes, and facing the consequences of their choices. The consequences of RUBBER WALLS have greater impact.

Cheryl begged me to let her walk home after school with her friends. She promised she would follow our rules—no stops along the way, come straight home, no rides from older friends or strangers. Several weeks later I learn that she rode home from school with several older kids from another school. I told her, "No way, kiddo! You'll have to ride the bus right to our door for two weeks, and then, maybe we'll try it again." After that she knew I meant what I said about following the rules, and we've had no more trouble.

—Rita, mother of Cheryl, eleven

IRON BARS are required when a girl is a risk to herself or to others. Her behavior is so out-of-control that she must have round-the-clock supervision by her parents, the school, Juvenile Hall, or a mental hospital. This is boundary-setting in the extreme, and we hope most parents do not have to enforce it. If girls fail to learn an internal sense of who they are, where they begin and end, what their responsibilities are to themselves and others, and how to regulate their own behavior, they risk facing IRON BARS. Out of fairness to our daughters we must clearly and firmly let them know what behavior is OK and not OK, safe and not safe, from the very beginning.

Fences in Action

Judy, single mother of Lisa, age 14, was surprised to get a note from her daughter's principal. For the last thirty days, Lisa had been skipping several classes each day. When Judy confronted Lisa, she said, "Yeah, I skip once in a while." "But, this note says you've been skipping every day. That's more than just once in a while." Lisa accused her mother of believing school authorities over the word of her own daughter, and Judy felt badly about that. She decided to write a note back to the principal, telling him she and Lisa were working on the problem and that things should be fine now. Lisa agreed to stop skipping school. (SPOKEN VERBAL AGREEMENT)

Two weeks later another note appeared in the mail, requesting Judy to come to the school, because of Lisa's "chronic absentee problem."

Lisa's skipping had now increased to missing entire days. Judy was surprised. Lisa had been easy to raise with few problems before now. After the meeting at school, Judy realized that reminding Lisa of her responsibility to attend school was not enough. She informed Lisa that she was grounded for two weeks, and that she would use that time to catch up on her missed school work. (RUBBER WALLS) Lisa protested, her mother listened, and her mother followed through. After two weeks, the school informed Judy that the skipping had been cut in half, but it was still at the level of suspension, if major changes in Lisa's behavior didn't take place. Judy knew stronger action needed to be taken. Lisa was put on total restriction on weekends. Judy took this opportunity to engage Lisa in conversations about her school, her friends, what she thought about things in general. She learned a lot about her daughter that she hadn't known before. Lisa shared that she was bored in school and had little respect for her teachers, who seemed to just be going through the motions of teaching, rather than trying to instill enthusiasm for learning and creative thinking. She felt that her time spent outside of school talking with her friends about real things in life had more relevance. Judy shared that she had very similar feelings when she was a teenager, and the two seemed to come to an understanding that Lisa would have to make the best of it, following the school rules. She promised she would allow Lisa to develop outside activities aligned with her interests. (PICKET FENCE)

To Judy's disappointment, their discussions did not bring about the necessary changes, and she realized that the school could not keep track of her daughter and make her go to class. Judy also knew that any change would have to come from Lisa and herself. Early one morning, Judy awoke from her sleep with a solution. She negotiated two weeks vacation from her work, and took Lisa off restriction for the weekend. Monday morning Judy announced to Lisa, "Let's go! We're due at school in ten minutes." "What do you mean 'we'?" Lisa asked suspiciously. Judy just said, "Come on. Let's go." Judy parked the car and got out with Lisa. Lisa shrugged, assuming her mother was coming in to talk with the principal again, because of her poor attendance. Instead, Judy walked with Lisa to her locker, smiling at the other students. Then Lisa noticed her mother was not wearing her usual work clothes, but was more casually dressed. "What's the deal, Mom?

You're gonna be late for work." Judy smiled and said, "Since you are having so much trouble going to your classes, I'm going to go with you all day." (IRON BARS) Lisa's response was memorable. She cocked her head to the side, like a dog does when it hears a strange tone, and said, "*What?*"

"I followed her from class to class all that day. I was sorry she felt so humiliated, but I knew this was what it would take for her to go to class. I sat in the back of each class. I even went to the bathroom with her. Since I set this up with the principal beforehand, I ate at the teachers' table during lunch. By the end of the day, Lisa knew she had met her match. Things were stone quiet at home that night.

"The next morning was comical. Lisa assumed that the purpose of yesterday was humiliation, and that it was over. As she got out of the car, she looked down, saw my tennis shoes, and moaned, 'Oh, no, not again!' I told her that until she can go to school herself, I would be with her. That night she promised to go to her classes and begged to be given another chance. I gave in, but I told her that I'd be checking each day at lunch and again after school to see if she had been in class. If she had trouble again, we'd start all over. During the rest of my vacation, I checked on her each day with no misses. The Monday I went back to work, she skipped four out of seven periods. I was furious. Later I found out she had called my work to see how long my vacation actually was. She stayed in school until I went back to work. This was much more serious than I had thought.

"When she came home from school that day, I didn't mention it. After she went to bed, I put together the final iron bar of the fence, and the next morning I put my piece of work on the wall—a color-coded calendar from that day to the end of school When Lisa asked what it was, I told her to look closely. She asked me why her grandfather, grandmother, two uncles, or my close friends' names were on each day of the week. I then dropped the bomb. 'Today, I am taking a day off from work to go to school with you. Since I have to work and support us tomorrow,' I said, pointing with my pencil at the next day, 'Grandpa has agreed to be with you all day at school. The calendar goes to the end of the year. I have a day for each person except for the last week of school.' Lisa was stunned. I went to her school that day. That night she said she wanted to try again. I said, 'Okay, after Grandpa has a turn for one day.'

"Grandpa came and went to school. After that, Lisa did not miss one class and ended school with better grades than I had expected. I learned that some problems require total focus, commitment, and some pretty tough boundaries from both people in a relationship. School isn't always fun, neither is a career nor a relationship. I love my Lisa. I will be her parent, whether or not it is convenient for me."

This story illustrates each "Fence" in action. We saw that as the boundaries increased, more action, time, and attention by the parent is required. More conversation is needed. When one level doesn't work, it is increased until the daughter understands what is required of her to regain her former Verbal Agreement or Picket Fence privileges. The parenting team we spoke of in Chapter Five is needed at the higher fence levels. One or two parents cannot do it all. Many teenagers figure that out quickly, and maneuver their transgressions around the limitations of their parents' schedules. From pure exhaustion parents let children continue behaviors that are harmful, dangerous, and symptomatic of deeper problems. Once a child knows there are others who care about her by firmly yet kindly setting limits, she finds more creative options that work for her rather than continue the destructive behaviors that worked against her.

"Lisa is now sixteen," says Judy. "I trust her to drive because we have become much closer since the school attendance thing. We talk a lot and disagree a whole lot. And we work out more room for her to grow as she shows me she can handle it. I think we won't need the Iron Bars anymore. We can talk things out and reach a compromise now before things gets to that level of seriousness. She now knows I'm in charge at home, and that I'll do what's necessary to help her shape up. Gradually, I'm seeing her become more able to set her own personal boundaries. If she can make wise choices from her own internal boundaries when she is ready to leave home, I will have done a good job in helping her become a healthy adult."

Fence-Setting Guidelines

Good fences invite connection. Although fences separate one neighbor's yard from another, the clear boundary often facilitates cooperative connection. We know where our property begins and ends, and this knowledge gives us more confidence in relating to our neighbors. The image of women, hanging out the washing, stopping every now and then to lean over the backyard fence and share the latest news of the day comes to mind.

> *Katy lost the privilege of going out at night for two weeks after she came in three hours late twice in a row. The first time she had a good excuse; the second night, her excuse was ridiculous. So, instead of going out last weekend, she went with me to visit my sister. The four-hour drive was getting long when we started talking about her boyfriend and how much she missed him. This led to talking about our recent conflict. I was amazed to hear her say she deserved to lose her privilege of going out at night. "I wouldn't have respected you, Mom, if you hadn't done that," she said. I was even more amazed to hear myself tell her that I wouldn't respect her if she didn't take a good risk now and then to learn more about herself, the world, and how far I will let her go! We laughed. It's funny how close we became after she knew I meant business but still respected her need to be herself.*
>
> *—Jessica, mother of Katy, fifteen*

Fences support healthy personal boundaries and protect a girl's access to her inner guidance system. As we talk with her about the how's and why's of her behavior, we help her sort out her inner voices and urges. Seeing her choices clearly laid out before her enables a girl to learn the structure of the decision-making process and her power in each situation. She learns she doesn't have to act immediately in relation to an inner whim or idea; she doesn't have to take the advice of an inexperienced friend; nor does she have to succumb to the urgings of a peer's challenge or dare.

Setting appropriate fences at the right times may appear to merely intensify the conflict and distance between us and our daughters. If our goal is to help girls create clear personal boundaries, we are bound to hear our daughters' side of things, and that's not always easy for parents! *Good personal boundaries make us distinct from one another and connect us at the same time.* Persistently setting the right consequence eventually yields more understanding between parents and daughter and develops a daughter's ability to use her own good sense. She will come to understand that our consequences are not given to show her she is a bad person. The fence and its consequence mark where we connect, whose actions are who's, and who is responsible for what. As parents we are responsible for setting the best possible limits we can. Our daughters are responsible for either following these limits, requesting a change, or going around them and dealing with the consequences. This is how girls get to know themselves—how to discern what inner voice or feeling to follow. In the process, they learn our values about life. Fences and consequences foster connection and trust, making the journey through rough times together easier.

Good consequences relate as directly as possible to the break in the fence.

⇒ *JEANNE* | Before setting a consequence, I find that a "break in the action" is helpful to make sure I don't regret what I choose. I finally realized that I don't have to react immediately—you know, the silly feeling that as a parent I must always know what to do? When my daughter was little and misbehaved, I learned that saying, "I need to think about what will best help you remember to put your toys away," gave me time to choose something that directly related to what I wanted her to learn. Knowing I could stop before doing anything diminished the urge to swat out of anger, too, which never really teaches our children how we want them to behave.

"That's not fair, Daddy. Not getting my stories tonight has nothing to do with eating those yucky green things," my daughter wisely said to me one evening after I had lost my patience with her dawdling at the dinner table.

—*Jeff, father of Liza, seven*

Daughters usually resist what doesn't make sense. Their resistance can be an open invitation for us to forge ahead, whether our actions make any sense or not, like waving a red cape in front of a bull. Sadly, this gives a girl the indirect message that she is wrong, that her observations are not important. Feeling in the wrong breeds resentment and anger, as do shaming, humiliating, and blaming. Consequences that fit the broken fence resonate with a girl's sense of justice. A fair consequence may still be hard to face, because we've put up a barrier to what she had in mind, but our daughters won't have to also deal with the injustice of it all. Protect her ability to see things clearly. Take time to cool off and find a better consequence. Tell her she's right. Story time is more about refusing to get ready for bed. Eating "yucky green things" relates to the privilege of getting dessert. She will balk at that too, but somewhere inside her, she will feel reassured. "Yes! My parents are in charge and do know what they are doing." Girls need this reassurance perhaps more than anything else.

Good fences focus hard on the issue and easy on the person. All too often family members take each other's behavior as personal assaults, and it is hard not to believe that our children are not sometimes just out to get us. Why else would they act the way they do? "Why *do* they act the way they do?" is the question we need to ask ourselves when we are setting fences and choosing consequences. Focusing on the inherent messages in the behavior often leads us to the real problems.

> *I used to get so upset at Jenny when she cried and carried on in the grocery store. I'd think, "Why is she embarrassing me like this?" Then I'd realize she was tired or hungry, so her cry was for my help, not to embarrass me in public!*
>
> —*Judy, mother of Jenny, four*

When our focus is misdirected toward our own discomfort or inconvenience, we miss a unique moment of connection with our daughters. Please do not misunderstand what we are saying here. We do not advocate parent masochism, nor child tyrants, but misbehavior is usually a child's plea to a grown-up to feel safer, to be taken care of, or to be noticed. When we see the muddy footprints on the kitchen floor as our daughter's intentional act to create extra work for us, we risk dimming her adventurous spirit and miss a science lesson in how to mix soap and water together to mop the floor; or an art project to create a colorful box to catch muddy shoes before coming into the house. Fences and consequences require great creative thinking from parents. Fatigue, stress, and lack of time dull parental senses, leading to harsh words and consequences that fail to achieve our purpose of shaping self-reliant, responsible daughters. All children want to please their parents, want to feel capable, and want to experience competence at the tasks they are asked to undertake. Taking time to focus on behavior and what is needed to change it, rather than on personality faults, "You're so messy!" "You never think!" "Why can't you remember to take off your shoes? I've told you a dozen times (Dummy!)!"—eliminates power struggles and enhances connection between us and our daughters.

Destructive Cultural Fences

Earlier we discussed hidden beliefs about girls and boys perpetuated by our culture through the media, our educational system, and so on. The following story told by Ruth, a government social worker, beautifully describes how fences and consequences help us avoid the pitfalls of the "good girl/bad boy" cultural stereotype that keeps children of both genders locked into limiting roles they do not deserve.

"I stayed with Debbie and Jimmy for sixty days while their mother was in the hospital. Jennifer took special care to warn me about Jimmy, age 7, and to praise Debbie, age 8. She was right. Jimmy was a hellion from the beginning. Because I had worked in Juvenile Hall, I knew how to handle tough guys like him. I showed him that I was the boss, and that if he crossed my boundaries, he'd get a consequence. I gave him lots of positive attention, focusing on the good things he could do, and he bloomed like a flower.

"Debbie was another matter. As the 'angel' in the family, she had never been made to follow the rules and pretty much did anything she wanted. She ran into a big barrier when she ran into me. I think girls need to be made responsible for their actions, too. Well, the first night

Jimmy had been getting lots of positive attention from me, and when Debbie thought I wasn't looking, she hauled off and slugged Jimmy, taking his sandwich. When I walked over, Debbie started crying and claimed that Jimmy had hit her. I got down beside her and said, 'No, Debbie, you hit him. Give his sandwich back.' Sweet, little Debbie went ballistic. I had betrayed a fundamental rule in this house: Jimmy is bad, and Debbie is good. She was the angel; Jimmy was the devil. Jimmy was punished for everything; Debbie always got off clean.

"For two weeks, Debbie did everything she could to re-establish the status quo—she is always good, Jimmy is always bad. She threw temper tantrums, ignored my existence, refused to speak to me. She staunchly held to her position of being above accountability for her actions, even though she wanted to let it all go, and join me in making things work. Because of the limited role she had in her family, she could see no other way to be. I continued to hold her responsible, to talk about her feelings, to set logical consequences that related directly to her behavior, to show her what I wanted from her, and to be as fair as I could.

"In the third week, I told her she could ask me to teach her to use my laptop computer. Quickly she said, 'I'm ready!' She sat on my lap, played a computer game with me, then leaned back, and cried her heart out. That was the turning point. She still tested me to see if I would follow through, but she took her consequences, voicing her disapproval all the way. By the end of my stay, Debbie was cooperative, assertive, fair, and pleased about her new-found strength. When her mother returned, she said, 'Mom, Ruth says I'm just as bad as Jimmy!' Her mother was appalled."

Believing that girls should be nice overlooks their need to test limits. Girls need firm boundaries that are flexible enough to allow experimentation to find out what happens *when*. What happens when I say what I feel? What happens when I say "No"? What happens when I lie? What happens when I don't do what I am told? Learning that someone else will act out for them is a dangerous lesson. Girls need self-reliance and competency to thrive. These gifts are hard-won in the tussles of everyday dealing with fences and consequences, making choices and facing what happens next. In the fray girls learn to be accountable for the personal responsibility that common sense and ethical behavior demand.

When others—a brother or a sister—act out for her, a girl learns either that she is the only responsible one and others don't have to be, or she learns that everyone is responsible but herself. These two positions disconnect her from personal accountability. Through being held accountable for our behavior, we learn to listen to our inner guidance, to know what is right, to trust our ability to act, to follow through on what must be done. We become self-confident and self-reliant. We take a stand for what we truly believe. Without these resources we become like Debbie. Because she could only see herself as an angel, she was limited in her choices of behavior, felt powerless in most situations, and missed out on genuine connections with others.

During the teenage years, a girl becomes more at risk if she believes she transcends personal and legal boundaries. A false sense of power, or the other extreme, a false sense of her powerlessness, weakens her common sense in the face of the hard choices of adolescence—whether to use drugs, what peer group to join, who to date, whether to become sexually active, the importance of academic performance, and so on.

Fences that encourage a healthy sense of when she is responsible and when she isn't make room for a girl's soul to emerge. This is most dramatically seen in therapeutic work with adult women who have been sexually molested as children. "Sexual molestation of a young girl is one of the most fundamental violations of her life," reports Dr. Francine Shapiro, Ph.D., originator of the powerful and highly effective Eye Movement Desensitization and Reprocessing (EMDR) method for resolving post-traumatic stress. "What is so personal and private becomes distorted by an adult who is supposed to be modeling healthy, personal boundaries and teaching what is okay about behavior and what isn't. One of the most important tasks facing any victim of molestation is to reset her boundaries between herself and the other. This helps with the inevitable question: 'Whose fault is it?' The victim almost always takes responsibility for an event that was out of her control. She continues to take on responsibility for outside events in her adult life, unless and until the trauma is resolved and healthy personal boundaries are developed."[7]

Setting Fences in Stepfamilies

Stepfamilies are difficult. Knowing this from the beginning makes the experience easier. Rather than denying the difficulties, we can seek support, education, and encouragement from others in similar situations. Stepfamilies are no longer a rarity. By the year 2000, stepfamilies will be the dominant family configuration.[8] Although our family patterns are rapidly shifting, our attitudes towards stepfamilies are slow to change. *The American Heritage Dictionary* defines "stepchild" in the following way: 1. a spouse's child by a previous marriage 2. something that does not receive appropriate care, respect, or attention.[9] We have tried to change prejudices against this nontraditional family situation by using the term "blended family." This name is misleading, however, because it implies smooth, interwoven, and peaceful. Families with children from more than one marriage are anything but smooth. *Challenging, ever-changing, meaningful*, and *frustrating* are more apt descriptions. Relabeling stepfamilies is only giving them a "new coat of paint." Starting a stepfamily is building a family from the ground up. No simple blending occurs. A complete reconstruction of a foundation must be accomplished by two very dedicated people. With a strong foundation, family pride and coherence can be built. In his excellent book, *Making Peace in Your Stepfamily*, Harold Bloomfield writes, "A stepfamily is a remarried couple with children who are taking steps toward becoming a family...becoming a family takes time. You have to take many steps, one step at a time, but as long as you remain on the right path, you will arrive at a wonderful goal."[10]

When setting fences in a stepfamily, the following suggestions will be helpful:

We are pioneers. We have no cultural guidelines for stepfamilies. When children lost a parent in premodern tribal cultures, they were absorbed into another family, or the remaining spouse took another mate. That was it, and the entire tribe adhered to these customs. Today, every family has its own view of right and wrong, social graces, and life values. Even within marriages, parents may be deeply divided on critical issues affecting how the home is managed, how children are expected to behave, and the purpose of family life. Modern stepfamilies cannot look to the past for wisdom and guidance. Today's parents of stepfamilies are pioneers and must rely on our own reflections and lived wisdom in the process of building new family foundations.

The biological parent must lead the way in discipline. Stepchildren need time—lots of time—to begin to trust a stepparent. To smooth the way, it is important for the biological parent to take the lead in discipline. As mentioned earlier, most children need three to five years before they respond positively to the discipline of the nonbiological parent; therefore, clear communication between partners is crucial. The primary thoughts in a daughter's mind are, "Who is in charge? If you are not my own mother or father, you are not the boss until you earn it!" Behind closed doors, both partners must learn how to communicate their concerns to each other, so they can cooperate in relating to their children. Each stepfamily has different needs in the area of discipline. Starting with the biological parent and expanding the direct authority of the stepparent over time builds a realistic approach to the sharing of this most important parenting function.

Both parents need room to complain and be heard in private. Communicate, communicate, communicate! Even in the strongest of relationships, the stepparent can feel like the "odd person out." In bringing a stepfamily together, the potential for discipline problems does not double; it increases geometrically. In the heat of arguments, loyalties tend to divide according to biological lines. Biological parents are often stuck between their new spouse and their children; not a comfortable position to be in. Both partners need ample room to express frustrations and to renew their love and commitment to each other in private. Psychotherapy, stepfamily support groups, and even friends who share similar situations can help strengthen the bond of the remarried couple and provide outlets to vent feelings.

In a divorced or stepfamily situation, our daughter may spend considerable time in the home of her "other family." Discipline styles may vary widely, and it is helpful to provide as much consistency as possible. The following points may help in dealing with differences in rules and expectations:

Find out how the "other family" sets fences and chooses consequences. Learn about our daughter's other situation and keep those rules in mind when setting fences at home. Dealing with two different sets of rules can be confusing and frustrating for divorced parents. If it is to a daughter's advantage, she may not let us know that rules we set in our home are more lenient than with her other family. Very likely she will subscribe to Napoleon's famous saying, "Never interrupt your enemy when they are making a mistake."[11] If possible, try to discuss with her other parent how to standardize things, such as bedtime, curfew, overnight privileges, driving, and other rules. Agreement may be impossible, but making allowance for differences and understanding what is expected of our daughter helps her know where she stands and makes it safe for her to come to us with her frustrations.

Count to one hundred and drink five glasses of water before giving consequences. We are not kidding! This allows time to calm down before setting a consequence we might later regret. Time to think gives room to consider how this consequence will affect our daughter's life in her other family, as well as at home. We can remain clear and calm in the face of our daughter's distractions and avoid possible cross-purposes with our ex-spouse. Understanding, flexibility, and clear communication of what we need are vital to the well-being of everyone concerned.

Fences in Single-Parent Households

Single-parent families and stepfamilies share similar frustrations. There is one big difference—one parent must shoulder it all. Single parents face many additional wrinkles in the family scene, such as increased economic pressures, reduced resources for child care—especially when a child is ill—the effects of a parent's dating on the children, the remarriage of the former spouse, the addition of stepbrothers and sisters, and not having someone else to talk things over with. We urge single parents to remember that it is important to ask for help. Check for resources listed in the "Help!" section of Chapters Nine through Eleven under "Fences." Consider the following suggestions when setting limits with daughters as a single parent:

Be the boss and a friend, in that order. "In the absence of a partner, parent and child often relate as friends. So the single-parent family ends up with no real hierarchy of power. This puts the parent in a bind around issues of discipline," asserts Shoshana Alexander, single parent and author of *In Praise of Single Parents*. "The solution seems to lie in developing good communication skills as well as establishing clear guidelines about what is expected of the child. This covers both aspects of the relationship. In the role of friendship, clear and respectful communication is essential. In the role of parent, you as the authority make clear what is expected of the child. The more clearly the child knows what is expected, the easier it is to talk about problems when they come up. The child feels secure knowing you are in charge and also open to discussion. In that order."[12]

Ask for help. "You can't do it alone," says single parenting expert and family counselor, Liz Hannigan. "You have to ask for help. This is the first time in recorded history we are trying to raise children alone. Asking is the hardest thing you will have to do, so if you can't do it for yourself, do it for your child. In my case, I was going to have to change my daughter's preschool for the third time in a year, and I didn't want to put my three-and-a-half-year-old through yet another change. I finally got up the courage to ask the school for help with fees, and even though the school had never done it before, they said OK! I was shocked. It pays to ask. Now, years later, I have given back a thousand fold. When you're on your feet again, you can give back and more. When you're struggling is the time to reach out and ask—for your sake and for your child."[13]

Develop a parenting team and be quick to consult. Single mothers and fathers need feedback and information about current trends in their daughters' lives—age-appropriate behavior, fashions, peer group choices, and so on. Single fathers may need advice about clothing styles, tattoos, curfew times, and protocols for overnights at friends' houses. Single mothers may need to get perspectives on how to enforce chores, homework, financial assistance, discipline and other problems. Close friends, family members, neighbors, ministers, church and temple members, counselors, teachers, and daycare staff are all potential support for a parenting team.

Major corporations do not hesitate to consult a professional for assessment and recommendations when faced with important decisions. Single parents must break down their walls of isolation and reach out to others when in doubt about parenting. Then trust your inner guidance system about what is best for you and your children.

Bold and Audacious Parenting: New Community Fences for a New Era

Many parents feel overwhelmed, not only by the surprising behavior of our daughters, but by the complicated tangles of modern lives: divorce, single parents, and stepfamilies, overcrowded schools and overloaded teachers, understaffed police and overscheduled judicial systems, and neighborhoods where few of us know the people who share our street. Life becomes even more complicated in the teen years when the parents of our daughters' friends remain mysteries, because of differences in race, income level, religion, business, or lifestyle preferences. Staying in close connection with our active daughters, within the confines of our busy work schedules and family activities, presents a challenge staggering to even the most energetic and organized of us. Unless we set clear, appropriate fences, our daughters will make choices they aren't ready for, and what looked like freedom will quickly become a prison devoid of life choices. How do we set limits that work for our daughters as well as for ourselves? Here is a wonderful story about how a group of brave and audacious parents in Indianapolis, Indiana, did it.

"When our daughter became a freshman at Arlington High, her father and I worried about the violence at her school," says Linda Wallace. "The first football game of last year's season had to be stopped because of a riot. We both work and could have moved to another neighborhood, but our daughter hated to leave her lifelong friends, and our son was a senior, so we decided to stay and work to make some changes in the school.

"Conditions at the school were really in a terrible state. Most social events were canceled because of gang interference. Then the school decided to try a talent show and asked several teachers and parents to be monitors. My husband and I went. We parents and teachers each took a section of the auditorium, standing in a visible position. The event was a success with little trouble. I noticed an important thing that night. Of all the sections, my husband's was the best behaved and seemed to have the most fun. I had an idea: why not get a group of fathers together, have T-shirts made that say 'Security Dad,' and have them show up for football games? I was amazed so many dads liked the idea and were willing to sign up for duty.

"The first football game of that season was against our biggest rival. Last year's game ended in a riot. The police were ready for the worst. This was our first big test. Twenty 'Security Dads' arrived early, planned their game strategy, and spread out in the stands. The mothers ran the concessions. It worked beautifully. The chief of the Indianapolis Police Department thanked us for the best game he had ever enjoyed. My son, now graduated, complained, 'Why didn't you do this when I was in school?'

"Our success continues. After four years our graduates and their parents come back for dances, parties, talent shows, and games to be in on the fun and join in the work. Most parents want to do something more than bake cookies, so I established a Parent Center that's open every day. The men especially enjoy making a difference. 'Security Dads and Moms' come to school weekly, walking the halls, and sticking their heads in classes. We plan the school events calendar with the principal, make phone calls, and have fun together. You would think the kids would be upset with so many parents around. The opposite is true. At that first talent show I saw my husband treat the kids with respect and leadership. They respected him in return and assumed leadership for themselves. I overheard one senior boy bragging that his father helped in the school library. He was proud that his father was there to help, instead of being there because his son was in trouble."

Linda Wallace and the "Security Dads" [14] are excellent examples of community fence-setting at work to make our children's environments safe and fun places to be. Around the country, parents are joining together to model healthy boundaries in community. The "Security Dads" project took Linda Wallace's ingenuity, commitment, persistence, organization, energy, and time to become the effective organization it is today. It also required the cooperation of the school administration, teachers, and concerned parents to do the work of raising money for T-shirts, phoning, scheduling, and planning. Linda Wallace found that parents and schools are more than willing to help when they have a clear plan of action and a specific role to fulfill. The people in Linda Wallace's community became bold enough to stop the violence threatening their children's school and audacious enough to try solutions that had never been tried before. Their daughters were in on the process of taking action from a sense of purpose and commitment from the beginning. They demonstrated that schools and communities don't have to remain victims of violence and abuse.

"My daughter is the real winner in all of this," says Linda Wallace. "She now attends a school that's safe, whose kids are proud to be there. Someone from the student body thanks us everyday, and they are part of the team, too. We have a real partnership."

Fences: A Quick Summary

Good fences make good neighbors.

Spoken Verbal Agreements	Spoken agreements kept between parent and daughter that carry no consequence. Reminders are rarely necessary, and there is care shown on both sides to keep the agreement. When the agreement is broken, amends and apologies are made swiftly. The motivation to keep verbal agreements is inner-directed and comes from a sense of commitment to the relationship, so they work best with girls after age nine.
Picket Fences	Reminder is enough to alert the daughter to her agreements and participation in the family. Picket fences are used to promote basic household functioning. A girl may occasionally hop over it or forget, so a reminder, minor consequences, or negotiation may be necessary.

Rubber Walls Not able to set own limits, so they are set for her. She needs something to bounce off of, to feel safe and to learn responsibility. The consequences have greater impact.

Brick Walls Tough consequences needed to get the daughter's attention. She needs to immediately change her thinking and behavior, or she will put herself in trouble or danger. The goal is to take care of the problem within the family before an outside authority must intervene.

Iron Bars At risk to self or another, daughter requires twenty-four hour supervision by parents, school, Juvenile Hall, or a psychiatric hospital. Daughter could be in legal trouble. Free movement is limited. She must show serious intent to do good before regaining freedom, privileges, trust, and responsibilities.

Endnotes

1. Don Elium and Jeanne Elium, *Raising a Son: Parents and the Making of a Healthy Man* (Hillsboro, OR: Beyond Words, 1992), 1.

2. Gerald Manley Hopkins, as quoted in "Maintaining Personal Boundaries in Relationships," David Richo, *The California Therapist*, Jul./Aug. 1990, 40.

3. Jean Baker Miller, *Toward a New Psychology of Women* (Boston, MA: Beacon Press, 1986), 40.

4. The "How Healthy Are Your Personal Boundaries?" quiz was adapted from the article by David Richo, "Maintaining Personal Boundaries," 41.

5. Sherry Glueck, interview with Don Elium, Danville, CA, 27 Mar. 1993.

6. Harriet Goldhor Lerner, *The Dance of Anger* (New York: Harper & Row, 1985), 124.

7. Francine Shapiro, a lecture given as part of an EMDR training, Sunnyvale, CA, 23 Apr. 1993.

8. Harold H. Bloomfield, *Making Peace in Your Stepfamily* (New York: Hyperion, 1993), 3.

9. *The American Heritage Dictionary* (Boston: Houghton Mifflin, 1992), 1761.

10. Bloomfield, *Making Peace*, 5.

11. Nelson DeMille, *The Gold Coast* (New York: Warner Books, 1977), 279.

12. Shoshana Alexander, phone interview with Don Elium, Minneapolis, MN, 28 Sept. 1993.

13. Liz Hannigan, M.A., interview with Don Elium, Touchstone Counseling Services, Pleasant Hill, CA, 28 Sept. 1993.

14. Linda Wallace, originator of "Security Dads," a community parents organization, phone conversation with Don Elium, Indianapolis, IN, 27 Jul. 1993. To contact Linda Wallace for more information about "Security Dads," call (317)226-4006.

CHAPTER SEVEN

INNER GUIDANCE SYSTEM: FEELING, THINKING, AND WILLING

There is something in every one of you that
waits and listens for the sound of the genuine
in yourself...the only true guide you'll ever have.
And if you cannot hear it, you will all of your life
spend your days on the ends of strings that
somebody else pulls.[1]

—Howard Thurman, Graduation Speech,
Spelman College, 1981

The Powerful Trio

Our cultural gauge of competence measures whether or not we can make decisions, solve problems, and contribute as productive members of society. Stereotypically, men are valued for their rational thinking and problem-solving abilities. Women have been considered less intellectually capable—more susceptible to getting lost in their emotions—relying on their intuition to get them through. Because we place heavy emphasis on the intellectual, rational mind as a problem-solver, few of us realize our decisions are made from the vital partnership of three powerful, guiding forces—feeling, thinking, and willing. We are warned not to get stuck in emotions, and that intuition is suspect and perhaps doesn't even exist. Because of cultural conditioning, most of us rely on our intellects to "figure things out." When we teach these beliefs to our daughters, they learn to make choices without engaging their entire inner guidance systems, and we deny them their birthright of personal power.

The powerful trio of feeling, thinking, and willing gradually awakens with our daughter's psychological development. In the beginning, she soaks up her environment through her body's five senses. She tastes, touches, looks, listens, and smells every aspect of the world around her. At the same time, her intuition, what some call the sixth sense, infuses all her knowing, as she is more attuned to the heavenly world she came from than this earthly one she now inhabits. We call intuition an *involuntary sense*, because its wise messages come through to our conscious minds unbidden. We have no control over them. We just know something without knowing how we know it—that Aunt Lula is going to call, that an important letter will arrive tomorrow, that our daughter is in trouble. Our tiny daughter's intuition is based on her knowledge of the natural world's own mysterious language, and it enables her to perceive things we no longer see. We must not distract her from this knowing; we do not want her to forget these numinous mysteries too soon.

> *How like an Angel came I down!*
> *How bright are all things here!*
> *When first among his Works I did appear.*
> *O how their Glory did me crown*
> *The world resembled his ETERNITY*
> *In which my Soul did walk;*
> *and ev'ry thing that I did see*
> *Did with me talk.*[2]

—Thomas Traherne, *"Wonder"*

After the change of baby teeth around ages seven to nine, a girl develops the rudiments of conceptual thought. Unfortunately, most of us fail to recognize the gradual awakening of this function of the rational mind, believing our daughter capable of thinking the way we do long before she is able. We give her mixed messages about her ways of knowing; too early we expect her to understand our reasoning and yet are surprised when she knows things we didn't realize she knew.

> *Before her dad and I split up, Janie began having these terrible nightmares about being left in a huge, dark place all alone. We were very careful not to discuss anything about a divorce in front of her, and we really didn't fight out in the open all that much. During the day Janie was really clingy to both of us. It was as if she knew, even before we did, that we were going to end our marriage.*
>
> —*Irene, mother of Janie, three*

The dichotomy between what girls perceive as real and what we tell them is real causes great confusion. When daughters learn to deny vital information-giving parts of themselves, they begin to doubt their own knowing. This doubt festers and spreads, eating away at a healthy self-esteem. Around adolescence, phrases such as "I don't know" and "What do *you* think?" creep into their conversations, as they look to others to fill in the missing information they learned to deny.

One remedy for the common loss of self-esteem among adolescent girls is to instill confidence in their powerful trio of knowing—feeling, thinking, and willing—from their moment of birth. Allow room for emotions by listening, honor intuition by making room for the possibility that what they sense is true, enhance thinking skills by offering choices and challenges when they are ready, and encourage their engagement of will to achieve their dreams.

The Feeling Life

The feeling life is a girl's soul life, her heart—her intuition, her emotions, and her feelings. Acknowledging these ways of knowing is vital for the development of a whole, healthy woman.

Feeling and emotion are used interchangeably in our language. We offer the following explanation to simplify the differences between these two extremely complex human responses. Emotion is the pure rush of love, hate, joy, sorrow, fear, and so on, without the involvement of thinking or willing. We experience an emotion as an immediate reaction to an event, a memory, a perception. For example, a dramatic sunset, the picture of a lost loved one, or a familiar piece of music may immediately move us to tears. It is only later, when our tears have dried that we can voice how we felt about hearing that particular song again; that we were reminded of our high school prom and felt the bittersweet sadness of people and time gone by. This later expression of sadness is a feeling, a message from the heart, beginning as raw emotion and eventually refined by thinking. Therefore, feeling is an emotion that has been worked on by thinking. We feel a surge of rage; then later are able to explain that we felt angry.

A healthy girl makes decisions and acts from her own inner guidance system, rather than someone else's. She learns to listen to her inner voice for signals to what she likes, what she wants, and how others are affected by her behaviors. She comes to understand her inner urgings and whether to act upon them. Using her feeling life as a barometer to what is happening around her gives a girl the power to be who she truly is. She learns to be appropriately responsive to others and to set boundaries by saying "No" when necessary. She is able to live her own life, rather than living only to please others.

Traditionally, females have been given the responsibility for carrying the feeling life. To the detriment of all, modern culture isolates men by stimulating their aggressiveness and intellect while suppressing their emotions and feelings. We are just now coming to realize that men must reclaim their hearts, or they spend their lives seeking to conquer and own the feeling-hearts of women. Any chance of a satisfying relationship with a woman is killed by a man's lack of knowing his own feeling nature. A woman's fulfilling relationship with a man is dependent upon how well as a child she learns to access and listen to her own heart, how confident she is in following her own inner messengers. Two people in touch with their feelings provide the crucible in which love can grow.

Although we sanction females as the bearers of feelings, we limit their emotional repertoires. Because some emotions and feelings are not allowed, we render them partly feeling-blind, charting a journey with great expectations, only to end up someplace else, with someone else's map, taking care of someone else's travel needs. With this partial awareness, a girl is destined to say "Yes," when she means "No," "No," when she means "Yes," and "I don't know," when she really knows but is afraid to say. Our daughters need to know their whole hearts.

How Feelings Work

The *how* of feelings has a simple theme and follows a predictable path. The Feeling Curve below illustrates this path.

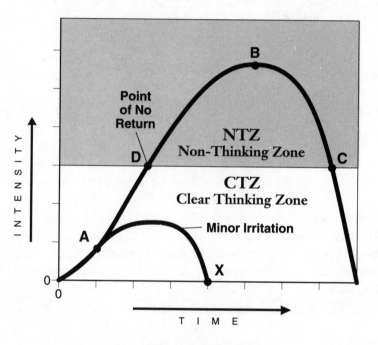

The Feeling Curve

An emotion starts and increases in intensity (A). If the emotion is not very strong—we are only slightly irritated, for example—it is quickly released, and we revert to calm (X). "He really bugged me for saying that, but it wasn't that big a deal." The emotion is a small "blip" and quickly released, often without our noticing.

When an emotion is much stronger, however, it increases in intensity, until it hits what we call the PNR, or Point-of-No-Return (D). "I couldn't believe my brother. After telling him three times when and where to meet me, he didn't show, and I had to ride the bus again!!!!!" The emotion is now so intense that until it hits its peak (B), it is extremely difficult to release (C).

The PNR is an important moment. Before this point, conversation, discussion, and even disagreement are all possible. Our intellect, or rational mind, is operable. At the PNR, however, an emotion rushes headlong up and over the top of the curve, oblivious to any rational thought or word from others attempting to stop its mad course. Warning! Logic has no power here. "I hate it when you keep telling me I shouldn't be so upset!!! I'm mad at you!!!" says Debra, aged thirteen. Reasoning with her only causes irritation and makes her emotion even stronger, because she has entered a different dimension called the NTZ, the Non-Thinking Zone.

In the NTZ, we only experience the fullness of emotion. "I try not to yell at you, Mom, but it just comes out of me!" says Kiki, age eight, after she calms down. Clear, rational thought is totally impossible. The course of the NTZ is carved in stone. Once emotions reach the Point-of-No-Return, we enter the Non-Thinking Zone, and our emotions go only in one direction—up and over the Feeling Curve.

When we allow our emotions to naturally follow the full Feeling Curve, they are released, and we enter the CTZ, the Clear Thinking Zone (C). Here, and not before, are we able to reflect on the meaning of what we felt. "OK, I see your point, but I don't want to stop using my fingers to add. I'm afraid I'll make a mistake, if I don't," admits Kelli, aged nine, after screaming at her father to get off her back about math. As her father waited patiently for her emotions to subside, Kelli became thoughtful and more flexible, where only seconds before she said she hated him and never wanted to talk with him again.

When taken by our emotions to the Non-Thinking Zone, we are incapable of stating our feelings clearly, describing our position, or making decisions. These come later from the Clear Thinking Zone. What we say from the Non-Thinking Zone can change, and probably will. "One second she says she hates me," reports Ben, father of Andrea, sixteen. "The next minute she agrees to go along with my request. Sometimes I feel as if I'm talking to a girl with two personalities!"

How can we know when our daughter's emotions have progressed through the NTZ to find release in the CTZ? This takes careful listening and patience. When her logic is fuzzy, she says she "doesn't know," she responds to our comments with nasty retorts, or she keeps repeating herself, we can be fairly certain she is not yet ready to discuss her position. She still needs time to fully experience her emotions. We recommend taking a break, letting everyone cool down, and coming back to the matter later.

Time varies for emotions to rise, peak, and release into thoughtful feelings. When emotions are allowed to follow their natural course, the shift from the Non-Thinking Zone to the Clear Thinking Zone happens rapidly. Moving too quickly into problem-solving, however, denies a girl's natural timing and starts the Feeling Curve cycle all over again. "He doesn't give me time to get my emotions out. He just jumps right in, giving me advice about how I can fix my problem, without even really understanding how I feel about it first! That makes me livid!"

How to Navigate the Non-Thinking Zone

Listen and leave room for expression. Listening without interruption gives a girl the support she needs to let her emotions evolve into expression of feelings. This process invites discussion and compromise in older daughters (eight and over) and cooperation in younger daughters (two to seven). Sometimes a girl's emotions naturally follow the cycle of the Feeling Curve, and sometimes she needs help moving out of her deep emotions.

> *My daughter's natural seriousness and tendency to brood about things are sometimes frustrating for me. She can cry on and on over a hurt or disappointment. Recently, she sat on the floor of her room, sobbing because her friend couldn't spend the night. I said, "I'm sorry, sweetheart. I can't help you out of this one. You're just going to have to do it yourself." She cried, "But, I don't know how to get out of it myself." I asked her whether she wanted some help. When she nodded, I advised, "First say to yourself, 'I feel really bad about this right now, and there's nothing I can do to change it.' Then say, 'What can I do to help myself feel better right now?' It may be something you do for yourself,*

or it might mean doing something for someone else."
She looked at me with half-lidded eyes for a moment,
and then turned to amuse her baby sister.

—*Laura, mother of Elizabeth, seven*

Having an emotion, expressing a feeling, and committing violence are three entirely different acts. We can let emotions run their course, naturally peaking and releasing, without expressing them if we so choose, or we can express feelings, after we have had time to think about them, by voicing them in a personal way, such as "I feel so sad," "I was angry," or "I feel abandoned."

Emotions do not hurt people, unless they are cut off, suppressed, denied, or ignored. When we interrupt our daughter's emotions and feelings by saying, "It's not that bad," she either tries to please us by stuffing them or explodes on the spot. Stuffed emotions and feelings usually come out at us later, so either way, we create an eruption we might have avoided. Making judgmental statements, such as "Can't you just stay calm, for once?" giving advice before she is ready, such as, "You should have done such and such," and using logic, such as, "If you had used the smaller scissors, then you wouldn't have been as likely to slip and cut a hole in your new dress," provokes the same explosion or withdrawal as we get when we make light of her feelings.

Parents need not tolerate physical violence, verbal abuse, and critical character assassinations from our children. When girls are free to follow their emotions up and over the Feeling Curve, are given time to think about how they feel, have their feelings heard, valued, and understood, and if necessary helped through them, violence of any kind is less likely to occur.

Be slow to problem-solve and quick to listen to all of her feelings. What appears to us to be a small rock in shallow waters, may be the tip of an iceberg to our daughter. The longer we listen, the more understanding we have about what lurks beneath the surface of her deep ocean of feeling life. From this vantage point, we can help her chart a straighter, safer course.

We do not have to agree with her feelings. Sometimes parents worry that acknowledging a daughter's feelings without judging them implies we agree with her. Describing what we observe, is not agreeing, and we avoid making her feelings right or wrong. "You sound angry when you talk about what your friend said," describes what we observe and tells our daughter that we are relating to what she is sharing with us. Whether we understand why she feels the way she does, or whether we would feel the same way, too, are different matters and not important now. What nourishes her feeling life is that we give her our focused attention, we listen, and we describe her experience as closely as we are able.

Consider what she really wants to know. Sometimes we ask questions when we are really sharing feelings. When a girl asks, "What would you do if the teacher yelled at you?" we might take it as an open invitation to relive our own painful school experiences. If we respond with, "You sound angry," instead, we have opened the way for her to explore her feelings. She may then feel able to say, "Yes, I'm angry, and embarrassed, too!"

Be empathetic, but don't overdo it. "My dad really tries hard to listen and to understand me, but sometimes he nods his head up and down so much when I'm talking, he reminds me of those dogs some people have in their cars with the springs in their heads," laughs Juliet, aged thirteen. It is better to err in this direction, however, than to jump into problem-solving, patronizing, or talking her out of her feelings. Responding with, "I just don't know what to say, except that this sounds really hard for you," lets a daughter know we support her, whether or not we share her feelings.

We must beware of overusing reflective listening—the practice of rephrasing what we hear someone say—because in our efforts to comfort a daughter, we may lose sight of what she is telling us she needs. Sometimes we are unaware we are trying to soothe a fear or hurt that is within us, rather than within her. Being overwhelmed by her feelings is a clue for us to step back, slow down, or take a "time-out."

Give advice sparingly. Our daughters do need to hear our opinions and often want our advice. Make sure they are out of the Non-Thinking Zone and proceed with caution. With good timing and understanding, our wise words will become a cornerstone of confidence in our relationship. Our daughters will come to us when they really need our help or advice.

Forgiveness and perseverance are essential. We are only human, and the path of parenting is full of ruts and potholes. We only fail, however, when we give up trying. Being easy on ourselves when we miss a chance to listen models forgiveness for our daughters. The road to a successful parent/daughter relationship is bumpy. Our ups and downs are sure signs we're on the right road.

Parenting from the Non-Thinking Zone

In a memorable scene from the old Bill Cosby show, Daddy Huxtable goes upstairs to his daughters' bedroom and says in a tightly controlled voice, "Your mother told me to come up here and killlllllllll you. Do you want to know why before I killlll you?" Huxtable knew the worst time to set a consequence is when parents are upset and frustrated. More than likely, the consequence we set in this mood will inconvenience us more than it will teach our child anything about self-regulating behavior. The following list of the Top Four Parenting *Faux Pas* from the Non-Thinking Zone was offered by fifteen parents waiting in line at our local supermarket. Many of us can probably add our own favorites.

Top Four Parenting *Faux Pas*

1. I'm grounding you for the rest of your life!

2. Go to bed and don't ever get up!

3. You will sit there until you eat every bite!

4. I will never, ever _____ *again!*
                        (You fill in the blank)

Set consequences in the Clear Thinking Zone. We laugh about our parenting *faux pas* years later, but at the time we feel inadequate and silly. We also make it difficult to follow through, because snap judgments from the Non-Thinking Zone are difficult to back up. Our daughters learn that we do not really mean what we say.

I had the terrible habit of acting first and thinking later, until I realized that my daughter didn't believe anything I said. I had given her crazy consequences enough times that she knew I would have to back down, while she got away with murder! I finally got a grip on my anger and can cool down now, before I slap an outrageous consequence on her. The other day I told Kathy and her friend that if they didn't pick up the toys now, they would go in a box in the garage for a day. I overheard Kathy say, "Let's do it; he means what he says." She remembered when it happened last week. Thank goodness we can both change our ways.

—Ned, single father of Kathy, nine

Good timing allows clear thinking. Setting limits and consequences from the Clear Thinking Zone avoids unnecessary confusion, conflict, and anxiety.

⊰ *JEANNE* | When I realized I didn't have to respond immediately, on-the-spot, I was able to give more thought to what my daughter's behavior was all about. I could consider what interventions were required to help her regulate her own behavior. After the heat of the moment passed, I was also able to relate to her with less criticism and judgment about what she had done. When she was really little, of course, she needed me to respond sooner, because the anxiety would be too great for her to wait long. As she grew, we could both agree to come back to something after we had both cooled off.

Suppression of Emotion and Feeling: Short-Term Storage

The Feeling Curve is, of course, an oversimplified picture of how emotional energy works in the human being. Emotions do not always rise and fall into thoughtful feelings as neatly as the diagrams imply. Emotions follow these predictable patterns just often enough for us to believe we have them all figured out. Then we observe something new in our daughter's behavior, and we are at a loss as to what to do next.

The feeling life is more complex than the predictable rise and release of emotion, because we can express emotions, suppress them, or repress them. Emotions that climb the Feeling Curve and release into the Clear Thinking Zone are conscious feelings. They are emotions that have been worked on by thinking. They let us know we are alive, connected, and relating. They also tell us when we are in trouble, in love, or lost.

Often, our emotions rise and subside in situations where we cannot appropriately express and deal with our feelings. Alicia, company project manager, moans, "I am so frustrated with my boss. She is making this project twice as hard as it has to be. But, I have to focus on the deadline now. Later, I'm going to tell her how I feel!" We have all been in Alicia's place. We feel strongly about our experience, but we have to set our emotions and feelings aside for the moment to accomplish the task at hand. This act of temporarily setting aside our emotions and feelings is called *suppression*.

We still feel strongly, we know our emotions are there, but we have consciously stored them away to concentrate on what needs to be done first. When the time is right, we can retrieve them from their temporary "storage," think about them, express them if we choose, and deal with them.

> *Sharrie woke up this morning, wailing that she hated school and doesn't want to go anymore. I found out that her teacher has shortened the free play time, so what Sharrie looked forward to with joy she now dreads. She tried to make the best of it at school, but her feelings poured out at home where she feels safe.*
>
> —*Karen, mother of Sharrie, seven*

Sharrie did not feel comfortable expressing her feelings with people at school. Her inner guidance told her on some level of her awareness that she could wait until she got home to let her emotions out. This emotional delay is helpful, because we cannot always express our emotions at the time we have them. Suppression allows children to get through overwhelming situations, surviving as best they can until they are safely home in our comforting arms.

Suppression, therefore, is an emotional delay. The emotion or feeling is consciously put in a temporary emotional/feeling storage area, until the time is appropriate to allow it to complete the Feeling Curve. Clear thinking about the issue or event can then occur.

Emotion/Feeling Delays Have Their Down Sides

We use a lot of energy to suppress our emotions and feelings. Consider a can of shaving cream. Trying to stop an emotion or a feeling is like trying to stop the shaving cream from coming out of the can. Once we push the button, it just seems to flow out on its own. After the effort of suppressing an emotion/feeling, we feel tired, irritable, or restless. If we leave it in cold storage for too long, we risk a blow up or overreaction to something trivial. Eventually, the suppressed emotion/feeling festers and grows so big or painful that we are unable to concentrate on anything else.

When we try to ignore this "beast" inside us, it spills out unexpectedly during an argument, at bedtime, or in innocent conversation. Suppressed emotions/feelings have a timer on them, and they remain closed away only so long. Emotions/feelings by nature must be released and digested. Whether we wish it or not, they will sneak out into the light of day, demanding our attention. Storage is only temporary. Time will run out.

The ability to suppress emotions/feelings differs according to age. Our younger daughters from birth to seven automatically experience their emotions with little ability to set them aside. Their emotions literally explode out of them. When Jenny, aged two, was left in the car in plain view of her mother, she immediately burst into huge tears. When her mother got back in the car sixty seconds later, Jenny continued to cry. Her emotions of fear or abandonment shot up and over the Feeling Curve, until she was assured her mother would not leave her there again. Only serious shock and abuse can stop the emotions of a young child from being expressed. Even at age seven, emotions are free-flowing.

Older girls have longer emotion/feeling delays while adjusting to difficult situations. They may act fine and say they are fine, but they are unable to as yet express what is in their hearts. It is important for us to check in once in a while to offer them the opportunity to express any leftover emotion/feelings from a difficult event. Suppression is a survival function of a healthy human being, enabling our daughters flexibility and choice in matters of the heart—the home base of feeling. If we have proven ourselves to be open and understanding, they will eventually confide in us.

How to Deal with Suppressed Feelings

Be open to rapid changes in a daughter's emotional states. Our daughter's days are filled with events we often know nothing about, and we must trust her to bring her troubles to us. Most of us know immediately when something is bothering her, but her responses change as she grow up.

JEANNE | When my daughter became a teenager, it became more difficult for her to put her feelings into words. Remembering how I felt at that age helped me understand how frustrating and confusing it all was. At times I was literally swamped with emotion, usually contradictory and not making much sense. Trying to put any of it into words was beyond me. I usually ended up yelling at my mother that she just didn't understand me. And it was true! My poor mother. She told me years later that during those assaults, she just went into her bedroom and cried.

Be a model for dealing with emotions/feelings. The best way to learn how to get emotions/feelings out is to watch our parents do it. Strong emotions/feelings about important things are released in stages according to our inner, emotional timetable. When we are ready, safe, or full-to-bursting, our emotions come out. Watching others express feelings when they are ready, gives a girl permission to share on her own inner time schedule.

⊰⊱ ⊰⊱ *DON* | When I work with young girls in therapy who have a secret about something, I'll often say, "Don't tell me your secret [long pause] until you are ready. Don't worry about interrupting me. Just blurt it out. But, don't tell me until you are ready." Usually by the end of the session, they tell me—in their own timing.

Repression of Emotion and Feeling: Long-Term Storage

re-press (ri pres')

5. Psychoanal. to reject (painful or

disagreeable ideas, memories, feelings,

or impulses) from the conscious mind.

—The Random House Dictionary
of the English Language

Unlike conscious and suppressed emotions/feelings, repressed emotions/feelings are not available to the conscious mind. They are tucked deeply away in the unconscious, where their frightening or horrible demeanors are hidden from our awareness. We all have repressed emotions/feelings from events and patterns in our past that were too painful to bear at the time. We were too small, or too burdened to work on our emotions with thinking.

The psyches of young children repress intense anger and other threatening emotions, because their emotional bodies are not mature enough to deal with the intensity. They are like 60-watt bulbs with 320 watts running through them. They feel much safer putting on a smile and acting as though nothing has happened. Unless a parent or other trusted adult helps them get the emotions out in the open, their emotions are buried alive.

The repression of the fear or pain of a traumatic event allows us to cope with situations too unbearable to deal with. Emotions/feelings lie deeply buried until an event joggles them awake; then they surface in bits and pieces or in a full force of memory. Like a bottle of wine, whose bouquet is as aromatic after many years as the year it was bottled, the repressed emotion/feeling of anger or panic is as strong as the day of that lost event, hidden from our consciousness in long-term storage.

Many of us live for years with repressed emotions/feelings. What we do not realize is that they affect our everyday lives without our knowing it. We could say that we live with a powerful dictator hidden inside of us, who controls us like a puppet on a string. We may not want to react the way we do sometimes, and we may plan to act differently next time, but the next time comes, and we cannot help ourselves.

> *Whenever my husband gets angry, I tremble and want to run.*
>
> *—Vicki, thirty-five*

> *I'm fine when a man-friend gives me a friendly hug, but let him want to take me to bed, and I'm gone!*
>
> *—Cindy, twenty-eight*

> *If my oldest son so much as lays a finger on his little sister, I get so enraged that I can't be held responsible for my actions.*
>
> *—Vera, forty-one*

> *If I make any kind of critical comment to my husband about how he did something, he comes unglued.*
>
> *—Loreen, twenty-two*

Thirty-five-year-old Vicki began therapy to deal with her anger toward her four-year-old daughter. "I get so out-of-control over such little things with my daughter," she confessed. "I find her clothes lying on the floor or her toys not picked up after I've asked her, and I snap. I yell and even come close to slapping her. Afterwards I shake and can't calm down for hours; and I feel so guilty. I can't seem to control myself. What's really strange is that when my husband gets angry at me, I feel like I imagine my daughter must feel; really small and helpless—and bad."

During the course of therapy, Vicki uncovered repressed memories of her childhood. Her father, troubled over losing his job and not adequately providing for his family, gave in to frequent bursts of anger while he cared for five-year-old Vicki and her younger brother. Whenever Vicki cried and asked her father to stop yelling, he ridiculed her weakness. His moods were so bitter and so much out of character from the usually gentle father Vicki counted on, that she denied his attacks on her, acting as though nothing unpleasant was happening. She put on a smiling face and became extremely helpful and cooperative around the house. Consequently, she remembered very little of her early years at home and was thoroughly puzzled over her behavior toward her daughter and her reaction to her husband's anger. When her memories came flooding back, she found compassion for the little girl she had been, who was frightened of her father's anger and criticism.

Vicki's inner guidance system was malformed around her repressed emotions/feelings and memories. Her emotions of fear and panic were too great to bear, and her father refused to deal with them; therefore they were buried in the long-term storage of repression.

The Feeling Box

We use Vicki's childhood experiences to illustrate the concept of a Feeling Box. Imagine we all carry a box inside of us. Emotions/feelings fit either inside or outside the box. Those emotions/feelings we were allowed to feel as children go inside our Feeling Box, and we have easy access to them. Those emotions/feelings our parents did not allow, for all sorts of reasons, fall on the outside of the box, and those emotions/feelings are difficult for us to acknowledge. Fear, panic, and weakness were not allowed in Vicki's family, and she relied on smiles and helpfulness to survive. She learned two responses—to be helpful or to become angry. "I was either a wimp or a tyrant," she laughs. "I cringed around anyone I thought knew more than I did, or if they were smaller or weaker than me, like my daughter, I completely overran them." Vicki's Feeling Box looked like this:

"Therapy helped me understand why I couldn't feel my fear and panic. Now when I become overly helpful, I know it's a clue that I'm either feeling fearful or I'm angry at somebody. I can stop my old smiling act and use my new assertive self." After recovering her repressed feelings, Vicki's Feeling Box looks like this:

Teach Girls to Respect Anger

Anger is an emotion frequently left on the outside of our familial feeling boxes. With the cultural dictum to be nice, girls often need help learning to listen to and express their anger in constructive ways. Because biological and psychological influences turn them instinctively toward relationship, many girls learn not to jeopardize connection by showing uncomfortable and conflicting emotions and feelings. Rather than being angry, many daughters learn to be sad or compliant, denying the important inner signals anger offers them. Anger says, "This is important to me!" "This has meaning!" "Something is wrong here!" Recognizing the roots of a girl's anger empowers her to take care of herself or to ask for help from others. Identifying and respecting our daughter's anger builds a healthy inner guidance system.

Unfortunately, stuffing and ignoring strong feelings, such as anger, can lead, in mild cases, to such physical symptoms as tummy aches and headaches. Young girls sometimes develop excessive eye blinking, nail biting, or bed-wetting in more serious situations. Older daughters may act out their anger by not eating, breaking curfews, being chronically ill, and becoming depressed. These symptoms *do not* always suggest unexpressed anger, but they *do* indicate underlying feelings a girl believes she cannot express for fear of being punished, judged as bad, or getting someone else in trouble.

The best way for girls to learn about anger is to live with others who model a healthy, direct expression of feeling, that is emotion that has been worked on by thinking. When girls see anger expressed in cruel or mocking ways, they learn to be cruel themselves, or they try to avoid being the brunt of it through compliance. When anger is considered a natural emotion to be listened to and carefully used, girls learn to respect its messages and act constructively to change or improve the relationship or situation. The following suggestions are helpful in teaching our daughters about anger:

Learn about anger. Most of us could use some guidance about expressing our own anger and dealing with the anger of others. As children many of us learned to react with anger when we were hurt. The anger covered up our hurt, and striking out at others helped us feel less vulnerable. Many adults continue to use anger to cover up feelings of hurt and vulnerability. We need to do some reading, take classes, and perhaps even explore our feelings concerning anger in therapy. Conscious practice in listening to what our own anger tells us and whether, when, and how to share it, makes us better models for our daughters.

Look for what is wrong in the relationship, rather than for what is wrong in our daughters. Saying, "I feel angry when you say you will put your shoes away, and you don't," carries a much different message than saying, "How many times do I have to tell you to get those shoes back in your room?" The first statement clearly implies a problem between us and our daughter. The second one infers she is stupid for not doing what we asked of her. In a culture that still considers females "less than," a girl will feel ridiculed by our indirectness. Using "I feel angry when you _____" statements provides opportunities for open exchange of feelings and helps a girl learn to share her anger clearly, directly, and cleanly without the need to hide, to hurt others, or to defend herself.

Anger does not equal violence. Many of us fear anger, because in our past experiences, it led to violence. Spanking a girl out of anger is not discipline; it simply teaches her to feel small and helpless against adults and to hit when she is angry. Seeing their parents become angry and then work it out together serves as a model for daughters that anger does not have to become violent. Girls especially need to see their mothers stand up for themselves by sharing their angry feelings clearly and honestly. Being willing to work things out by listening to all feelings—both positive and negative—and valuing the relationship and the people involved, takes the sting out of angry situations.

Provide a safety zone for anger. The old expression about anger, "Seeing red," like the bull and the red cape, aptly describes the emotion of anger before we have time to think it over. Sometimes the emotion goes so deeply that all we see in front of us is red, red, red! In these instances, we need a white flag, time-out, or safety zone to retreat to while we cool off, count to ten, or collect our thoughts. When emotions run high, it may be wise to establish some family rules about anger in order to prevent emotional hurt or physical violence. When parents become angry, we can call a halt to the interactions by saying we need a break for awhile or by simply walking away. When a daughter becomes angry, we can help her manage her anger by providing a quiet space, near us but apart, where she can cool down. She gets the message, "We all need a break, but we are staying in relationship." She learns that anger comes and goes, that anger is an emotion to respect, and that relationships stay intact in the face of it.

When Traumatic Events Happen

"Life is difficult," writes best-selling author M. Scott Peck, M.D. In *The Road Less Traveled*, he asserts that by embracing the difficulties, life becomes easier.[3] After seeking to avoid pain by choosing as much pleasure as we can, many of us discover that life has lost its meaning. We feel empty inside. Dr. Peck advises that embracing the difficulties and suffering of life is not an exercise in choosing between pleasure and pain, but a choice between meaningless suffering and meaningful suffering. When we let go of those activities that are meaningless to us and choose to participate in enterprises that have heart and meaning for us, our lives suddenly take on a purpose we did not feel before.

For Strength

The soul's longings are like seeds,
Out of which deeds of will are growing
And life's fruits are ripening

I can feel my destiny and my destiny finds me.
I can feel my star and my star finds me.
I can feel my aims and my aims are finding me.
The World and my soul are one great unity.

Life grows brighter around me
Life becomes harder for me
Life will be richer within me.[4]

—*Rudolf Steiner*

We all want to protect our daughters from harm and find we cannot always ease their pain. The suffering of life inevitably interferes with our best-laid plans. When we show our daughters how to face the bumps in the road by choosing the meaningful paths, we empower them to live life actively, rather than constantly reacting to what happens to them. Choosing a meaningful life sometimes means marriages must dissolve, jobs must end, schools must be changed, and secrets must be shared. If we learn to approach traumatic events open to the full range of human emotion, we find meaning in the midst of anger, grief, shock, and painful suffering. When traumatic events happen in our daughters' lives, the best way for us to support them is by helping them find meaning in their experiences.

Immediately listen to her feelings and the truth of what happened.

⟨≈⟩ ⟨≈⟩ *DON* | During my work with school children after the 1989 San Francisco Earthquake, I learned that the more they were able to talk about, act it out, and draw what they experienced, the fewer aftereffects they had. Those who were, for various reasons, unable to retell their stories suffered the common symptoms of trauma—nightmares, sleep disorders, and behavior problems both at home and at school.

Inner strength is developed through felt experience. A divorce, the death of a loved one, a change in school, a debilitating illness, a radical shift in lifestyle, and so on are traumatic events from which we wish we could protect our daughters. Our best protection, however, lies in our open support and validation of their struggles to understand these difficult events. By providing opportunities for them to release their feelings through art, play, conversation, and comforting, we lessen the need for repression of feelings and increase the likelihood of a healthy adjustment.

The degree of repression is in direct proportion to age. The younger our daughters, the more quickly they repress frightening emotions and feelings. Thank goodness for the human psyche's natural protection of babies. Their nervous systems are too sensitive to process the myriad of events occurring in their little lives, most of which do not seem traumatic to us, but are to them. They block out most experiences by sleeping through it all, and when they have slept their fill, they relieve their trauma through crying and moving.

> *I was puzzled why every time I took Belinda to the mall with me, she cried for hours after we got home. She loved the mall, or so I thought. She gazed around at everything, her eyes large and round. Then I read* Raising A Son—*the part about protecting our young children from too much stimulation, like bright lights, loud noises, harsh colors, too many people, machines, and such, and then I understood why Belinda had to cry when we got home. She had to work out all of that sensory bombardment. Now I leave her with Dad when I go shopping! We're both much happier.*

> —*Sally, thirty-one,*
> *mother of Belinda, sixteen months*

After girls develop the ability to verbalize their feelings, we are more able to assist them in the processing of traumatic events. They can deal with more intensity; they don't feel as bombarded by events as infants do. Our babies are calmed by walking, rocking, and holding. Our older daughters, while they also need hugging and rocking, are comforted by our listening, supporting, and validating their feelings. "You were frightened by that mean, ugly dog!" "You hated being embarrassed by your teacher in front of your class." "Losing your first love hurts your heart."

Dreams, Nightmares, and Night Terrors

Repressed emotions/feelings, suppressed emotions/feelings, and the stressors of daily living all come alive in a girl's dream life. Dreaming, a vital function of the unconscious mind, manages the incredibly complex world of the soul—emotion/feeling/intuition. Dreams are part of our inner guidance, resolving those emotions, feelings, and experiences which are too threatening for our conscious minds to contemplate. Through our dreams, we process our daily anxieties, fears, and challenges. Dreaming lessens the negative intrusion of our repressed memories and emotions/feelings of the past. We find it comforting to know that a wise, unconscious part of us is working at night for our benefit to heal the traumas of our waking experiences.

When a girl's sleep is disturbed by overactive dreaming, her unconscious is signaling there is too much material in long-term storage to be handled by the dream world alone. She may not remember the dreams that awakened her, but she is afraid to go back to sleep. Nightmares thunder through her sleep, frightening her awake, forgotten in the morning, only to return the following night. Night terrors, even more terrifying than nightmares, continue after she is awakened, and it takes a patient parent to comfort her back to sleep. Sleep disorders, sleep walking, nightmares, and night terrors often originate in unresolved, repressed emotions/feelings.

How Parents Can Help

Dreams are an important part of the inner guidance system. Sleep problems indicate that the unconscious is trying to heal itself but needs some extra assistance. These guidelines help us value the positive intent of nightmares, sleep disruptions, and night terrors and offer constructive ways to assist our daughters' natural, inner healer.

Ask those in charge of a daughter's care about any current problems she is having at school or day care. Small changes in routine can deeply disturb a girl without our realizing it. Other people who spend time with her, and whose opinions we value, may offer insights into the cause of her bad dreams.

Become better informed about sleep problems. Check the library and local bookstores for information about sleep disturbances in children. Keep in mind that many sources offer conflicting advice, but knowing more about the problems will better enable us to understand what is happening with our daughters. Some solutions work better at certain times than at others, depending upon a girl's age and what has disturbed her.

Listen. Let the dramas of a girl's dreamscapes unfold slowly as she remembers them, at her own pace and in her own words. Knowing we are open to listening to anything she has to share, makes it safe for her to reveal experiences that may be painful and terrifying. She may feel guilty about the pictures she remembers, or confused. Getting them out into the light with an understanding parent works wonders for lessening her trauma.

> *As long as one person in the world can really hear us, really feel with us; it can be endured.*[5]
>
> —Adele Faber and Elaine Mazlish,
> *Liberated Parents Liberated Children*

Stay with her dream language. Sometimes we adults are too quick to attach literal meanings to the images of dreams. If a girl shares that the sky was red, we must refrain from contradicting her, instead nod our heads and say, "Umm hmm." She is seeing in the language of dreams, messages from what is happening deep within her, and the symbols of that world are not usually realistic.

Do not interpret her dream symbols. Only the dreamer knows the meaning of her dreams, and if she doesn't know it on a conscious level, that's okay. Sometimes the telling of the dream is enough to clear the repressed material from deep storage. We can be assured that the unconscious is doing the work that needs to be done, and this can seem slow and tedious.

Observe a daughter's imaginative play. Girls reenact the experiences of daily life in their creative play. Like the work of dreams at night during sleep, daydreams and fantasy play help a girl adjust to the difficulties in her everyday life. Themes that we hear played out over and over are clues to hidden, troubling contents of the unconscious mind. By acting them out among her toys, she has more control over them; what was terrifying in the night, becomes more manageable during the day in her play.

When Lia's beloved Grandpapa died, I worried about how she would cope with the loss. For days she played with one little doll that had always reminded me of a clown. She would act one little story over and over. "And now the little girl goes to her Grandpapa's, and they go to the circus, and then he dies." Only later did I realize that the little doll reminded Lia of a clown who had large tears on her face she and my father had once seen at the circus!

—Margaret, mother of Lia, five

Help her keep a dream journal. After the age of eight, a dream journal appeals to many girls, and can be a wonderfully insightful way to work with disturbing, as well as vivid dreams. This record can be written in words, a combination of words and pictures, or simply pictures. Taking time to record and embellish a girl's dreams relates how powerful and important we consider them to be. Together we honor the work of her inner guidance system, using the nightmares and terrors as great healing gifts and potentials for growth.

Marcie woke me up crying from her bedroom. It was 2 a.m. I stumbled to her room, and while I held her, she told me her bad dream, the third this week. After she was able to go back to sleep, I, now sleepless, wrote down what she had told me of the nightmare. The next morning, we talked about her dream, and I shared what I had written with her. We decided to do a dream journal. For a seven-year-old, she did very well. What she had dreaded each night, became fun and something we both looked forward to completing together. Each morning before breakfast, she drew pictures of her dreams and told me their stories. Often they made absolutely no sense to me, but she was really enthralled by the process. Her concentration and commitment amazed me. She began recording all of her dreams, not only the disturbing ones, and after about three weeks, her nightmares stopped. We didn't uncover what they were really about, but she made it through, and now has a wonderful tool that she calls her "dream book" to help herself.

—*Esther, mother of Marcie, seven*

Help her dream the dream onward. The famous psychologist Carl Jung believed that giving an ending to an unfinished dream or making a troubling dream into a story was helpful in completing the dream work. When a daughter is willing, help her tell the story of the dream in the style of a fairy tale. Fairy tales follow a general format. They usually begin, "Once upon a time...."; the characters are introduced, "...there lived a..."; the problem is described; and the problem gets too big to solve, and all seems lost. "Then one day..." comes along, and a surprising resolution appears to end the story. An important dimension of a fairy tale is that there is always a helper of some kind who assists in bringing about the desired conclusion—a fairy godmother, a gnome with magical powers, a mythical beast, a magic stone. She is reassured she is not alone in her difficulties. Fairy tales fit so well with the resolution of troubling dreams because they use the language of the soul.

Consider allowing her to sleep with us when she needs to. Humankind, until recently, has always slept together for warmth and safety. It is lonely and scary to be tucked away from everyone else in our beds in the dark, if we are little. When nightmares awaken us, it becomes especially difficult and frightening to think of going back to sleep all alone. We encourage understanding when girls crawl into the big, inviting, warm, safe, cozy bed between their parents. This may not work for all families. Sacrificing sleep is no small matter for any adult these days, and we all have our limits. But, when possible, it may do a world of good for our daughters. Remember how comforting it was?

When Our Best Efforts Fail

Sometimes no matter what we do, our best efforts have no affect on life's circumstances and the problems our daughters encounter. A father we know had helped his daughter, Moleta, cope well with her nightmares. His ability to comfort kids who are upset or scared impressed us. Yet two years after his wife's death, his only daughter could not sleep through the night without problems. "Every evening she gets panicky before bed," related Manuel. "She says scary thoughts keep going around and around in her head. She stays up late, because she's afraid someone is going to take her away. When she finally does sleep, her nightmares wake her up in terror. She is so afraid, she won't even try the things we used to do when she had trouble sleeping." Finally, Manuel decided that Moleta's problems were beyond them both, and he sought the help of a professional.

How to Use a Therapist for Sleep Problems

Choose a therapist carefully. Ask others—teachers, ministers, school counselors, and so on—for referrals to therapists who have a successful history treating sleep disturbances in children. Ask them to share some of their success stories.

Choose a therapist who uses methods congruent with dream language. There are many effective approaches for working with nightmares, night terrors, and such. Those most successful with young children include the use of art, sand play, storytelling, imagination, and other methods that access the unconscious, such as EMDR[6] or hypnosis. These mediums are effective, because they speak directly to the dream world, where unresolved feelings are more easily available.

Be willing to be part of the therapy. One family member is never the whole problem when difficulties arise. During traumatic situations facing adults such as a divorce, loss of income, serious illness of a parent or child, job changes, and so on, our daughters experience our stress and may develop sleep disorders as a result. Children often act as barometers for what is happening emotionally in the family, and their behaviors are clues to us to seek outside help to deal with life's difficult times. Working together as a family, rather than focusing on a daughter's sleep problems, for example, will bring more immediate relief and more lasting results.

Intuition: The Sound of the Genuine

There is sort of a spirit world that
coexists with the world of empirical
observation, and you have to get in touch
with that world....You don't use a crystal ball,
though I'd like one that worked—
but you do clear your mind and listen to what
isn't said and see things that aren't there.[7]

—Paul Brenner, detective,
The General's Daughter,
Nelson DeMille, 1992

Although we tend to put the involuntary sense of intuition in a class by itself, it is actually part of the feeling life that has gotten a bad reputation. Out of one side of our culture's mouth we say, "Yeah, right. I'm gonna intuit my house payment this month. The bank will love that!" Out of the other side, we wonder, "How did I know to call her when I did?" Too often our culture discounts intuition as "flaky," witchcraft, a female "thing," or a New Age fad. Intuition is really a human being thing. If we are really honest with ourselves, it's something we have all experienced. The *Old Testament* describes it as a "still, small voice" that comes from God.[8] Some of us call it a hunch or a gut feeling. Often we preface telling friends about our intuitive feelings with the words, "You're gonna think I'm crazy, but..." Whether or not we knowingly follow our intuition's messages, it daily speaks to us in its still, small voice.

Messages from our intuition come in various forms. Some of us are hit with a flash of knowing; others experience strong physical sensations; many of us "see" pictures in our mind's eye; still others dream our messages.

I had this really strong feeling that I should check on my brother. My body just took me to his room. He was trapped under his toy box, and I pulled him out!

—Aleana, fourteen

Our physics teacher decided to introduce quantum physics ideas to my class. Some of the boys got it right away. I'm usually very good at that kind of thing, but I just couldn't get it, you know, that energy can be both a particle and a wave? Then, in a flash I could picture it in my mind.

—Lea, sixteen

I was really worried about going to a new school. You know, afraid I wouldn't make new friends, that I'd get lost trying to find my classes, the whole thing. The night before school started, I dreamed that I went to a new supermarket and found all kinds of new foods that tasted great. I ate and ate and ate. Then I woke up. It sounds weird, but I felt a real peace about my new school. I knew it would be okay. It hasn't been exactly easy, but I don't feel worried any more, and I have made a lot of new friends.

—Lana, thirteen

Intuition is an internal knowing. Intuition usually comes through a foggy notion or vague but strong sensation. It is best described by metaphor. "It takes me a while to figure it out sometimes," says Natalie, seventeen, "But it's like a bubble coming up from the bottom of a deep lake. If I reach and try to grab it, I get nothing. If I wait and listen, it pops to the top with a gurgle, and then I'm clear about what I want to do. I sometimes have to go on long walks, or lock myself in my room, listen to music, or draw. If I am patient, I just know what I need to do."

The word *know* is an important one. Intuition is an internal *knowing* that sometimes has nothing to do with the facts in front of us.

Thinking lags behind intuition. "They all agreed the map said to go right," says Mavis, aged fourteen, "I didn't even look at the map and my gut said left. Everybody went right, while I went left. And there it was, the house we were looking for. I backtracked to find the others, still consulting the map. Come to find out, they were reading it upside down!" Sometimes we just *know*, in spite of the facts and the opinions of others.

Intuition connects us with something greater than ourselves. We call this *something* spiritual, universal, morphogenetic, or an ocean of energy. Our intuition tunes in to messages we couldn't know simply by analyzing the facts before us. The telephone rings, and we know it is Dad; talk about an old friend, and the next day we get a letter from her in the mail; sit down a moment with our daughter, because we sense she needs us, and she breaks into sobs. Psychologist Dr. Carl Jung called these events synchronistic, meaningful happenings of illogical but purposefully, coinciding events.[9] When a girl is in touch with her intuition, she is in touch with the unseen worlds of meaning and connection. She is connected to something greater than herself.

Intuition is a girl's best friend. "I knew my boyfriend was seeing another girl," says Maureen, sixteen. "I knew it in my bones, but the facts didn't add up; my girlfriends said I was crazy. I felt badly about not believing him, but the feeling wouldn't go away. Now I know why. He was writing to an old girlfriend from his hometown. Boy, was I dumb." The difficult part of intuition for westernized minds is that it may never be verified. We just feel the way we do, because we do. When our daughters learn to dismiss their inner knowing to please others or to go along with the crowd, they end up being hurt and confused. A very important part of them needs our respect and support.

Intuition is a truth teller. Even when parents try their best to keep difficult circumstances out of their daughters' lives, on some level of her awareness a daughter knows something is amiss. When a girl is eventually told her parents are divorcing, that Daddy lost his job, or that Grandpa is gravely ill, she often says, "I knew something was wrong, but I was scared to think what it might be." Once she knows the truth, we can help her deal with what her intuition was warning her about. Although the truth hurts, she can rely on us to support her through whatever it is.

Intuition is self-validating. When girls learn from experience that they have a deep source of inner knowing, they begin to trust themselves, to act with confidence and courage. They develop competence from knowing and acting from their own inner truth.

Thinking: The Other Part of Knowing

Our feeling life—emotions, feelings, intuition, dreams—keeps us in touch with the world around us. Through these unseen forces we feel alive and intimately connected to life. We cannot live fruitfully in our feelings alone, however. Good decisions and purposeful actions come from the guidance of both feeling/intuition and thinking. Girls need finely-tuned thinking skills to solve logical problems, achieve perspective, develop action plans, and create order out of chaos.

In her provocative book, *The Female Advantage: Women's Ways of Leadership*, journalist Sally Helgesen quotes an old Chinese proverb: "Women hold up half the sky." She interprets this wise saying to mean that women perform half the thinking and half the work in the world. She writes, "For the sky to be complete, both halves must work together...."[10] We believe the same is true about the dynamics *within* each of us. For our lives to be complete, both parts of our beings must work together, feeling/intuition and thinking.

Girls and women seem to naturally think in terms of the group, concerned with how individual members are doing and what needs to be done to benefit the whole. Much of a female's information about the group comes through her feeling/intuition functions. Her strategizing, planning, and carry through to meet personal needs and complete household tasks rely on *diffused* thinking, thinking that takes in various sensory input at once. This explains why women can accomplish several things at one time. They can talk on the telephone, while bouncing the baby on a hip and stirring a pot of soup. They can look for errors in an important memo, while responding to their secretary's question about scheduling appointments and repair a broken nail. In Chapter Five we called this diffused thinking *group mind*. It requires thinking and acting with the group in mind, flexibility, care, and a relational focus, that is, an attitude that makes connections between people primary.

Strategic Thinking

Strategic thinking or *strategy*, is rooted in the Greek *strategos*—a general, *stratos*—an army, and *agein*—to lead. Current business still follows a strategic, military-like, chain-of-command structure, with a general at the head who conducts a campaign and maneuvers an army.

Many career women have been told that to successfully enter the business world, they must leave their feeling/intuition at home and assume a general-like, strategic mode of thinking. This approach is out-of-balance. Closing off feeling/intuition leaves brittleness, rigidity, single-mindedness, and aloofness. Men, as well as other women, often use these terms to describe their female bosses, who capitulated to the belief that success in business requires that we leave our feeling/intuition at home.

Diffused thinking is most effective when balanced with focused, or strategic thinking. Many females are seen as incompetent in activities required outside the home, because they fall short on strategic thinking.

Getting from Point A to Point B

Getting from point A to point B may sound easy to many of us. Men are trained, encouraged, challenged, and praised as boys to learn to master this feat through participation in sports, higher mathematics courses, business, mechanics, computers, and so on. Some girls are adept at getting from A to B, because they were lucky enough to be given opportunities to learn how. All girls need experiences that teach them how to take care of themselves without relying on or waiting for others to take care of them.

⇢ ⇢ *DON* | So often, my women clients in their forties and fifties facing divorce feel incredibly panicked about taking care of themselves—how to have the car repaired, how to change the oil, budgeting their money, balancing a checkbook, making sound investments, doing their taxes, and so on. I am struck by how the old, rigid male/female roles no longer work, are even dangerous in these times. These women believe that losing a partner prevents them from living a full, happy life.

How Do Girls Learn Strategic Thinking?

Girls need basic, problem-solving skills. We must allow them to struggle with the problems they face, while we cheer them on with support, advice when they ask for it, encouragement, and praise. Showing a girl how to think strategically about a problem, empowers her to act. "Our daughter got a B in a high school class that she knew should have been an A," says Karen Lassell, mother and family therapist. "She fretted about it all summer, and we encouraged her to talk with her teacher, but she resisted.

"Finally, I sat down with her and mapped her dilemma out in black and white. First, what did she want? What was her objective? She wanted to get her grade corrected. How was she going to accomplish that? What was her strategy? She decided to collect her past work, talk with her teacher, and ask him to cross check the grades in his book. Stating clearly what she wanted and having a step-by-step plan gave her the courage to see her teacher. Sure enough, he had made a mistake in his record-keeping. It was too late for a grade change, but it changed my daughter. She has the tools to confront any problem that faces her. I'm not only proud of her; I'm hopeful that she will use both her intuition and her thinking skills to accomplish whatever she desires."

Watch first, act later. Particularly when our daughters are young, we want to rush to the rescue whenever they come up against an obstacle, especially if we perceive they may be hurt. Watching to see whether they can manage the challenge before we come swooping in, allows them room to discover their own solutions and to reap the benefits of thinking it out for themselves.

My three-year-old was riding her tricycle on the patio. Suddenly, the front wheel got stuck between the lawn and the stone of the patio, and she tipped over. My first instinct was to rush over and tip her upright to see if she was all right. Before I could act, she rolled over, got up, and slowly righted her tricycle. She worked the wheel back and forth, finally releasing it. And she was so proud. "Daddy, see what I did!" We beamed at each other.

—*Harold, father of Debra, three*

Team sports offer training in strategic thinking. On a team there is an overall game plan, a goal to work for, individual positions, and clearly defined roles to carry out step-by-step tasks. Learning to hold onto the overreaching goal, while focusing on individual tasks, requires discipline to master the principles of strategic thinking skills.

Rachel hated soccer at first, but we encouraged her to stick with it. We thought the game would teach her skills she will need to compete in the work world—to think in terms of strategy and single-mindedness of a goal. In soccer you can't be kinda' a goalie and kinda' a halfback. You have to apply yourself. She is required to think clearly, know her role, know the bigger picture, and move forward as a team to reach the goal. Once she got over her fear of getting hurt and not being able to play well, she mastered that way of thinking. It carried over into other aspects of her life, too. She plans better for school, getting papers done on time without a last minute all-nighter; that kind of thing.

—*Hilda, mother of Rachel, thirteen*

We all need to grapple with any doubts we might have about our daughter's thinking abilities. Do we unconsciously believe the old stereotypes that females cannot think as logically and rationally as males can? That girls can't do math? That women shouldn't be rocket scientists? Or heads of state, because their emotions render them unstable in precarious situations?

We must view with a fresh eye the possibilities—both traditional and nontraditional—in our daughters' lives. Our good friend Penny learned plumbing, wiring, and carpentry as a girl from her mother as they remodeled their house together. Known for her careful, safe, and high-quality installations and repairs, Penny is one example of the many girls and women who excel in areas that were in years past considered only a man's domain. "How do you check the oil?" asks Heidi, twenty-one, as her stepfather checks under the hood before a family car trip. "Guys always know those things, and girls get left out." We have a responsibility to imagine what our daughters need to be competent in their lives so they do not always have to rely on someone else to do things for them. They will be less likely to grow up blaming others—men, Mom, Dad, Fate—for what happens in their lives. Knowing how to think for themselves is one of the best gifts we can give them.

Small is the number of them that see with their own eyes and feel with their own hearts.[11]

—Albert Einstein

Willing: The Call to Action

will, n.

a. the mental faculty by which one deliberately chooses or decides upon a course of action; volition.

b. self-discipline; determination; deliberate intention.

—The American Heritage Dictionary

Our daughter's feeling life guides her relationships, personal preferences, passions, and hopes for the future. Her thinking life enables her to think things through, make her own plans, and choose her own moral and ethical positions. Without the third partner of the powerful trio, however, she is unable to act on her dreams. The willing life gives her the ability to take a course of action with deliberate intention and see it through to the end.

The Will: Four Aspects

The will surfaces most powerfully during the years from birth to seven or eight. When we consider the powerful early childhood drive to master the art of walking, the following descriptive qualities of will come to mind: dynamic power, intensity, mastery, control, discipline, concentration, attention, single-focus, determination, decisiveness, resoluteness, persistence, courage, and daring.

One of the masters of modern psychology, Roberto Assagioli, M.D., states in *The Act of Will*, that there are many aspects of the will. He writes, "Most misunderstandings and mistakes concerning the will arise from the frequent misconception that the strong will constitutes the whole will. Strength is only one of the aspects of will, and when dissociated from the others, it can be, and often is, ineffectual or harmful to oneself and other people."[12] We often hear parents describe their daughter's *strong will*.

> *My daughter is relentless. When she wants to finish an art project, she won't stop, no matter what I want. She yells until I give in. When I do give her more time, she accomplishes something really wonderful. But, I can't run a home around the strong will of a four-year-old girl. What will she be like when she's sixteen? I can't imagine how to live with her obsessions.*
>
> *—Michael, father of Angelina, four*

A strong will needs protection and development in balance with the other aspects. Parents must walk the fine line between setting firm limits to shape a strong will and squashing it. For willful Angelina in the previous story, her father must firmly hold the boundaries of a rhythmic family life, helping Angelina trust that there is a time and space for everything, and gently leading her from one transition to the next. We often make the mistake of matching a strong will with an even stronger one, which most of us have found only leads to colossal power struggles. Next time strong-willed Angelina sets up roadblocks in her father's path, he might try meeting her resistance with a *t'ai chi* move, that of *going with* her resistance.[13] This does not mean *giving in*; rather it allows the strong-willed girl to have room, within predetermined limits, to act on her own terms.

Mandy is like me—she has a mind of her own, and it is definitely a struggle to convince her of anything otherwise. We have the most trouble over getting ready for bed or to go somewhere in the mornings. Force doesn't work; both of us just end up in angry tears! Finally, I told her, "I get it! You want to be in charge, so here's what must be done, and you have plenty of time—thirty minutes—to do it." Together we made a list of pictures of what she had to do to get ready for bed, and I set a timer for thirty minutes. As she completed each task, she checked the box with a big red X. At the end of one week, if all boxes were checked without any struggles between us, we agreed to do something fun together. The amazing thing about this process is that it now takes her ten minutes to get ready for bed! She feels proud and powerful, and I feel peaceful and relieved.

—Janice, mother of Mandy, five

Another important component of will described by Dr. Roberto Assagioli is the *skillful will*. This is "the ability to obtain desired results with the least possible expenditure of energy."[14] For our daughters this means knowing themselves—their abilities, their needs, their habits, their limitations. They learn about themselves by trial and error. We have mentioned before how important it is for girls to be allowed to take risks, to attempt something new, and to learn from their mistakes. They need practice in putting their own talents and resources to work in efficient ways. We do not recommend throwing them into the river to sink or swim, however. We all learn best through the example of someone more skilled than we are at what we are trying to learn. Parents are a daughter's best model for developing a skilled will.

My daughter and I have loved working together in our garden since she was tiny. We both relish getting dirt on our hands. We can even put aside those mother/daughter dramas when we plant, weed, and water in the evenings. I must admit I had an ulterior motive in mind when I taught Melissa to garden. My mother taught me about life through gardening. She taught me how to work "smart." When I was six, she asked me to move a pile of dirt from one side of the garden to another. Being such a strong-willed child, I immediately set about the task, taking one shovelful after another to a new pile twenty yards away. My mother stooped down to hold me with one of her generous hugs, and whispered, "I'll show you the secret way, if you want." Of course, I did. In silence, she pulled out a wheelbarrow, shoveled it full, and dumped it on the other side of the garden in graceful movements. That was the beginning of learning to work "smart." My daughter also learned this in the garden, and she uses this ability in whatever she has to do—homework, household chores, art projects, errands, and so on.

—Dorothea, mother of Melissa, fourteen

As our daughter watches us do household tasks and favorite projects, she catches our enthusiasm for a job well-done, an art well-crafted. She learns to work "smart." When we encourage her to try sweeping the floor, brushing the cat, painting a picture, or hammering a nail, a girl gains competence in her skills and pride in being an active member of the family. The strong will and the skilled will go hand-in-hand. Strength combined with skill empowers girls to determine the course of their own lives.

A strong and skillful will can be used for good or for evil, as many historical figures confirm. Dr. Assagioli writes that "the will, to be fulfilling, must be good."[15] To awaken to a healthy womanhood, capable of living a good life, a girl must develop a *good will* to choose goals that support her welfare and the common good of others. Mentors and role models greatly influence a girl's choice of goals. She gains inspiration from her parents, her teachers, the stories she is told, the books she reads, and the spiritual traditions her family follow. We emphasize here the overwhelming influence that television has on development. Too often the underlying messages we see are that we must cheat to get ahead, we must look a certain way to be admired, and violence is the way to settle our differences.

I visited my first rest home when I was thirteen. I remember I didn't want to go, because I thought I'd be bored. Bob, our youth director at church, insisted that our group of ten teenagers accompany him one Sunday evening. The first person we visited was an eighty-five-year-old woman, who looked like she had not had a visitor in years. When all ten of us came trooping in behind our leader, her eyes got real big. Bob pulled up a chair, introduced himself, and took her hand. He asked her what she had done when she was the age of these teenagers. She told some of the funniest stories I had ever heard. Bob teased her about making up tall tales; she pinched his cheek and kissed him. We all laughed until we cried. When we left that room, Bob said, "OK, let's go to the next room, and I'll show you one more time how it's done." We all told him, "No way. We want to do it on our own." Two hours flew by as we heard stories that brought both laughter and tears. That was sixteen years ago. Bob and that experience inspired me to get my master's degree in aging and geriatrics. Today, I am regional director for a senior citizens' corporation. Bob did more than show me how to relate to older people. He gave me a life's purpose with meaning. I hope to pass that on to others.

—Cindy, twenty-nine

Like Cindy, young girls need experiences where they are called upon to use their gifts and talents to find the delight in genuinely helping and empowering others. Through example and encouragement our daughters develop a good will.

With a strong, skillful, and good will, a girl can create a meaningful life with others. Dr. Assagioli wrote of a fourth aspect of will that goes beyond the common, personal, accepted parts of the will into the life of spirit, the vital principle or animating force within living beings.

"Though many are unaware of it and may even deny its existence, there is another kind of awareness....In the past, it was generally considered the domain of religious, or 'spiritual,' experience, but it is now gaining increasing recognition as a valid field of scientific investigation."[16] Dr. Assagioli called this awareness the *transpersonal will*. Those who follow the Tao call it "The Way." Christians might say, "Holy Spirit." In the Jewish tradition it is called, "Ru-ah." Native Americans refer to it as "The Great Spirit." Members of Alcoholics Anonymous call it a "Higher Power." Whatever the tradition, whatever the wording, and whatever the form, the will does not reach true balance and wholeness until it is connected to a greater power beyond the personal.

When asked how they stay in touch with "spirit," members of a women's group shared the following: "I feel it in nature. I seem to come back to what's meaningful," says June. "When I sing, I feel connected to something more glorious and greater than myself," responds Becky. Mavis shares, "When I remember to pray, I feel myself back in touch in a deeper way." "Yoga and meditation keep me connected," says Lucille. "My daily time, late at night, when I read and think helps me stay in tune with a greater force," replies Margaret.

Helping our daughters find their own special way of connecting with powers beyond themselves can take many forms. Setting aside family time for ritual and worship, spending time together in nature, reading stories that inspire, praying before bedtime, and using the imagination to send out angels for safekeeping are just a few of the numerous ways we guide our daughters' development of the transpersonal will.

When our daughter was seven, she began having nightmares. It was a particularly bad time for all of us, until she told me that a bright bird came to her in her imagination and agreed to eat all her bad dreams. Each night she saw the bird in her mind before going to sleep, and the nightmares stopped. Together we thanked the mystical bird for its generous, loving assistance, and Ellie continues to ask for its help when she is frightened or worried. The change in her is wonderful. She seems to have a trust of herself and the

*world that she didn't have before the glorious bird
came to her.*

—Janis, mother of Ellie, nine

Again and again, we teach our daughters by our own example, and developing the will is no exception. If we have the habit of allowing ourselves a few moments of quiet time, away from the stress of daily living, or if we regularly seek experiences in nature by walking, gardening, or simply sharing space with a tree, our daughters will learn the essential practice of opening to the wonder of creation and the force behind it.

Great souls have wills; feeble ones have only wishes.

—Chinese Proverb

A Balanced Inner Guidance System

The powerful trio of feeling, thinking, and willing are expressed differently by each of our daughters. One girl may have strong opinions about what she wants and how she wants it, but she has difficulty taking the necessary steps to achieve her desires. Another girl may see the issues clearly and know how to deal with them, but lacks the goodness of heart to realize her goals without hurting others in the process. Still another girl may clearly figure things out, but become overwhelmed by her feelings and unable to take the right action for fulfilling her bright ideas.

It is important to remember that at each age of development the focus of our daughter's growth changes. Although each component of the inner guidance system is developing and functioning, there is more emphasis on willing from birth to seven, on feeling from eight to twelve, and thinking emerges in more complex forms in the teen years between thirteen and seventeen. Knowing these tendencies enables us to better understand the convoluted development of our daughter's inner awakening into a healthy woman.

Endnotes

1. Howard Thurman, as quoted by Marion Wright Edelman, *The Measure of Our Success* (Boston, MA: Beacon Press, 1992).

2. Thomas Traherne, "Wonder," in *The Norton Anthology of Poetry*, ed. Arthur M. Eastman (New York: W. W. Norton, 1970), 166.

3. M. Scott Peck, *The Road Less Traveled* (New York: Simon & Schuster, 1978), 15.

4. Rudolf Steiner, "For Strength," in *Prayers and Graces*, collected by Michael Jones (Edinburgh, UK: Floris Books, 1987), 77.

5. Adele Faber and Elaine Mazlish, *Liberated Parents Liberated Children* (New York: Avon Books, 1974), 27.

6. EMDR, Eye Movement Desensitization and Reprocessing, was developed by Dr. Francine Shapiro and found to be especially effective with victims of trauma—Vietnam war veterans, victims of accidents, sexual assaults, robberies, adults with early childhood problems, nightmares and sleep disorders. EMDR is still an experimental method and is more widely used in veterans' hospitals, emergency rooms, rape crisis centers, and other facilities working with trauma victims. We suggest choosing a therapist carefully. Make sure she or he has experience using EMDR with children and was trained by the EMDR organization. For more information about EMDR, call the office in Pacific Grove, CA: (408)372-3900.

7. Nelson DeMille, *The General's Daughter* (New York: Warner Books, 1992), 90–91.

8. 1 Kings 19:12.

9. C. G. Jung, *Memories, Dreams, Reflections* (New York: Random House, 1963), 139, 197.

10. Sally Helgesen, *The Female Advantage: Women's Ways of Leadership* (New York: Doubleday, 1990), xxi.

11. Albert Einstein, as quoted in *Correct Quotes* (Sausalito, CA: WordStar International, Inc., 1990).

12. Roberto Assagioli, *The Act of Will* (New York: Penguin Books, 1976), 15.

13. Al Chung-liang Huang, *Embrace Tiger, Return to Mountain* (Noab, VT: Real People Press, 1973), 12.

14. Assagioli, *The Act of Will*, 16.

15. Ibid.

16. Ibid., 17.

CHAPTER EIGHT

THE POSITIVE INTENT

...suppose you...read a person's life backwards....Suppose we look at the kids who are odd or stuttering or afraid, and instead of seeing these as developmental problems we see them as having some great thing inside them, some destiny that they're not yet able to handle. It's bigger than they are and their psyche knows that. So that's a way of reading your own life differently. Instead of reading your life today as the results of...[mistakes] as a child, you read your childhood as a miniature example of your life, as a cameo of your life—and recognize that you don't really know your whole life until you're about eighty—and then you're too old to get it in focus or even care to.[1]

—James Hillman, Ph.D.

P arenting is not logical. If it were, we would never have to read a book such as this, never need a family therapist, and never feel the urge to call a close friend late at night for support after a particularly trying bedtime scene. Logic classes would solve all our problems, especially with our children and our marriages. But, parenting is not logical. We have moments of logic, but life is run by a much larger force. Life is filled with disagreement, opposition, illusion, irrational thinking, miracle, meaning, surprise, and wonder.

We all face these maddening problems; daily occurrences that slowly consume our energy until we question our ability to parent anybody. Eventually, these impossible situations that logic cannot solve wear away our resistance to trying something new. Albert Einstein is reputedly to have once said that we cannot solve a problem on the level that it was created. We need to approach these frustrating, problem behaviors on a new level.

This new approach, what we call looking for the *positive intent*[2] of our daughters' behaviors, allows us as parents to set aside the personal involvement we feel—guilt, anger, or helplessness—in power struggles with our daughters. *The most frustrating behaviors we encounter with our daughters are young expressions, or seedlings, of their future, their unique destinies. They are not to be eliminated. They are to be worked with, developed, and they will be—whether we like it or not.*

The Seeds of Her Destiny

Within each girl are unique possibilities, little seedlings holding the promise of future gifts, talents, and resources. When she is small, her budding potentialities may be difficult for her to manage. She has these mighty impulses within, but she is not mature enough to direct them. They are now stronger than she is, and they control her more than she controls them. In fact, these potential gifts may be the very things that frustrate us the most about parenting her.

> A girl who whines and complains all the time that nothing is just right, may become an eye surgeon, dedicated to delicacy and precision.

> A girl who argues with everyone about every little thing may become an attorney, defending those unable to speak for themselves.

> The bossy little girl who orchestrates the activities of her group of friends may become a corporate executive, creating confidence by delegating tasks and authority to her staff.

> A daughter who draws on her walls with crayon after we have tried everything to dissuade her, may be a future mural artist, spreading lovely colors where once only dismal drabness existed.

The girl who insists upon order and beauty in her dress and environment, may become a community organizer, creating order out of the chaos of misunderstanding and poverty.

The daughter who constantly talks on the telephone with so many friends we can never keep track of them all, may become a world leader, able to inspire others to cooperation and greatness.

Not until a girl reaches her middle twenties does she begin to understand her unique gifts and start to discover their true purpose. When we look for the positive intent beneath her behaviors while she is little, allowing it room to grow, giving it just enough light, pruning it when necessary along the way, a girl naturally grows toward her purpose in life. Like our prevailing, gender-biased culture, we can squash her talents, discourage her yearnings, or force her voice underground, but her true nature will always strive to peek through to the surface of her being. When we are at cross purposes with her budding talents, however, we stunt her development into a healthy woman, a woman in touch with both her feminine nature and her innate competence.

She has always argued relentlessly with me. When she was little, she would sometimes forget her point, but that didn't faze her. She just shifted the subject and pounded onward. At one point I thought she was possessed.

—Karen, fifty-two, mother of Marlene

I remember those times, and I did feel possessed. A power came into me, bigger than me, and I was on a high. My poor mother was on a roller coaster. I can control it now and direct it for my clients. I have realized I have turn it off around my daughter. She's better at it than I am. I understand it now, and I must say, I have a lot more compassion for my mother. My daughter is as relentless as I am!

—Marlene, thirty-two, trial attorney

A young girl's quirks, obsessions, and most difficult behaviors wait to mature into the talents and resources she needs to follow her mission in life. During her years in our care, we are the gardeners of her gifts—feeding, staking, trimming, and encouraging her to grow into her true nature, whomever that may be.

Listening for the Positive Intent

"So are you saying I should let my daughter do whatever she wants, because of this 'bud' thing?" challenges a father attending a *Raising a Daughter* workshop. Listening for the positive intent of a behavior changes the interaction between us and our daughters from adversarial to understanding. We do not mean to imply that we no longer set fences and enforce consequences. Our guidance is extremely important to our daughters. Limits and consequences allow them to look inward, to develop their own internal boundaries, to become healthy and loving women.

> *My daughter just learned to drive, and recently she asked to go to a friend's house. I let her take my favorite car. Unfortunately, she went too fast on a wet road and slid, hitting the bumper of my vintage auto. My old way would be to ground her for life. When she told me the facts, I could see that she felt awful about hurting my car and had learned her lesson about driving too fast. Later that night she very shyly asked if she could go to a movie with a friend. I thought a moment, and said, "Sure, go ahead." She looked stunned. "You aren't going to ground me for crashing your car?" I replied, "No, you did the best you could. I know you are trying to be a good driver. Everybody makes mistakes." She looked at me as if I were crazy. "Shouldn't I be grounded?" she asked. I didn't catch how stunned she was at my new response. "I don't think so." "Okay," she said. "I really am sorry for*

crashing it. I love you, Dad." When she left, I cried.
She hadn't said that to me in years.

—Richard, thirty-eight, father of Julie, sixteen

We set limits and consequences to guide our daughters into maturity. What limits and consequences we choose depend upon our daughters' behaviors. To find age-appropriate limits and behavior-appropriate consequences, we must tune into our daughters' worlds; we must truly listen to their feelings; we must seek to understand their positions. When we shift from wondering when they will do something wrong to listening for the positive intent of their behaviors, we change assumptions about our daughters. No longer assuming they argue with us because they don't care about us, or wreck our cars to get back at us for being too strict, by listening for the positive intent we assume there is a good reason when they get off track. The event is a signal that something needs our attention.

I thought about this positive intent business and my daughter, Loreen. She gets so mad when I ask or tell her what to do. Now, at fourteen the smallest of things set her off. The other night she was mad when I asked her to pick up her clothes in the hallway. I said, "I know you want to run your own life. You must hate it when I keep nagging you all the time." She said, "That's right! I do, and I do hate it when you go on and on and on about things. When I grow up, I'll put my things where I want them!" She stomped off with her clothes. Later we calmly talked about other things. Since then we've had an understanding. Who knows if it will last, but she seemed to change her attitude just a little when I shared how frustrated I felt with her behavior. When I named her motivation as "wanting to run her own life," I think she really felt I had seen her. Isn't that what I want her to be able to do anyway? I still have to ask her to pick up clothes. We joke more about it, though, and she still gets mad. But there's still this "understanding" between us.

—Joyce, mother of Loreen, fourteen

When daughters hear their behaviors framed in a positive way, they shift their self-perception from, "I am doing this because I am bad," to "I am doing this for an important reason." Having pride in their reasons is a good thing, because they can then adjust their way of doing things without crushing the young, seed-like expression of their deeper natures. Who knows where Loreen will take her steadfast persistence to do things her way. As this quality matures, she may use her ability to discover a cure for AIDS or to find solutions to homelessness and poverty. While she is young, we want her to know that doing things her way is a good thing, *and* that there are times when she will need to adjust *how* she goes about doing it "her way." Hopefully, we can encourage her to adjust without having to give up her self.

The following graph portrays Loreen's positive intent beneath her anger at being told what to do:

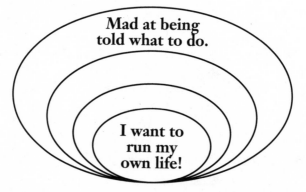

By acknowledging our daughter's underlying intent and by naming it as something good, she will be more willing to be flexible. Most people become extremely rigid when we miss the "why" of their behavior, seeing only the "what". When we accurately name what a girl feels, she heaves a visible sigh of relief, her body relaxes, and her soul shouts an unconscious, "YES!"

Self-Esteem and Soul

The most precious gift we can give a child

is a positive and realistic self-image. Now how

is this self-image formed? Not all at once,

but slowly, experience by experience.[3]

—Dr. Hiam Ginott

≪≫ ≪≫ *DON* In my therapy practice, I work with many parents and daughters. One mother had particular difficulty understanding the idea of the positive intent. She complained, "Lauren does great, and then she screws things up by not showing up on time or something else. No matter how much we ground her, we can't break that pattern in her." I thought in silence for a second and said, "She is committed to doing things her way." Her mother smiled and said, "You bet! She always ends up doing things her way." I turned to the daughter in the room, "Is this right? You are committed to doing things your way?" She nodded her head and grimaced. "So, I guess the new question is, how can you continue to do things your way," I paused as her parents visibly stiffened, "in a way that doesn't get you in so much trouble?" The daughter liked that. The parents did too, after they started breathing normally again. Instead of having a problem behavior that needed breaking, Lauren and her parents could view her ability to do things her own way as a positive quality. With her self-esteem intact, we could now help Lauren find ways to do things her way that fit with family needs. Rather than trying to eliminate her determination, she and her family will nurture her soul quality into a future resource for the benefit of Lauren herself, her family, and her community.

Here is a picture of Lauren's troublesome behavior and the positive seed that lay within:

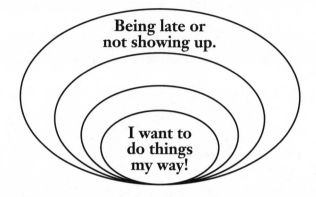

Being late or
not showing up.

I want to
do things
my way!

Self-esteem plays an important part in how our daughters approach the ups and downs in their lives. Lauren can now be more flexible, because her pride is intact. Her so-called problem behavior has a self-assertive and positive purpose. Doing things in our own unique way gets us far ahead of the many who do what they are told to do without thinking about it. Lauren can be more flexible, because staying out of trouble by considering how doing things her way will affect others, gives her more of the freedom she seeks. She may not realize it now, but she gets more than freedom. She has a new, positive self-esteem and confidence in her behavior. She later explained, "I didn't really know why I always screwed things up until Mr. Elium said I was committed to doing it my way. Now I understand myself better. I don't like it when my folks assume I'll do things their way. They don't even ask. But, I do consider what they want and why, and then I do it my way, if it works. I like having that freedom to choose. I have friends who say they could never question their parents. It seems natural for me. I guess I'm lucky my parents support my judgment. When I'm off, they tell me. It's a lot better than the yelling we used to get into."

Lauren's behavior pushed her beyond her capabilities to be responsible for her actions. Naming the underlying positive intent of her behavior prodded Lauren to wonder about "her way." What is it? How does it affect others? How does it serve me? Why is it so important? Understanding brings the power to choose our behaviors, to anticipate and act on that anticipation, rather than simply waiting and reacting.

When we stop treating our daughters as "delinquent teenagers" or "difficult toddlers," we acknowledge them as people with potential gifts, whose capable minds of their own are leading them toward a healthy womanhood.

Guidelines for Naming and Developing the Positive Intent

Children see themselves primarily through their parents' eyes. They look to us to tell them not necessarily what they are, but what they're capable of becoming. They depend upon us for a larger vision of themselves, and for the tools to implement that vision.[4]

—Faber and Mazlish, *Liberated Parents Liberated Children*

Parenting skills must mature with our daughters. Girls constantly change and mature, requiring us to continually alter our parenting approaches and techniques. What worked well at one age may totally backfire at an older stage. A successful approach with one daughter has no effect with another daughter. Each daughter has a destiny to live out, and the little branches that needed room to grow in when she was five may need pruning at thirteen. Patience and persistence are required to name the positive motivation beneath a girl's frustrating behavior. She needs us to stick with her. Awakening a girl to her future destiny as a woman is neither a simple nor a predictable endeavor.

Parents have a positive intent, too. As parent gardeners, we are called upon to be flexible, forgiving, ingenious, and understanding. Not an easy job. When we are not up to it and fall back into anger, judgment, or impatience, looking for the positive intent behind our slip-ups saves our parenting self-esteem. We shouted at our daughter, because we care so much, or we came down hard on her, because we are judging ourselves too harshly. Sometimes we have darker reasons, as well—we are too tired, too hurried, too self-preoccupied, and so on. Understanding we have our limits frees us to be authentic models for our daughters, compassionate yet real about how we are affected by their behavior.

Listening for the positive intent is part of setting fences and choosing consequences. Developing inner personal boundaries, learning to trust her inner guidance system, and listening for the positive intent behind her behavior deepen a girl's understanding of herself. From this understanding comes the confidence and competence to use her gifts, talents, and resources throughout her life. A girl best achieves an understanding of herself if she is guided by clear fences and consequences that recognize and nurture her positive intent.

We are still amazed at how pinpointing and accurately naming a behavior's purpose changes a relationship dynamic. When it happens, everyone involved immediately relaxes, steps back from their frozen positions, yields a little, breathes deeper, and becomes more willing to hear all sides and opinions. The positive intent behind some of our daughters' behaviors may be hard to identify. If at first we do not succeed, we must try, try again, because it is worth the trouble. Finding that magic word or phrase frees a girl to grow. The following list of positive intent ideas may be helpful in redefining the problem behaviors we have all experienced in girls. We start with the young, immature behavior and grow it into the gifts and talents it will become.

Immature Form	**Possible Mature Form (Positive Intent)**
temper tantrums	self-assertion
pouting	thoughtfulness
whining	compassion
laziness	rich inner life
stinginess	conservation
fearfulness	protectiveness
aloofness	independence
bossiness	leadership abilities
dawdling	carefulness, methodical way of working
picky	discernment

Immature Form	Possible Mature Form (Positive Intent)
giddiness	zest for life
moodiness	inner searching
secretive	keeps healthy boundaries and privacy; able to say "No"
conformist	teamwork

Exercises: Learning to Name the Positive Intent

The key to listening for the positive intent beneath our daughter's problem behaviors is to ignore for the moment what she is doing. We often get so hung up on how *what* she is doing looks to others we miss the meaning of the behavior. "Oh, no! My two-year-old is having a temper tantrum in the grocery store. All these people must think I'm a terrible mother, because I can't control my daughter! Bad girl!" Although it is hard for many of us to believe, it really does not matter what other grocery shoppers think of our mothering abilities in that moment. What is important is what has led up to our daughter's tantrum. The grocery store is often the last stop in a long list of errands, and our child has reached her limit. She has had it, and she tells us the only way she knows how. The positive intent behind her positively embarrassing behavior is, "Mom, I'm tired and hungry, and I need to go home to be rocked where it's familiar and peaceful." She is expressing her needs—immaturely, but effectively.

To practice finding the positive intent in problem behaviors, we have included a list of common situations we all experience with our daughters. Write a response for each one that recognizes the positive intent behind the words. We completed the first one as an example.

Statement: Watch me, Mommy. Watch Me, Mommy! Watch ME, Mommy!! WATCH ME, MOMMY!!!!!!

Positive Intent: *I need your attention. I need to know you are here for me.*

Statement: I won't wear that silly dress!

Positive Intent:

Statement: I hate you! You can't make me do what you say.

Positive Intent:

Statement: You're not being fair. All my friends are going.

Positive Intent:

Statement: I will not clean up my room.

Positive Intent:

Statement: I'm so fat and ugly!

Positive Intent:

Statement: I'm never going to play with Jessie again. She's stupid!

Positive Intent:

Like learning any new skill, hearing the positive intent requires practice and perseverance. The more we do it, the better we become. Our older daughters may even begin to help us understand what they are really trying to tell us.

Do These Sound Familiar?

How often have we said we will never treat our daughters the way our parents treated us, and then watched ourselves do just that? Old habits die hard, and we easily slip into the power-struggle situations with our daughters we hoped to avoid. The following are examples of missed opportunities, moments we can all remember, when we wished we had known to say something else. We offer them, not to instill guilt, but to encourage us all, knowing we always have another chance to listen better next time.

I won't wear that silly dress!

That dress cost a lot of money, and you'll wear it whether you like it or not!

I hate you! You can't make me do what you say.

I've had enough of your back talk. Go to your room until I say you can come out!

You're not being fair. All my friends are going to the concert.

Life isn't fair, and it doesn't matter about your friends. You are not going!

I will not clean up my room.

You march in there right now, young lady, and don't come out until it's finished.

I'm so fat and ugly!

That's a terrible thing to say about yourself. Of course, you're not ugly. If you would just lose a little weight, you'd be beautiful.

I'm never going to play with Jessie again. She's stupid!

It's not nice to say things like that about your friends. You'll feel differently tomorrow.

We can all imagine what these responses would elicit from our daughters—angry retorts, pouting, sullen looks, stomping off, stony silences. Try the following possibilities to foster communication and understanding between parents and daughters.

I won't wear that silly dress!

You want to choose your own clothes.

I hate you! You can't make me do what you say.

This really means a lot to you.

You're not being fair. All my friends are going to the concert.

You really want us to trust you more. Give us more information, and let's talk.

I will not clean up my room.

You hate it when I tell you what to do. You want to do things your way.

I'm so fat and ugly!

Tell me more about how you feel, because this sounds really important.

I'm never going to play with Jessie again. She's stupid!

Sounds like maybe Jessie hurt you, and you need some help with that.

Responding to the positive intent behind our daughters' behaviors and statements requires us to be more conscious in our responses. The same old words our parents said to us no longer fit. We must find new, more appropriate ways to let our daughters know we understand their positions, or that we want to, but we just need more information about what they are trying to tell us. The following blanks provide space for the typical statements your daughters make, your old responses, and new ones you might try to hear their positive intent.

My daughter says

_____

I used to respond

_____

My new response

_____

My daughter says

_____

I used to respond

_____

My new response

_____

My daughter says

_____

I used to respond

_____

My new response

_____

My daughter says

_____

I used to respond

_____

My new response

_____

Endnotes

1. James Hillman, "Is Therapy Turning Us Into Children," *New Age Journal*, May/June 1992, 64.

2. Positive Intent is a phrase used by Vernon Woolf, Ph.D., in an "Unfolding Potential" seminar, San Rafael, CA, 17–19 Aug. 1990.

3. Adele Faber and Elaine Mazlish, *Liberated Parents Liberated Children* (New York: Avon Books, 1974), 54.

4. Ibid., 120.

Part III:

From Cradle to Career

CHAPTER NINE

THE "WATCH ME!" YEARS: FROM BIRTH TO SEVEN

The unborn child is a person
no one knows.[1]

—Lennart Nilsson, *A Child Is Born*

W hen we look at a sleeping baby, a smile begins at the corners of our mouth; we become quiet inside; our gaze softens in wonder; we take in the creamy skin, fine hair, curled fingers, pudgy toes, soft breathing. Then we ask, "Boy or girl?" Even before we ask, we hazard a guess from the colors of the blankets, the clothes, the delicacy of the features, the amount of hair.

Conversation between two newborns:

High Voice: What do you think I am?
Deep Voice: You? That's easy—you're a boy.
High Voice: Are you sure?
Deep Voice: Of course I'm sure....
High Voice: Gee, I don't feel like a boy.
Deep Voice: That's because you can't see yourself.
High Voice: Why? What do I look like?
Deep Voice: Bald. You're bald fellow. Bald, bald,
*   bald. You're bald as a ping-pong ball. Are you bald!*
High Voice: So?
Deep Voice: So, boys are bald and girls have hair.
High Voice: Are you sure?
Deep Voice: Of course, I'm sure. Who's bald, your
*   mother or your father?*

High Voice: My father.
Deep Voice: I rest my case.
High Voice: Hmmm. You're bald, too.
Deep Voice: You're kidding!
High Voice: No, I'm not.
Deep Voice: Don't look!
High Voice: Why?
Deep Voice: A bald girl—blech!—disgusting!
High Voice: Maybe you're a boy and I'm a girl.[2]

—Peter Stone and Carl Reiner, "Boy Meets Girl"

No matter how hard we try, we cannot escape our gender destinies. The early years from birth to seven are spent discovering who we are in relation to others and the outer world. Who we are begins with whether we are girl or boy, and from the inside out, our gender flavors all our experiences. In broad strokes, let us consider who our daughters are from birth to seven, keeping in mind that we are viewing them from the outside in. Like butterflies emerging from their cocoons, they unfold before us, compelling us to watch their wondrous flight.

Developmental Tasks

What is important for us to know about the developmental stages of growth in girls that we have not already studied in college courses or gleaned from the hundreds of parenting books we've read? Mostly, parenting materials are written about children in general, rather than about girls specifically. In many ways babies are babies with similar needs and developmental tasks to accomplish. Young children, however, get it straight very early in their lives which they are—girl or boy.[3] This gender identity is very important to them, not to know how to behave, but to know who they are. We see small girls and boys regularly crossing over stereotypic gender roles, while steadfastly maintaining their own gender identities. Girls and boys develop in very similar ways during some stages and very differently in others. It is important to value and uphold the differences and the similarities.

Growth during the years from birth to seven is rapid and body-centered, laying the physical, social, and emotional foundations for later intellectual development. According to philosopher and founder of Waldorf Education, Rudolf Steiner, the natural focus of development in the early years is in the body and in the emergence of the will for both girls and boys.[4] Learning to walk, to talk, and to think are the giant leaps taken from birth to seven, and they are accomplished in that order.

Ideally, both girls and boys complete these tasks in their own internal growing time. We caution parents about paying too much attention to the charts and standards of growth to which doctors and other experts are compelled to compare our children, because western culture has the tendency to urge children out of infancy too soon, to awaken the intellect before the body has had its full growing season. Allowing our daughters to *unfold* like buds may be an overused cliché, but we recommend this method over the artificial forcing in development we are tempted to try, such as baby exercise classes, toys to enhance motor development, programs to teach early reading skills, and so on.

The tendency of our head-oriented culture to explain to, to give reasons for, and to admonish our small daughters is another way we push them to develop too early. We begin reasoning with them the moment they learn to talk, mistakenly believing they understand. The thinking of a three-year-old is much different from the nine-year-old and miles away from an adult's. Their questions and statements are not yet rational, and reasoning does little to change a girl's behavior.

> *I used to tell Lila twenty times a day to put the lid back on her clay, because air dries it out, and then she won't be able to play with it anymore. I carefully explained this to her, but she never remembered. Now I realize I have to help her put it away over and over until she remembers to cover it on her own.*
>
> —*Sheri, mother of Lila, three*

Piaget's studies of children's development show that rational thinking does not evolve until the age of ten or eleven.[5] Pushing understanding before the capacity or need is there, only serves to frustrate parents and overburden little ones, whose energy is best focused on body development, not reasoning ability. Some studies show, and many parents experience, that girls tend to develop concrete operational thinking sooner than boys do, but just because the budding capacity is there is no reason to push it. Remember this old joke? "Never try to teach a pig to sing. It wastes your time and annoys the pig." Similar thing. Rudolf Steiner taught that any activities taking energy and focus away from the body should be postponed until after the change of the baby teeth, around the seventh year. We believe this is a good measuring stick for all children from birth to seven. As the following conversation implies, Dr. Steiner recommended distracting, rather than discouraging.

> *Proud parent: My four-year-old Sheila is already trying to read.*
>
> *Waldorf teacher: Perhaps you could interest her in baking bread or planting a garden.*

Appropriate play during the infant years involves clapping, peek-a-boo, singing silly songs, bouncing, and crawling after desired objects. Simple toys are best—a soft ball made from natural fabric, wooden rattle, and a plain, stuffed animal or doll. Older babies find great amusement in household objects, especially what is found in a bottom drawer of the kitchen—metal bowls, wooden spoons, cups of various sizes, and so on. What all babies love most is physical contact with their parents. They never tire of playing face to face, with noses, hair, puffed-out cheeks, and silly expressions with mouth and tongue.

Play for the toddler is centered around repetitive games with large physical movements, such as climbing, running, hopping, throwing and catching a ball; building with large blocks; manipulating clay; imaginative play with small, wooden figures of people, gnomes, and animals; and the imitation of household chores: sweeping, dusting, washing dishes. The years between two and seven are spent perfecting these physio-motor skills.

Children also need great amounts of time in water play, cloud gazing, and the testing of time and space. Remember how a baby drops her spoon, peas, mashed potatoes, anything within reach over the side of her highchair? A budding Galileo, she approaches everything with the Zen beginner's mind; therefore she finds fascinating the everyday things we have long since stopped appreciating.

⊰ *JEANNE* | I remember taking newly-gathered eggs from their wire basket and dropping them one by one, amazed at how the sharp white shell shattered, as the brightly colored yolk spread across the floor.

Girls grow within relationships of ever-increasing complexity. The infant girl's first explorations begin with her own fingers and toes and ripple out to ever-widening circles around her. Our daughter's first lessons in relationship come from us, her parents. Her first glance is focused intently on our faces. Her first smile is for us alone. Her attention is directed to the relationship between us; she is ever-alert to the changes in our focus, our mood, our reactions to her efforts to communicate. Her entire being is a highly-tuned sensory organ, soaking in every nuance of our interaction.

Later, her attention widens to include the natural world around her, whose lessons she soaks in through touch, taste, sight, and smell. She lives in her surroundings, taking in the voices of flower and tree, stone and grass, water and soil through senses we adults have, somewhere between then and now, forgotten how to use.

Gradually, simple objects, such as a ball, her doll, and the toy box, come to inhabit a girl's small world. She views these objects as living beings that exist in relationship to herself. During the years from birth to seven, a girl begins to recognize the permanence of these playthings—to know they will be where she left them and will respond in the accustomed ways—and she learns to assert her will upon them. She learns to trust us, her parents, as well, to provide the care she needs and, most importantly, to be involved in this great, ever-widening, ever-fascinating game we call *relationship*. Her growth is not aimed toward separation, but toward an enlarged ability to relate in ever more complex connections with others.

Girls develop as beings-in-relationship.[6] The popular and long-standing theory of self-development involves the eventual attainment of independence and autonomy; that is, children must separate from their parents, or more specifically, from *mother*. We put great emphasis on this sense of "separate self" for boys and push them in this direction, but somehow, girls never seem to measure up. They are rarely seen as independent and as capable of making their way in the world as boys are. Why? Because our understanding of normal growth for girls has been skewed by research done primarily on boys: We have mistakenly assumed that girls and boys are the same.

Child-development studies infer that girls develop a sense of self the way boys do, through ever more separate and independent acts. From her insightful research, Jean Baker Miller, M.D. finds that infants of both sexes sense themselves as interacting beings. Culture, however, diverts boys away from this relational sense of self to a sense of a separate being, alone and independent. Girls are encouraged to develop their abilities to be tuned to how others feel, to remain in relationship with others. Dr. Miller describes a girl's sense of self as reflecting "what is happening *between* people."[7] Dr. Miller believes that to feel related to another person and to care about her well-being enhances a girl's self-esteem, rather than threatening it. Her sense of competence and power is heightened, rather than diminished. A girl feels, "This is how things should be. This is how I like them to be."

How does this new understanding of development help us parent girls from birth to seven? Most importantly, how can we more consciously value and nurture the seed of our daughter's destiny as a female being-in-relationship? There are hazards along the way that parents must consider. The most common mistakes we make in raising girls are to unconsciously or unintentionally teach them 1) to overcompensate when care is lacking in a relationship, 2) to give care inappropriately, and 3) to care at all costs. All three of these tendencies entrap girls and women in limited roles and behaviors.

Feeling, caring, and nurturing are considered feminine skills in our culture. We therefore often demand that girls and women fill up the empty spaces in relationships to overcompensate where care is missing. This overcompensation causes numerous unfortunate problems for all of us, both females and males. When girls and women assume sole responsibility for the caring, they may eventually become overburdened, burned out, and resentful. Girls and women want and need to be given care in return. It is the mutual exchange of care within relationship which enlivens connection and nurtures the participants.

When boys and men leave the responsibility for care-giving to females, they fail to develop this human capacity vital for a healthy life. Their hearts and feelings shrivel from lack of use, and we all lose out, especially within our families. Men feel they do not belong, and women feel they have to do it all alone. Teaching our daughter to give and receive care, to say "No" when she wants to, and to ask for what she needs from others, helps her achieve a more balanced relationship of care. Parents do this best by modeling these behaviors in our own relationships, as well as with our daughters.

Because females naturally seek connection, daughters develop the art of giving care very early in their lives. Our vital job is to teach them to give care appropriately. We do that by being clear about our own boundaries, and helping our daughters remain children, rather than expecting them to provide what they are not mature enough to give. This is what happened for Alessandra, six years old.

> *When we divorced, Paul seemed the logical parent to take Lessa, because he worked at home. She's lived with him for two years now, and I'm shocked I haven't realized before now how much like a little wife she's become. She tells me about his work, his trouble with his girlfriend, his worries about money, and everything he used to tell me; well, almost everything. She's only six years old! I try to get her to lighten up when we're together; you know, play make-believe, be silly, pretend we're someone else. It's beyond her. She mostly wants to talk, and she wants to know things about me and my life I don't think is appropriate for a child her age. I'm not a prude or anything. I just think kids should be kids and not have to worry about adult stuff. They get there soon enough as it is.*
>
> *—Lea, thirty-nine, mother of Alessandra, six*

When a girl learns that she must care about others no matter what, at all costs, those parts of her that do not care must be kept hidden. What is she to do when she feels hatred, rage, or fear towards others? A good example is when a small daughter has been the only child for several years, and a new sister or brother arrives. A girl naturally feels animosity toward this intruder, but she is usually admonished to be nice, to love, and to *care for* her new sibling. It is important to know that having the freedom *not to care for* allows room for connection without dictating the form of the caring. Being honestly angry at someone we love and telling them without blame or judgment can be a form of caring and often strengthens the connection between us. When we allow our daughter's full range of feelings, she learns to make and maintain connection in her relationships as a full human being.

A girl must allow others to share the responsibility for care, thus enabling others to care for her. She must learn how to care in ways appropriate to her age, her desires, and her needs; she then acts with authenticity. She must be allowed the freedom not to care; she then has access to a wide range of feelings and is able to care more fully. When healthy boundaries guide our daughter, her relational way of being in the world gives her strength and self-confidence. She can know, "I am a capable human being, because I care about others and attend to their feelings. And my parents understand this is my way. It is what helps me become a healthy woman with a full sense of self as capable of helping others grow." When this vital part of a tiny daughter is recognized and valued, she is free to develop her more masculine traits, as well. With a balance of both feminine and masculine talents and resources, she has a wider freedom in her life choices.

"In the first years of life, imitation is one of the most important functions that the child performs...."[8] Both the baby and the toddler spend their days imitating the people in the world around them. Unconsciously, they practice again and again father's lift of a brow or a pursing of the lips, until we recognize the gesture ourselves. At all stages of growth, but perhaps most significantly now, our actions teach far more than our words.

> *I worked with a woman whose noticeable limp could be linked with no known physical cause. We searched her childhood memories for any accident or illness and got nowhere. One day her mother, visiting from the Midwest, came to the appointment with her. Her*

mother had the same, noticeable limp, a remainder of the polio she had as a child![9]

—*Ann Grassel, physical therapist and Aston Patterner*

Not only our physical mannerisms but our moral postures, as well, are imitated by our little sensory detectors. Through our examples they learn how members of a family treat each other and how to relate to those in the outside world. Our facial expressions and tones of voice signal openness or caution, warmth or scorn, approval or criticism, adroitly perceived and imitated in their interactions with others.

I learned my love of gardening from my Granny and Granddad. They suddenly became more alive, more animated when we were in the garden. They never seemed to tire of weeding and calling out the names of tiny seedlings to me as we worked. I have the sense this was their true work, and I always feel better in my garden.

—*Moira, forty-six*

My dad hated loafers. No matter who it was, they were measured according to whether or not they were hard-working. To this day, I can't stand to see my husband lying on the couch when the grass needs mowing, or there are dishes in the sink.

—*Sandy, thirty-four*

The work of the home is always of great interest, and children want to be part of every activity, imitating the dusting, washing, cooking, and sweeping. Children copy what they see their parents doing, and home is where many lessons in sex-role stereotyping occur.

As I weeded my flower bed, five-year-old Greg from next door, paid me a visit. "Where's Mike?" he inquired about my husband. "He's in the kitchen, fixing our supper," I told him. With a shocked look he protested, "No! He can't be. My daddy never cooks! He's not supposed to cook!"

—*Linda, forty-two*

Play is the medium through which the developmental tasks of these years are manifested. Play is a child's work. Being allowed ample time to experiment with the elements of water, air, and earth provides the foundation for the later understanding of matter, time, and space—science, physics, geometry. As we discussed in Chapter Four, our selection of toys shape a young girl's developing psyche into the cultural mold or give her the freedom to grow according to her inner yearnings. Baby dolls, miniature ironing boards, and plastic kitchens prepare her for a life of care-taking for house and family. Those toys *plus* balls, and marbles, and blocks, and tiny figures, and colored scarves, and trains offer her the balance of choices her healthy growth demands.

Undisturbed play encourages concentration, follow-through, and creativity, builds self-esteem, and enhances cooperation and satisfaction. Constant meddling in a child's play creates a short attention span and the "What can I do now?" monster. After a child has thoroughly explored an object of interest or completed a task, she is ready and willing to participate in the family activities required of her. This is one of the most refreshing traits of a child in the "watch me" years. The uncooperative attitudes we see in our children often arise from their feelings of being constantly interrupted in their play. This is different, of course, from the ploys to prolong bedtime or the dawdling to avoid completing an undesirable task that we experience from an older child. A younger child is usually reluctant, because she has not finished an important piece of her work. Our understanding and consideration in easing our daughters through the transitions from one activity to the next avoids the power struggles that make family life so exhausting.

Needs

Babies need parents to be buffers between them and the outside world. Recent findings tell us the womb is not the quiet place we thought it to be. Common sense tells us the growing fetus probably hears what the mother hears, but in greatly subdued levels through the padding of skin, body fat, and lots of amniotic fluid. It's warm in there, too—and dark. We can imagine a newborn's first minute of shock out of her cocoon—the unfiltered noise, the bright lights, the cold, the hustle and bustle of medical staff. Practices are changing, however, to lessen the jarring impact of our world on a little one's delicate nervous system, and there is more we can do at home.

In the words of educator Rudolf Steiner, babies are "entirely sense-organ."[10] Without the adult ability to filter background stimuli, they experience the world all over and throughout their bodies. This stimulation is quite taxing and possibly toxic, and is one reason babies sleep so much during the early months. Their little systems need to be slowly awakened, to be buffered from too much stimulation. Babies especially need to be protected from loud, recorded music, harsh lighting, bright colors, television, and objects made from lifeless materials. They need soft colors and lighting, the nurturing feel of cotton, wool, wood, and other natural materials, and the soothing sound of silly songs and lullabies sung in their own parents' voices.

We expose babies too soon to the shopping mall, parades, the circus, the supermarket, the movies, and other technology. Childbirth and Waldorf educator Rahima Baldwin, whose wonderful book, *You Are Your Child's First Teacher*, explains that babies are resilient and should adjust to the ordinary sounds of the household.[11] We don't have to walk around the house on tiptoes, but neither must we subscribe to the mistaken notion that babies need to be prepared as soon as possible to cope with the harshness of real life. We advocate coddling the baby for as long as possible. She is only a baby once, and a gradual emerging from the quiet, dim cocoon is vital in the development of a healthy woman.

Babies need contact. We recommend "wearing the baby" during the first months of life. Native cultures around the world carry their babies constantly[12], passing them from adult to adult to older child, and so on, depending upon the activity, how many hands are needed, and the needs of the baby. The abundant, colorful slings and wraps from native peoples ingeniously keep the baby close to the wearer's heart and snugly, contentedly protected from cold and the unpleasant pull of gravity. This is probably as close to the environment of the womb a baby can get, except for floating in warm water, which babies love but is not practical for any length of time.

Cuddled and constantly carried, a baby develops a trust that her needs of warmth and companionship will be met. Within this soft cocoon, her body is free to adjust to this new, dry land environment without fretting about feeling cold, wet, and lonely. Her energy can go where it is needed—getting her respiratory and digestive systems, which so many babies have difficulty with, straightened out and functioning properly.

We know when this "in arms"[13] stage is complete, because our daughters begin to explore the world around them by crawling and climbing. We have a fear in this culture that our children will become dependent upon us—will always want to be coddled—if we carry them about and tend to their needs when they cry. On the contrary, they constantly cling to us when we do not give them the love, care, and undivided attention they need as infants. Our daughter's infancy is a very trying time, because her needs are constant, and caring for her consumes any time we might have had for sleep, a shower, time alone, a career, evenings out, and so on. Time invested during these early months of life, however, will come back full circle when our daughter's trust in us and in herself influence her decisions and behaviors during the crucial teenage years.

> *The most difficult thing I did in those early years was to surrender to my baby's consuming needs. When I took leave from my job, I thought I'd have all this time to complete those projects I'd wanted to do for years. No way! It was all I could do to get a shower in the morning and get myself dressed for the day. Then*

it'd be nursing, changing, rocking, sleeping while she napped. Then the whole routine started all over again. I look back on those months now as a blessed time. The outside world sort of stopped, and nothing else existed but me and the baby. I'd give anything to have even an hour of Kelly's undivided attention, but she trusts that she can come to me about anything on her mind. I'm so thankful for that.

—*Caroline, mother of Kelly, sixteen*

Sleep deprivation is a common complaint of parents during their children's early years. We either are up walking the baby, changing the baby, or feeding the baby, so the baby will go to sleep. Many wise parents have resorted to bringing the baby to bed with them, because everyone sleeps better. Of course! Only during this modern age of rugged individualism have we expected our children to sleep apart in the cold dark, isolated from the reassuring warmth and closeness of their parents.

Babies and young children need to be with their parents or other consistent parent figures. We very much applaud the parents who put family first in these difficult times by creatively negotiating work schedules that allow them to be the main caretakers of their children. Corporations and small businesses are beginning to realize that family is important to both mothers and fathers, and are seeking new ways to allow working parents to spend more time with their children. Job-sharing, more flex time, on-site daycare, maternity and paternity leave, and work-at-home time provide more options in the workplace. Here is another way we must be bold and audacious. By holding out for work schedules and benefits that support families, we can overcome our culture's destructive, downhill trend of ignoring the needs of our children. Look for a 1993 list of the 100 best companies for working mothers in the October, 1993, issue of *Working Mother* magazine. [14]

Two friends of ours, both marriage and family counselors, work from their home to share the care of their two daughters. One minds the kids and house while the other is working, and then they trade. This situation is not an easy juggling of clients, school schedules, errands, and household chores, not to mention social activities, but this dedicated couple make it work through their commitment to family life.

Single parents have the heaviest burden to bear in a culture hostile to families. It is ridiculous to consider job-sharing when the full-time jobs of many single parents barely cover living expenses, along with the high costs of adequate child care. Many single parents try family members first, then fill in the gaps with friends, neighbors, and child care centers.

> *I finally have a system that's working, but I don't know how long it will last, or how long I can keep up the pace. My mother is willing to watch Kris, but she tires easily, so she can't manage an active three-year-old for more than four hours. I drop her off there on my way to work, and on my lunch hour I pick her up and take her to my neighbor's house. My neighbor goes to work at 3:30 p.m., so she drops Kris off at a pre-school near my work until I'm off at 6:00. I can only afford the two hours per day. By the time we're home, I'm exhausted, and Kris is cranky from being carted all over the place. What else can I do?*
>
> *—Erin, mother of Kris, three*

There are no easy answers to the child care dilemma, and there are no hard facts about the effects on our children of being in day care. The reality is that parents have always worked and will continue to work to provide for their families and to fulfill the basic human need to be creative and productive. The increase of mothers in the workforce and in the numbers of single parents simply makes the child care crisis more glaring. Children's advocates call for "adequate child care," and the truth is that benefits for children have never been adequate in this country. A recent UNICEF study states that the poverty rate for children in the United States is more than double that of any other major industrialized nation in the world. "But what really distinguishes the United States from all these countries is that we started off with less generous benefits, and as we went through the 1980s . . . other nations got more generous and we got even less generous."[15]

We must all—parents, corporate executives, educators, members of Congress, retired citizens—work together to find healthy solutions for the care of our nation's children. The ideal day care situation is better than adequate. It is a warm, beautiful space situated closely and conveniently to a parent's workplace. The teachers and staff are open and loving, understand a child's point of view, and consider themselves partners with parents to provide the best possible care for each child. The group is small and intimate enough for each child to feel she can have the attention she needs when she needs it. There is a low staff turnover, which allows for the consistency and bonding young children need to become confident and secure. A detailed record of the child's day is available to help provide consistency between day care and home, and teachers and staff are always open to parents' visits and interested in their concerns and suggestions.

Community solutions for the care of our children will take various forms to suit our families. For example, four mothers in Folsom, California, joined together to creatively solve their child care dilemma by forming the "Mom Team."[16] They help each other out in other ways, too, by carpooling, being on call at odd hours for emergencies, and sharing their professional skills.

Young girls need to be protected from television. The evidence is in, and we are convinced television has no place in a young girl's life. We realize we are questioning a practice as habitual to the American public as brushing one's teeth, but we feel watching television is an insidious habit. Most of us don't realize how much we and our children really watch. A huge parental responsibility during the years from birth to seven is to help our daughters develop good habits. Television-watching is one they can do very well without.

We can imagine the alarm felt by those of us who, at some mad point on a crazy day when we thought we might lock ourselves in the bathroom, have used television as a babysitter just to get a few moments of peace alone. And what about those of us who use television ourselves to relax after a rough day? Won't we have to limit our own watching, if we eliminate TV from our daughters' lives from birth to seven or eight? Yes. We're afraid so. Is the sacrifice so great if we consider the harmful effects of watching television on our daughters' development?

> *Frankly, this discussion about whether or not to have television bores me. When others bring it up, I just tell them to put it away for two years, and see what a difference it makes in your children. That's the best evidence I need. You won't believe how well your family cooperates, how inventive your children can be in creating interesting things to do, how much time you have for all those projects piled up on your desk, what wonderful books are waiting to be read. I could go on and on.*
>
> —*Laura, mother of three,*
> *no television in the home for*
> *five years and no plans to have one*

We all have to find our own solutions to the television question—we "hide" ours in an old pie cupboard and don't subscribe to cable. But don't take our word for it, consider these shocking observations: Family psychologist John Rosemond asserts that for children of formative years, television-watching provides a deprivational experience. If a preschooler watches but twenty television hours a week—and surveys indicate that most watch much more than that[17]—by the time she enters the first grade, she will have spent four thousand plus hours staring at a flickering screen. Dr. Rosemond writes, "Four thousand hours of not exercising any competency skills has got to have negative impact on the child's learning abilities. During the first seven years of life, the environment imprints enduring patterns into the central nervous system. If a young child spends significant time staring at a fixed and flickering electronic field, is it not reasonable to assume that this experience is interfering with the establishment of key neural skills, including a long attention span and certain reasoning abilities?"[18]

Learning specialist Jane M. Healy, Ph.D., author of *Endangered Minds: Why Our Children Don't Think*, writes, "Research, overall, strongly suggests that fast pace and special effects can interfere with development of active learning habits....I am willing to make the leap and suggest, by inducing our children to habituate their brains to too much easy video pleasure, we may truly risk weakening their mental abilities."[19]

Another aspect of watching television just as disturbing as the physical effects is the influence of violence on our children. Constant exposure to violent imagery desensitizes us all to the pain others feel. "There's an extraordinary degree of violence in the language, and it's the window to the actual feelings and mores of the culture," says Dr. Robert Phillips, director of forensic services for the Connecticut Department of Public Health.[20] Our children do not invent violence; they are the reflectors of the violence they experience around them. On the average there are nine acts of violence during every hour of prime-time viewing and twenty-one violent incidents per hour in children's cartoons.[21] By the age of fourteen, the typical American child will have witnessed 11,000 murders on television.[22]

During the impressionable years, young children especially, have difficulty knowing the difference between what is real and what they see on TV. They learn to solve conflicts with others by using violent and destructive means. The incidence of violent crime perpetrated by girls is on the rise, and the experts who watch our culture's sociological pulse attribute this increase to violence in the media of television, movies, videos, sports, and video games, as much as the availability of drugs and guns.[23] Carol Nagy Jacklin, dean of the Division of Social Science and Communication at the University of Southern California, asserts, "It's so upsetting that, on the one hand, we seem to deplore this violence but, on the other, we are not stopping it in the ways that we know it needs to be stopped."[24]

More alarming to us than either the physical effects or the influence of violence is the erosion of a young girl's imagination. Waldorf teacher Karen Rivers writes, "Daydreaming and imaginative play promote a child's perceptual maturity, emotional growth, and creative development. Imagination is the capacity of the mind to project itself beyond its own perceptions and sensations."[25] Without imagination, we are unable to look outside ourselves with compassion for the suffering of others. Without imagination, we are unable to love.

The great secret of morals is love; or a going out of our own nature, and an identification of ourselves with the beautiful which exists in thought, action, or person not our own.... The great instrument of moral good is the imagination...[26]

—Percy Bysshe Shelley, *A Defense of Poetry*

Parents and educators have lost control of teaching cultural values to our daughters. This most important role has been usurped by TV. Have any of us considered what girls really learn from television? That most problems have to be solved through violence; that dressing in a sexy way makes one popular; that eating candy and soft drinks makes one happy; that shopping is a desirable pastime; that people from minority groups are either inferior, odd, or frightening; that you have to be "cool" to be "in" and if you're not, you're "out"; that sex-role stereotyping is OK; that alcohol and drug use are no big deal; that having sex is a given.

Ancient tribal cultures carefully chose the teaching stories told to the children, because they knew their survival depended upon a unity of cultural belief. The images and symbols of the stories graphically detailed expected behavior, and every girl knew what her necessary contribution to her community was. She sat, enraptured by the storyteller's voice, now loud and animated, now soft and persuasive. The described scenes became alive in her memory, dictating her behavior in the tribe.

We cannot return to the old ways, nor would we want the limited freedom of choice they allowed. However, we must stop to consider whether the teaching stories provided by television writers and producers are those that best teach our daughters to be kind, creative, inquisitive, caring, intelligent, and competent human beings. We strongly assert they do not.

We understand it is not easy to turn off the TV for good. It is perhaps simpler for those of us expecting a daughter or with daughters still too small to think they are missing something if we put the TV away. Many families have accomplished it with older daughters, too, and we include their helpful suggestions in the resources listed in the "Help!" section at the end of this chapter. Good luck!

Girls thrive within the rhythm of family life.

⊰ *JEANNE* | A new baby in the house brings a hush over daily activities. I moved slower and more deliberately, probably to keep from waking her. Colors softened, and life seemed hazy, somehow, perhaps from my lack of sleep. Whatever the explanation, if one surrenders to them, days with a baby take on a comfortable rhythm of bathing, nursing, rocking, sleeping, changing, nursing, rocking…

As she grows, Baby comes to trust and rely on these daily rhythms to orient her internal clock, to feel secure in the comfortable regularity of her day. She needs this slow, quiet time before the hustle and bustle of the outside world intrude upon her dreamy emergence from her cocoon.

Too often an infant's needs for a slow, regular pace collide with our adult needs for holding a job, keeping time schedules, and getting "things" done. The old debate about feeding an infant on demand or on a timed schedule so often leaves us confused about what we and our children need. John Davy, scientist and educator, learned from his experience of fathering his first son what to aim for in family rhythms: "Not the children making their demands on us; nor us making our demands on the children; but the art of finding the good rhythms for all our lives."[27]

"The art of finding the good rhythms for all our lives" is a challenge worthy of our thought, energy, and attention. Our frenetic pace separates us from the seasonal rhythms of nature, from the needs of our children, from the desperation of those in pain, from our own dreams. We lament our lack of community, of real connection with others who share our struggles, yet we rush through our days from one activity to the next, giving ourselves no time to consider what is really important.

When I was first building my therapy practice, I thought I had to keep evening hours for working clients. I hated missing my children before they were asleep. Finally, I decided I was giving up too much. They would be little for such a few short years. I still have a full practice, because clients arrange their schedules to see me. Putting what's important first made a big difference in how our family works.

—Alejandro, thirty-nine, marriage and family therapist, father of two girls

Somehow we must all find ways to bring more order to our frantic lives; as Dr. John Davy describes it, we need a "middle way, an art of living between mechanical routine and erratic whim."[28]

JEANNE | So often I've found that my daughter is the source of discovering the secrets of living a more fulfilling life. When she was tiny, her needs demanded I slow the pace of my activities, and I was rewarded with a "second sight," so to speak. I regained her baby's way of seeing the world for the first time, marveling in each miracle of bubble, bud, and crawly thing. Now her youthful insights renew my hope for an ailing planet, and I am again reminded to slow down and notice the simple, lovely things around me. Most of them cost nothing, require little, and give me incredible joy—my neighbor's antique roses, a sunset, my husband's softly bearded face.

> *A thing of beauty is a joy for ever,*
> *Its loveliness increases; it will never*
> *Pass into nothingness, but still will keep*
> *A bower quiet for us and a sleep*
> *Full of sweet dreams and health and quiet*
> *breathing.*[29]
>
> —John Keats, *Endymion*

The gift of family rhythms we give our daughters will be passed on for lifetimes to come.

An early, regular bedtime, free from TV and other stressors, provides the necessary rest required of a growing body and soul.

Bedtime rituals, such as lighting a candle, singing a song, saying a prayer, reading or telling a story, performed just the same way every night, help ease the transition from wakefulness to sleep and dreams.

Morning rituals, such as having the breakfast table set in a special way, singing a morning song, or using a regular morning greeting, help the family meet each day with a new heart full of expectation.

Celebrating the seasons with special dinners, decorating with collections gathered together on family outings in the woods, and observing the holidays with favorite family traditions all add to a girl's special childhood memories.

Creating little festivals out of routine chores turns potential power struggles into magical and artful acts. That wonderful scene in the story of Mary Poppins, when the children are instructed to clean up the nursery, and the toys fly into their places, brings all kinds of possibilities to mind that will delight and win the cooperation of any young girl.

In the process of providing rhythm and ritual in our daughters' lives, we ourselves reconnect to the source of aliveness and creativity within us. We can draw from that well of youthful anticipation and hope for the courage to carry on with a new *joie de vivre*.

Girls need activities, toys, and books that develop competence and confidence. Girls learn to speak through their play, and through language we connect with one another. Nursery rhymes, stories, and songs teach through their rhythms, repetitive beat, movements, and strong sounds. They naturally appeal to the young girl, who strives to learn about her world using all her bodily senses. The comfort of family rhythms and the fun of singing, speaking, rocking, swinging, moving with the sound, and riding on our knee, enhance her early development.

We earlier mentioned how the lack of competent female heroines in books for children negatively affects a girl's self-esteem. Our efforts to find books with strong female characters, positive minority group figures, and empathy for individual differences and capabilities will provide positive role models daughters need. We are not suggesting books be limited to only those with female heroines, because girls also love all the favorite books written about boys, too. It is never too early to begin reading such books aloud to nurture the imagination, feed a healthy self-esteem, and help make the bumpy path of life easier to negotiate. The "Help!" section of this chapter offers suggestions for how to find positive books for girls, plus all-around "good reads" for this age group.

In addition to the toys girls normally love, we recommend providing many choices among the following toys that enhance development of large motor skills, spatial-visual abilities, and problem-solving aptitudes:

> beads to string • gymnastics mats • knitting with wooden needles • mini trampolines • sewing projects with large needles • balls • blocks • walkie talkies • jacks • marble games • checkers • unusual pets, such as rats and lizards • chess • magnets • collections of leaves, stones, sticks • large pieces of silk in pastel colors • wooden puzzles • wooden figures of people and animals • wooden frames for house-building • large boxes

Our criterion for selecting a toy is to notice whether it will hold a young girl's interest. Is it greatly detailed, or is it simple enough to allow for creative play? A doll whose expression is fixed in a sweet smile, for example, will seem incongruent when she feels cross or sad. A plain cardboard box holds countless possibilities, whereas a plastic kitchen remains unyielding in its appointed use. We included toy sources in the "Help!" section to assist in finding well-made toys from natural materials that appeal to a girl's creativity and sensitive tactile and visual perceptions. Have fun!

Inner Guidance System

The "watch me" years can be confusing for both parents and daughters. Parents often make the mistake of expecting too much too soon, especially from the thinking aspect of the inner guidance system. Girls between birth and seven think symbolically and cannot be expected to logically understand a problem or execute steps toward a goal as adults do. They do not consistently remember family rules and must be reminded again and again. Young daughters do not understand why they feel the ways they do, and will not develop the insights to express what they are feeling until later, beginning around the change from baby teeth to permanent ones. Right now the focus is on developing the budding will.

Girls from birth to seven are engaged in a life of willing. They are actively driven to achieve mastery over their bodies and their environments. Learning to control their fingers, hands, feet, legs, bowels, toys, and relationships consumes their waking hours. The will drives them to become director of themselves and their world, one step at a time. To develop a healthy inner guidance system, girls in the "watch me" years need lots of activities to practice willful action; firm boundaries to shape the will; a rhythmic family life to guide the will; and support from parents to develop a trust in their own inner truths.

Age-appropriate activities and responses enable girls to grow in their own timing. We read a lot these days about girls growing up too fast, and they would perhaps be better off if we shielded them from the worries and cares of adult life. Praising a daughter for age-appropriate behavior allows her to follow her inner impulses, rather than drawing her out into a world she does not understand. Teasing about having "boyfriends," calling her "a little lady," and expecting her to behave in grown-up ways are often confusing and overwhelming at these ages. Trying to act and think beyond her years robs a girl of an essential trust in her inner wisdom of developmental readiness.

Respect a daughter's needs. In infancy, crying signals emotional or physical distress. The baby is wet, hungry, cold, angry, lonely, tired, or bored, and she needs our immediate concern and care. Between the ages from four to seven, crying becomes more complicated and may require discussion, but it still signals a daughter's need for our attention and assistance. When we respond to her cries for help, we indicate to her that we take her seriously, that her needs are important, and that we care about her. By teaching daughters it is okay to ask for help and that their needs are important, too, we thwart the female tendency to put others first to the detriment of oneself. We all benefit when girls learn that care goes out to others and comes back again to self.

Allow room for all emotion. The inner guidance system is the home of emotion, feeling, and intuition. When we deny our daughter's feeling life, we stunt her ability to know how she feels and to act from that place of knowing. By using responses such as "You don't really feel that way," "Don't cry, it doesn't hurt," "You're all right" when she isn't, and "That's just make-believe," girls learn from the people they trust not to trust themselves.

If we have difficulty with certain of our daughter's emotions, such as anger or sadness, and behaviors, such as whining or defiant determination, we can look to our own childhoods for understanding. Were we allowed to be angry or sad when we felt that way, or did we have to put on a smiling face, no matter what? Were we supported in engaging our wills by discovering how a new toy worked or by learning to open the cereal box unassisted? What was or was not allowed in our family's feeling boxes impacts tremendously upon our parenting approaches, and hindsight offers additional support in our striving to be more open, responsive, and supportive of our daughter's willful behaviors and strong emotions, feelings, and intuitions.

Instill a sense of wonder. The inner guidance system speaks to us through the symbols of our dreams, the ancient myths, childhood stories, and in nature. The voice of the soul is nourished through continuous connection with these sources. Early in our daughter's life we must begin to show her the wonders of nature and the beautiful truths of the old stories. They will provide her a constant well from which she draws hope, strength, courage, understanding, compassion, and goodness.

> *The child's wonder*
> *At the old moon*
> *Comes back nightly.*
> *She points her finger*
> *To the far yellow thing*
> *Shining through the branches*
> *Filtering on the leaves a golden sand,*
> *Crying with her little tongue, "See the moon!"*
> *And in her bed fading to sleep*
> *With babblings of the moon on her little mouth.*[30]
>
> —Carl Sandburg, *"Child Moon"*

Fences

It is helpful to view our daughters' behaviors in terms of making connections with others. Most behaviors—both positive and negative—are acted out by girls to test and define the boundaries of relationships between herself and others. "Where do I begin and end?" and "What are my responsibilities toward you?" are unconscious questions continuously checked out through a girl's actions. The limits we define and the consequences we choose for our daughters between birth and seven begin the intricate development of the internal personal boundaries that enable her to relate to the world around her with competence and courage.

Infants, toddlers, and preschoolers need constant supervision and assistance. Their endless stream of needs are both tiring and trying for the most patient and dedicated of parents. These years from birth to seven are often the most difficult, because parents must be on call twenty-four hours a day. We sometimes make the task more difficult for ourselves, because of a few mistaken assumptions about girls.

We must begin with iron bars. Girls are not little adults and will not understand what we want them to do or not do after the first telling. Girls from birth to seven think in pictures, not in concepts; therefore explaining the why or how of something has little meaning for them. We must do what is extremely difficult for all of us these busy days. We must get up from our comfortable chair or leave the task we are in the middle of, walk to our daughter, give her our full attention, and show her how it is done. For example, brushing her teeth for her the first few times and then with her over and over again, provides what she requires—connection. Basking in our focus on her, she is empowered to attempt the task herself, and from that success grows her ability to eventually do it on her own.

It is the same with behavior she must avoid, such as running into the street or putting noxious-looking red berries into her mouth. We must go to her, take her by the hand, lead her away from the street, and say firmly, "No! You must never cross the street without holding my hand." This requires constant reminders and reinforcement until she knows we mean it and that this behavior is forbidden. Our tone of voice, demeanor, and consistency carry even more meaning than our words.

Too many choices spoil the girl. We never give our daughters too much love, but at this age we give them too many choices. A little girl needs to know the rules and the routine and what is expected of her in relation to them. "What do you want for your lunch, today?" is too wide in scope for someone whose mind operates in pictures. Providing two selections to choose from, such as "Do you want an orange or an apple for your lunch?" may be managable for one girl but be overwhelming for another. Where we think we are teaching our daughters to make decisions, we are simply confusing them by offering them too many choices before they are capable of handling the intellectual processes required.

Until our daughters are six or seven, we must assume responsibility for deciding how our household will run, what's for lunch or snack, when it's time to brush teeth, go to bed, and so on. "Do you want to go to Melissa's house?" is a decision out of a young girl's realm. We have a duty to listen to her clues as to whether our daughter likes playing with Melissa, but it is up to us to choose happy, safe environments for her to play in.

Many of us will balk at this dictatorial approach. "What about her opinions and preferences?" we may ask, but we mistakenly consider the parenting of young girls to be a democratic process. When our decisions are given in a kind but firm and matter-of-fact way, we almost always elicit a daughter's cooperation, because she feels safe knowing we are in charge. Things, of course, will change as she grows older, as her concept of self enlarges, and as Piaget's concrete operational thought [31] emerges.

Adjustment studies of children raised with three differing parenting styles—the *authoritative, the democratic* and the *laissez-faire*—showed surprising outcomes. Authoritative parents make the rules, offer few choices, and expect their children to follow family principles. Democratic families operate from a place of fairness, consider how members feel, offer lots of choices, and place high value on cooperation. Children, whose parents are laissez-faire, are allowed to believe whatever they wish and to behave according to their own whims. This long-term study found that children raised in a laissez-faire fashion grew up to have difficulty cooperating and getting along with others. Those from democratic families found it hard to make decisions as adults. Those raised by authoritarian parents were the most well-adjusted adults, able to make decisions, follow rules, and cooperate with others.[32]

We carefully make a distinction between *authoritative* parenting and *rigid authoritarianism*, which could be classified as a fourth parenting style. These parents assert power through cruelty and abuse, with little regard for the needs, feelings, and well-being of family members. Children subjected to this style of parenting are less well-adjusted than any of the three other groups and are often the child abusers and mentally unstable adults of our society. While our daughters are between birth and seven, we recommend a *benevolent* authoritative parenting style, where we take charge with kindness, understanding, and empathy for our daughters' position. This stance assures them that we will take care of them and relieves them of having to be responsible for situations beyond their ability to handle.

Appropriate consequences enhance self-esteem. Consequences must fit the misbehavior and be carried out within as short a time-frame as possible. Probably the most common mistake made when setting consequences for young girls is to make them too big in scope or too far in the future. Sometimes we also fail to consider who really is responsible for the behavior. Let's consider the following example:

If our daughter fails to eat her dinner, and we say, "No more desserts for you!" her reaction will be helplessness or rebellion. We have given her no other choices. This consequence fails to address her underlying problem with eating her dinner, and it is too big in scope to bolster her confidence in her ability to change her behavior and regain the lost privilege.

There are many reasons why a young girl may not eat her dinner. Was dinner served too late, so that she was too tired to eat or past being hungry? Did she have a big snack too close to dinner? Were there stressors around the meal to make her too upset to eat? Was the meal really distasteful to her? We must take these factors into account before deciding on an action that will help her eat better in the future. If any of these circumstances affected her appetite, then we must take responsibility for what happened, because she is too little to be held accountable.

If she simply does not want to try a new dish that doesn't look good to her, we can use a consequence that appeals to her sense of fairness. The consequence we choose may be as simple as a rule that all family members must take at least one bite of any food. If they do not like it, they are not expected to eat it, as long as they take one bite to try it. This rule is easily followed, fair to all, and allows for some humor. Of course, a young girl will have to be reminded at every meal until she remembers.

Contrary to what many of us believe, we won't always know what to do at the time of our daughter's misbehavior.

… JEANNE | So often I was confronted by my small daughter's resistance to or insistence on something, and I didn't know what to do next. Telling myself I could think about this for awhile, or ask advice from my husband or a friend, helped me avoid getting angry and choosing an action I would later regret.

I marvel at my daughter Dale's ability to find ways to help Mandy learn family rules. When I stopped by recently for coffee, Mandy had just upset a potted plant in the living room for the second time. I could tell by her face that Dale was frustrated about having to clean up the potting soil again. This time she told Mandy, "I am upset that you knocked over the plant again with your ball. This time I will help you clean up the dirt, and your ball must go into its cupboard until we can take it outside to play." Mandy carefully spooned the soil back into the pot, and then happily skipped off to play in her room.

—Twila, mother of Dale, twenty-nine
grandmother of Mandy, three

Use "slow downs," not "time-outs." We prefer the idea of "slowing down" the action, rather than a "time-out," because, in our opinion, this popular discipline technique is misused. If girls' behavior is motivated by making connections—and we feel very strongly that it is—then separating them from everyone by shutting them in their rooms for ten minutes only succeeds in creating feelings of anger, resentment, helplessness, and rejection.

We all misbehave when things get out of our control, and our daughters do the same. Little ones are easily overwhelmed by the fast pace of our expectations of them. Insisting upon a quick transition from play to getting ready for bed, for example, automatically sets up a rebellion. A four-year-old does not want to go immediately to brush her teeth by herself, as we expect her to do. Being tired at this time of the day, she understandably wants to do it in her own leisurely time, and she wants company. Compounded by our own fatigue and desire to have some alone time, this situation holds all the elements of a freight train careening down the gorge toward destruction. If we catch it in time, all that is needed to avoid the crash is a "slowing down." Saying "Let's both brush our teeth," and perhaps taking her on our lap as we do so, slows down the freight train, gets the job done, and makes the connection we both need.

A time away from the action is sometimes helpful when a girl, having lost all control, refuses to be quieted by holding or rocking. We recommend she be placed in a quiet spot where she is distanced from household activity, but not closed off from it. Knowing we are nearby, continuing on with our affairs and being able to see what she is missing out on, gives her a personal reason to slow down the turmoil inside herself, rather than reacting against our rejection of her behind a closed door. The "slow down" becomes an empowering experience rather than a debilitating one. Over time, she develops an internal control over her own behavior that marks a growth toward maturity we all hope for in our daughters.

Sexuality

Many of us may begin reading this section of the "watch me" years and think, "Oh, no! Must we consider our daughter's sexuality already? She's too young!" In our opinion, this uneasiness is justified, because "sexuality" implies an adult consciousness and awareness of what it means to be sexual not present in our daughters from birth to seven. The term "sensuality" or "global physicality" perhaps better describes our daughter's early physical experiences of the world. The sensuous comfort of nursing from her mother's breast, cuddling in soft wool, floating in warm water, and kicking her chubby legs, all nurture the infant girl's budding sexual nature. Clothing that appeals to her sense of freedom and aesthetics, opportunities to stretch her growing muscles in running, climbing, and jumping, and being applauded by an appreciative audience all enhance the toddler's sense of belonging in her body. She develops a confidence in what feels good and what she likes. These are important lessons in the development of a healthy sexuality.

The sexual revolution may have drastically loosened our morals around explicit sex in the movies and on TV, and perhaps even in our bedrooms, but most of us gulp when we are faced with it in our daughters. We often put off thinking about it until they are older, but our attitudes about our own sexuality and how we handle their explorations and questions influence their early feelings about themselves and their bodies.

Feminine sexuality is inseparable from desire for connection and body image. Our daughters are sexual beings, and their explorations and curiosity are natural and normal. Like the butterfly emerging from her cocoon, a young girl's sexuality unfolds slowly within the context of her relationships with herself, others, and the world around her. Her early experiences and perceptions as lovable, desirable, and able to be in relationship with others have lasting effects on her feelings of self-worth, vital for a healthy sexuality. The early attitudes she receives from others about her body and its rightness contribute to her own feelings of satisfaction and pleasure. A positive body image greatly affects her development from its beginnings.

The widespread shame about our bodies experienced by most adults in our culture contributes to the dysfunctional sexual relationships many of us experience, hear our friends discuss, or read about in newspapers, articles, and popular books. Long term studies of sexual maturity and adjustment indicate that the degree of acceptance of one's body contributes directly to confidence, self-esteem, and a satisfying sex life.[33]

Most parents greatest fears for their daughters center around sexuality. Will she be abused? Will she be involved too early? Will she be hurt? Will she get pregnant? What are the chances of her contact with sexually transmitted diseases, like herpes and AIDS? Sex educators, Dr. Sol Gordon, Ph.D. and Judith Gordon, M.S.W., affirm that being taken advantage of is much less likely for anyone with high self-acceptance. In their thoughtful and provoking book, *Raising A Child Conservatively in a Sexually Permissive World*, they suggest that girls who don't value their own bodies or feelings may overvalue those of others and be more open to abuse, promiscuity, and early pregnancy.[34]

> *When my middle daughter was between two and four, she was always rubbing herself, down there. My husband and I were so embarrassed when she did it when company came. Our doctor said it was perfectly natural, but I had a hard time with it. I guess my parents were pretty strict about anything sexual, and I'm uncomfortable with the thought of my daughter's sexuality. Lia finally learned that rubbing herself like that was OK but something we do in private. I was very relieved.*
>
> —*Mara, age thirty-six, mother of three daughters*

Masturbation is normal. Just like everything else, infants take delight in discovering their genitals, those body parts usually covered by a diaper. Little girls soon learn that rubbing their genitals feels nice, and like Mara in the previous anecdote, we may find it embarrassing. Child-care expert, Dr. Penelope Leach, Ph.D., in her informative book, *Your Baby and Child: From Birth to Age Five*, advises us to treat the matter as we would if she were picking her nose—this is behavior acceptable in private.[35] Using shame or threatening statements does not stop masturbation. Our daughters will continue to masturbate and feel guilty about it. An exploration of what feels pleasurable and knowing how to pleasure oneself are both vital to the development of sexual satisfaction in adult life.

Other sexual exploration is normal, too. The natural curiosity young girls have about their bodies grows to include others, as well. First to come under her scrutiny are her parents and siblings. Many fathers may be surprised by a question such as, "How's your penis?"

When her inquiry is answered by a "Fine, thank you," we assure our daughter that we are open to talking about sexual matters and welcome her questions. She is simply trying to get the differences straight—Daddy has a penis; she doesn't. She has a vagina like Mommy.

What about *penis envy*? We agree with the idea that penis envy in girls ought not to be taken literally; between the ages of three to five, it is an expression of curiosity and a passing phase.[36] More crucial to our daughter's discovery of anatomical differences is how she perceives that her mother is treated by her father and how she, herself, is valued as a female. Subtle put-downs and definite sex-role differences in responsibilities, such as Mom keeps the house and Dad goes to the exciting Outside World to do Important Work, intensifies a girl's interest and attraction to the one with the penis/power. Never does a daughter switch her alliances from Mother to Father—a notion touted by early developmental theorists[37]—unless a mother is absent or totally inadequate. In normal situations, a girl maintains close ties with her mother and develops just as intense a relationship with her father.

During the early years, girls master sexual issues in the same way they make other discoveries about themselves and their world. As we mentioned before, their sexuality is better defined as a global physicality during these early years. Remembering that they think in pictures helps us to really try to understand what they are asking before we launch into a discussion of the intricacies of intercourse, and so on.

> *When Lucy asked how a baby gets into a mommy's tummy, I thought, "Oh, boy! Am I ready for this?" Then I realized she was not asking about sex, intercourse, or even the intricacies of the fertilization process. When I replied that a baby grows from a seed in a mommy's tummy, she said, "I thought so. That's just what Jenny said," and went skipping out the back door.*
>
> *—Allie, thirty, mother of Lucy, four*

When a daughter's questions or conversations indicate sexual exploration with a playmate, we must proceed with caution. We can probably all remember early incidents from our childhood when we also engaged in sexual play. Most often the discovery by a parent was the uncomfortable part of the affair, and the part that we most readily remember. Caught in the act, most of us were quick to assume blame for something we were probably made to feel we shouldn't have been doing. Child-care expert, Eda LeShan, whose readable book, *When Your Child Drives You Crazy*, which we highly recommend, advises to avoid shaming our daughters by explaining that we understand she is curious, but that when our adult friends come to visit, we do not take off our clothes, and neither should she.[38] A suggestion to go to the library or a talk with us to find out what she wants to know, focuses on her underlying motivation for the sexual play, rather than shaming her for doing it.

The possible danger inherent in our daughter's sexual play is that she might be taken advantage of by an older child, molested, and hurt. Many of us carry scars from early experiences we did not invite and were too little to know how to stop. Knowing she can bring any concern or scary experience to us to talk about, without fear of ridicule, punishment, or criticism, gives our daughter one of the best defenses against hurtful, sexual exploitation. Being taught to say as she walks away, "I have to go ask my mommy (or my daddy), first," settles the matter.

Each family must decide how to approach this delicate and scary subject without causing unnecessary alarm and paranoia in their daughters. Some parents find that reading stories for children about sexual abuse is helpful. Others play games, such as "What would you do if . . . ?", teaching family members what to do in threatening situations. Any method for enhancing a daughter's safety during the "watch me" years is probably most appropriate for girls between four and seven. For further discussion about sexual abuse and assistance in recognizing signs of abuse in our daughters, see Chapter Ten. For more information, check the "Help!" section at the end of this chapter.

Follow her lead in potty training. Before the age of three most children are not physically or emotionally ready to reliably accomplish the grown-up act of using the toilet without accidents.[39] Of course, there are individual differences in age of readiness, and we have discovered that allowing our children to stay a little ahead of us in their developmental steps enables them to achieve mastery of whatever it is they are ready for without undue stress upon them and unnecessary worry on our part. When girls are ready to use the toilet by themselves, they usually accomplish it easily and quickly with few accidents.

Choosing a potty chair, putting it in "her place" near the big toilet, and letting her use it when she thinks of it, whether she accomplishes anything or not, is a good way to begin. Eventually, she will connect the urge to use her chair with feelings of accomplishment and self-power, and will ask on her own to wear panties instead of diapers. Our praise of her achievement supports her progress, where pleading, scolding, or shaming may reverse the process.

Learning control of bladder and bowel is just that: learning control. Somewhere along the way, parents have mistakenly assumed the responsibility for *training* our daughters to have bladder and bowel control. This function is really an internal one, a natural capacity we all master when we are ready. If we expect control too early in our daughter's development or when we show frustration or disapproval of her inability to achieve it, we divert her attention from the development of an internal control to an outer power struggle with us. This diversion pitfall simply slows down the process.

We understand the reasoning of many preschools and day-care centers who require children to be out of diapers before they may attend, but trying to rush the process so a girl is ready by the time school starts puts undue pressure on the whole family. It is trying to teach that pig to sing all over again. Our daughter will balk at the affair or act out in other ways which make life difficult for everyone.

No matter how much we want her to measure up to a day-care center's standards, our sister's kids, or the neighbors, our daughter grows in her own good time, and we are wise parents who follow her lead, rather than forcing the bud to open before she is fully formed.

The Positive Intent

The positive intent behind our daughter's behaviors and statements comes from her soul. Viewing her misbehaviors, quirks, and obsessions as efforts that are immature, rather than bad, enables us to look beneath or beyond what she does, for a new understanding of who she is. These new insights guide us in shaping and channeling these inklings into her unique gifts, talents, and resources that fulfill her destiny. It is important to remember that between birth and seven, these preferences are stronger than our daughter is. No matter how many times we tell her, for example, not to touch Grandma's one-hundred-year-old vase, her soul's love of beauty compels her to caress it. The following are example behaviors and statements we can expect from our infant- to seven-year-old.

Behavior: Whining when we are busy.

Positive Intent: *You need more of my attention.*

Behavior: Screaming when something doesn't go right.

Positive Intent: *This problem feels bigger than you. Do you want some help?*

Statement: I hate my school.

Positive Intent: *You still feel like a stranger. Or, You love being at home. Or, You were upset yesterday when your teacher yelled at Jimmy.*

Behavior: Knocking over a full coffee cup.

Positive Intent: *You are very powerful to make the world move like that. Or, I need to put hot things out of your reach.*

Statement: I don't want to go to bed now.

Positive Intent: *If you are afraid that bad dream will get you again, we can leave the hall light on. Or, You find it hard to stop building that wonderful tower.*

Behavior: Not responding to our "No."

Positive Intent: *You're a big girl, and you want to act on your own. Or, You've been so lost in your play, you need help coming back to earth. Or, You're tired of hearing me say "No" every five minutes, so you're tuning me out.*

Behavior: Forgetting to do her simple chores.

Positive Intent: *You agreed to do these chores, but I forgot you're not big enough to remember them all the time. Or, You don't like these chores, because they are too hard for you. Or, You need some help learning how to do these chores. Or, My expectations of how well you do your chores is too high.*

When we have difficulty hearing or seeing the positive intent behind our daughter's actions, we may be stuck in an old belief-system. Do we feel that she is trying to punish us with her misbehaviors? Are we afraid of what others will think about her behaviors? Are we secretly resentful that she is more loved, has more clothes, is prettier, and so on, than we were as a child? A little inner searching often helps us understand and change our responses to our daughter's behavior.

Listening for the positive intent behind our daughter's problematic statements and behaviors becomes easier once we know that she is not being difficult out of spite, because she is a bad person, or to make life harder for us. All of her actions are to test her ability to make an impact upon the world around her, to make connection with others, and to stay in relationship with others. Keeping these motivations in mind, use the following spaces to examine your daughter's frustrating behaviors to discover the positive intent behind them.

Behavior:

Positive Intent:

Behavior:

Positive Intent:

Statement:

Positive Intent:

Behavior:

Positive Intent:

Behavior:

Positive Intent:

Statement:

Positive Intent:

Taking Action

The most rapid changes in both
mental and physical development
seem to occur in the first five years of life.[40]

—Irene P. Stiver, "Beyond the Oedipus Complex,"

Writings from the Stone Center

We parents have a busy time keeping up with our daughters from birth to seven. We think we are just getting to know who these little beings are, and then they suddenly make another leap in development, changing altogether. Following are a few suggestions for guiding our little butterflies on their curious flight through these exciting years:

Protect her infancy. Let infant daughters emerge slowly from their cocoons by keeping television, electronic music, and the frenetic pace of the outside world away for the first few months. Soft lighting, pastel colors, being carried in-arms, and the soothing sounds of her parents voices is what a little girl-child needs most in the beginning. Too soon she will be out trying her new wings amidst the harsh reality of daily living.

Sing, sing, sing! We know that keeping television and recorded music away from Baby seems absurd to most of us in this thoroughly technological culture. We hope the reader will consider the disturbing effects of these devices on her tender, developing sensory system, especially on a baby who is colicky and having trouble adjusting to this strange, new world. A quiet, gentle routine filled with the soothing rhythms of lullabies, silly songs, and old favorites sung in her parents' voices, will help even the most reticent butterfly land on earth.

Let the songs from childhood, ones our own mothers and fathers sang to us, come back. We can still teach our daughters our favorites from rock and roll, rhythm and blues, show tunes, pop, and even today's rap, if we're into that sort of thing, by singing them ourselves. If the lyrics are rusty, visit the local music store for songbooks, or listen to tapes or CDs while driving in the car, alone.

Children naturally respond to music and begin singing, moving their bodies, and making simple rhythms before they walk. To encourage a love of music that carries them through rough times later on, sing together and create a family band. First instruments are easily constructed from metal bowls and wooden spoons, oatmeal boxes, cardboard tubes, and beans. We know one family who, rather than watching TV after dinner, gathers in the living room for a song fest, accompanied by Dad on the guitar, every evening. Here are recommended resources to get you started:

American Folk Songs for Children, by Ruth Crawford Seeger, Garden City, NY: Doubleday & Co., 1948. A great collection of all our old favorites. Includes piano and guitar accompaniment and suggestions for improvisation and rhythmic play. Check bookstores.

Folk Song Encyclopedia, by Jerry Silverman, Milwaukee, WI: Hal Leonard Music Publishing, 1975. A super collection of more than one thousand folk songs from our American heritage of song. Check children's catalogs and bookstores.

Gonna Sing My Head Off!, by Kathleen Krull, New York: Alfred A. Knopf, 1992. Rich in sixty-two old-time favorites for young and old. Order from HearthSong catalog, a wonderful catalog filled with beautifully-made toys, books, games, and crafts. Write: 6519 N. Galena Road, P.O. Box 1773, Peoria, IL 61656-1773, or call (800)533-4397.

I'll Tell You a Story, I'll Sing You a Song, by Christine Allison, New York: Dell Publishing, 1987. A delightful parents' guide to the fairy tales, fables, songs, and rhymes we all heard in childhood but no doubt have partially forgotten. Local bookstores.

The Laughing Baby, by Anne Scott, South Hadley, MA: Bergin & Garvey, 1987. Full of well-loved songs and nursery rhymes. Local bookstores.

Music for Little People catalog. Full of musical selections from around the world; offers a large selection of books, gifts from many cultures, and musical instruments. Choices for all ages. Write: P.O. Box 1460, Redway, CA 95560.

The Reader's Digest Children's Songbook, Pleasantville, NY: Reader's Digest Association, 1985. A collection of 131 songs adapted from show tunes, movie classics, and American favorites. Includes simple piano arrangements and guitar chords. Available from local book or music stores.

Rise Up Singing, edited by Peter Blood and Annie Patterson, Bethlehem, PA: Sing Out, 1988. A spiral-bound giant of a collection of 1200 songs, including guitar chord accompaniment. Contains every kind of song under the sun! Available from Chinaberry, a catalog of "books and other treasures for the entire family." Write 2780 Via Orange Way, Suite B, Spring Valley, CA 91978.

Sing Through the Day, compiled by the Society of Brothers, New York: The Plough Publishing House, 1968. Offers ninety delightful songs about activities of daily life. For younger children and everyone who has a childlike heart. Ask local bookstores to order it or write to the publisher.

Provide age-appropriate toys, books, and experiences that nurture a girl's whole being. Start with simple toys—a wooden rattle, a soft, cotton ball, a sturdy board book, and a wool-stuffed doll are all she needs in the beginning months of life. As she grows and we discover who she is, provide her with choices of dolls and trucks, workbenches and stoves, marbles and jacks, soccer balls and jump ropes. She will also be adept at origami, tangrams, puzzles, and chess when we provide them at age-appropriate times and learn them along with her.

Stories speak to the soul of a girl and help ease the bumpy transitions of growing up. We recommend learning the lost art of storytelling. Simple bedtime stories set a comforting rhythm for the end of a busy day and help young children make the shift from their active, awake states to the quiet peace of sleep. Telling a story to our daughter without the encumbrance of a book, enables us to engage with her, face-to-face, nurturing her need for connection.

We are not at all against reading to our daughters, too, of course! It is especially important we select books considering their contents, messages, and illustrations when they are young. We hear from media experts that girls enjoy stories about boys, but boys don't like stories about girls. This explains why few books until recently featured strong, female characters and material of particular interest to girls. We question this theory, and we certainly believe girls and boys should hear stories featuring females who accomplish brave and daring deeds, aspire to noble causes, and show competency in accomplishing whatever they set out to do. Also important in the content of a story for girls is plenty of interaction among the characters. Who is related to whom and what they do together is always a focus of a girl's life; therefore, a story with these elements naturally feeds her soul. The following resources provide a place to start in looking for suitable books and toys for girls.

Chinaberry Book Service. A delicious selection of books for the whole family. Delightfully detailed descriptions of each item help in making choices. Problem is you'll want to read every one! To order a catalog, write: 2780 Via Orange Way, Suite B, Spring Valley, CA 91978, or call (800)776-2242.

Everyone's Kids' Books. Here's their description of their selections: "A catalogue of the best in nonsexist, multiracial children's books. We look for: books that teach creative, peaceful conflict resolution; books that help kids appreciate the value of diversity among people and nature; books set in all sorts of homes, neighborhoods, and cultures; nonsexist language and messages; interracial books; books that help kids feel empowered and motivated to build a more just world; low cost." To order catalogue, write 23 Elliot Street, Brattleboro, VT 05301, or call (802)254-8160.

HearthSong. Has won the "Parents' Choice Seal of Approval" for four consecutive years and is filled with beautiful, natural toys, games, crafts, and books for all ages. Many of the books listed as resources here and in the "Help!" section are available from HearthSong. For a catalog write, 6519 N. Galena Road, P.O. Box 1773, Peoria, IL 61656-1773, or call Customer Service, (800)533-4397.

New Society Publishers/New Society Educational Foundation. Offers books on topics timely for these desperate times, such as conflict resolution, living in the nuclear age, voluntary simplicity, ecology, nonviolence, reaching out to minorities, gender equity, and many more. Order newsletter from: New Society Publishers/NSEF, 4527 Springfield Avenue, Philadelphia, PA 19143, (800)333-9093.

The New York Times Parent's Guide to the Best Books for Children, ed. by Eden Ross Lipson, New York: Times Books, 1988. Contains nearly 1,000 titles for children arranged under these headings: wordless books, picture books, story books, early reading books, middle reading books, and young adult books. Short descriptions of plot are included. Check local new and used bookstores.

Reading for the Love of It, by Michele Landsberg, New York: Prentice Hall, 1987. The idea of reading a book about books may seem dry to some of us, but this delightful book is an exception. Chapter titles read: "Taking the Plunge," "Books to Encourage the Beginning Reader," "First Novels," "Liberating Laughter," "The Quest for Identity," "Adventure: The Great Game," "Fantasy," "Traveling in Time," "Growing Up," and "Girls' Books, Boys' Books, Bad Books, and Bias." Find it in local bookstores and enjoy!

Waldorf Student Reading List, ed. by Karen Rivers. "An invaluable resource for parents, teachers, grandparents, students, home schools, bookstores, and librarians. Contains lists of stories to read aloud to children, books appropriate for each grade level, and specialized lists for science and American history." To order, write: Michaelmas Press, 33 Serra Way, San Rafael, CA 94903.

Help! Is Out There—Where to Find It

We offer the following books, magazines, and organizations as practical guides in parenting to support the never-ending sources of creativity and wisdom within ourselves that often go untapped. We pass them on in hopes they will make the challenging job of parenting a little easier.

Developmental Tasks: Books

Beyond Sugar and Spice: How Women Grow, Learn, and Thrive, by Caryl Rivers, Rosalind Barnett, and Grace Baruch, New York: Ballantine Books, 1979. Explores the idea of competence and how to prepare our daughters to live in today's world. Libraries and local bookstores.

Children at Play: Preparation for Life, by Heidi Britz-Crecelius, New York: Inner Traditions International, 1972. A beautiful, sensitively written book offering practical guidance for parenting in the technological age. Available from the Anthroposophic Press, R.R. 4 Box 94 A1, Hudson, NY 12534, (518)851-2054.

Children Without Childhood: Growing Up Too Fast in the World of Sex and Drugs, by Marie Winn, New York: Penguin Books, 1984. An eye-opener concerning the demise of childhood, the conditions our children face in growing up today, and how we got here. Check new and used bookstores.

The Hurried Child: Growing Up Too Fast, Too Soon, by David Elkind, Reading, MA: Addison-Wesley, 1984. Relates how the pressures of growing up too fast affect our children. Local bookstores can order it, if they do not carry it.

In Their Own Way, by Thomas Armstrong, Ph.D., Los Angeles: Jeremy P. Tarcher, 1987. Encourages parents and teachers to re-examine such labels as "underachievers," "learning disabled," and so on. Invites readers to look beyond the accepted norms in education to what our children really need. Highly recommended. Local bookstores.

The Little Girl Book, by David Laskin and Kathleen O'Neill, New York: Ballantine Books, 1992. All about girls from birth through eight. Local bookstores.

Miseducation: Preschoolers at Risk, by David Elkind, New York: Alfred A. Knopf, 1987. Discusses what young children need educationally and why parents and preschools are "miseducating" them. Check libraries and local bookstores.

The Radiant Child, by Thomas Armstrong, Wheaton, IL: The Theosophical Publishing House, 1985. Chronicles the spiritual and psychological development of young children. Rich with resources for parents, educators, and children. Contact the publisher, if it isn't available locally.

Raising Black Children, by James P. Comer and Alvin F. Poussaint, New York: Penguin Books, 1992. Written by two medical physicians, using a friendly question-and-answer format, this thorough book covers many of the issues facing black children in our society. Local bookstores.

Women's Growth in Connection: Writings From the Stone Center, by Judith V. Jordan, Alexandra G. Kaplan, Jean Baker Miller, Irene P. Stiver, and Janet L. Surrey, New York: The Guilford Press, 1991. A collection of "works in progress" by outstanding theorists and practitioners of the Stone Center, Wellesley College. Offers progressive therapeutic models more realistically reflecting experiences in women's lives. Local bookstores and university libraries.

You Are Your Child's First Teacher, by Rahima Baldwin, Berkeley, CA: Celestial Arts, 1989. If you can buy only one parenting book, we recommend this one. Any baby whose parents follow the guidelines of Rahima Baldwin is off to a wonderful start. Ask local bookstores to order it, if they do not carry it.

The Young Child: Creative Living with Two to Four-Year-Olds, by Daniel Udo De Haes, New York: Anthroposophic Press, 1986. Written by a grandfather, lovingly involved with children. Emphasizes language development and appropriate teaching stories for young children. Available from the Anthroposophic Press (previously listed, p. 258).

Your Baby and Child: From Birth to Age Five, by Penelope Leach, New York: Alfred A. Knopf, 1977. A practical baby guide to everything. Local bookstores and libraries.

Needs: Books

Birth Without Violence, by Frederick Leboyer, New York: Alfred A. Knopf, 1975. A beautiful guide to childbirth. Libraries and bookstores.

Born Dancing, by Evelyn B. Thoman and Sue Browder, New York: Harper and Row, 1987. Helps parents trust their parenting know-how. Check library, new, and used bookstores.

Breaking the TV Habit, by Joan Anderson Wilkins, New York: Charles Scribner's Sons, 1982. Offers insights and suggestions for dealing with family viewing habits. Libraries and bookstores.

Children Without Childhood: Growing Up Too Fast in the World of Sex and Drugs, by Marie Winn (previously listed under "Developmental Tasks," p. 258).

The Children's Year, by Stephanie Cooper, Christine Fynes-Clinton, and Marye Rowling, Stroud, Gloucester, UK: Hawthorn Press, 1986. Seasonal activities, directions for making simple toys, dolls, and animals, recipes, and poems. A lovely guide to celebrating the cycles of life. Available from *HearthSong* and the Anthroposophic Press (previously listed, pp. 257, 258).

The Continuum Concept, by Jean Liedloff, Reading, MA: Addison-Wesley, 1975. A natural parenting style based on the wisdom of so-called primitive South American tribal cultures. Check library or bookstores.

Do What You Love, the Money Will Follow: Discovering Your Right Livelihood, by Marsha Sinetar, New York: Paulist Press, 1987. Our work can support our families and ourselves financially and emotionally, too. Bookstores and libraries.

Earth, Water, Fire, and Air, by Walter Kraul, Edinburgh, UK: Floris Books, 1989. Includes playful explorations in the four elements for children from six to twelve. Available from *HearthSong* (previously listed, p. 257).

Endangered Minds: Why Children Don't Think and What We Can Do About It, by Jane M. Healy, New York: Simon and Schuster, 1990. Here are the facts about the effects of TV and video games on the development of the human brain. Bookstores.

Festivals Together, by Sue Fitzjohn, Minda Weston, and Judy Large, Stroud, Gloucester, UK: Hawthorn Press, 1993. A guide to multi-cultural celebrations, songs, things to make, customs, and recipes. Available from HearthSong and the Anthroposophic Press (previously listed p. 258).

Four Arguments for the Elimination of Television, by Jerry Mander, New York: Morrow, 1978. Gives a provocative account of how program content is chosen and its effects on viewers. Local library and bookstores.

How to Raise a Healthy Child in Spite of Your Doctor, by Robert S. Mendelsohn, M.D., New York: Ballantine, 1984. A wonderful guide for the family with children of all ages. Local bookstores.

In Praise of Single Parents: Mothers and Fathers Embracing the Challenge, by Shoshana Alexander, Boston, MA: Houghton-Mifflin, 1994. An indepth guide for both single fathers and single mothers with hopeful solutions to real-life problems. Local bookstores.

Lifeways: Working with Family Questions, edited by Gundrun Davy and Bons Voors, Stroud, Gloucester, UK: Hawthorn Press, 1983. A collection of wonderfully insightful essays written by parents about the often perplexing issues in family life. Available from the Anthroposophic Press (previously listed p. 258).

Models of Love, The Parent-Child Journey, by Joyce Vissell and Barry Vissell, Aptos, CA: Ramira Publishing, 1986. Includes the spiritual side of parenting. Ask local bookstores to order it, if the library doesn't have it.

The Nature Corner, by M.V. Leeuwen and J. Moeskops, Edinburgh, UK: Floris Books, 1990. A beautiful beginning place to open the world of nature to a young child. Offers directions and ideas for creating a special, seasonal table in the home. Certain bookstores can order it; don't give up trying to find it, because it is worth the trouble.

Raising Black Children, by James P. Comer and Alvin F. Poussaint (previously listed, p. 259).

Roots and Wings, by Allen and Allen, Cleveland: Pilgrim Press, 1992. A guide for creating stability and order (roots) and nurturing imagination and love (wings). Woven in and out are lovely suggestions for celebrations through rituals and festivals. Local bookstores.

Special Delivery, by Rahima Baldwin, Berkeley, CA: Celestial Arts, 1986. A helpful guide for expectant parents, including pregnancy, birth, and the postpartum period. Available from Informed Birth & Parenting Books, P.O. Box 3675, Ann Arbor, MI 48106.

The Spirit of Community: Rights, Responsibilities and the Communitarian Agenda, by Amitai Etzioni, New York: Crown Publishers, 1993. A re-evaluation of what our children need to thrive in these times. Highly recommended. Local bookstores.

Teach Your Children Well, by Christine Allison, New York: Delacorte Press, 1993. A glorious collection of stories and fables for the entire family. Local bookstores.

To Dance with God, by Gertrud Mueller Nelson, New York: Paulist Press, 1986. Offers wonderful stories, activities, and insights into family ritual and community celebration following the Christian calendar. Local bookstores can order it.

What to Do After You Turn Off the TV, by Frances Moore Lappé, New York: Ballantine Books, 1985. Full of wonderful ideas for the whole family to enjoy together. Check libraries and bookstores.

101 Great Ways to Keep Your Child Entertained (While You Get Something Else Done), by Danelle Hickman and Valerie Teurlay, New York: St. Martin's Press, 1992. A fun-filled book of activities. Local bookstores.

Needs: Magazines and Newsletters

Family Affairs, a quarterly publication by the Institute for American Values. Write: 1841 Broadway, Suite 211, New York, NY 10023.

Mothering, a quarterly journal filled with wise and wonderful parenting support. Order by writing: P.O. Box 1690, Santa Fe, NM 87504, or calling (800)424-3308.

SingleMOTHER, the newsletter of the National Organization of Single Mothers. For a free copy, send a self-addressed, double-stamped envelope to P.O. Box 68, Midland, NC 28107-0068.

Welcome Home, a publication of Mothers at Home, an organization to support mothers who choose to stay at home with their children. Write: 8310A Old Courthouse Road, Vienna, VA 22182.

Working Mother, a monthly magazine filled with helpful articles, parenting tips, recipes, recommended books, and lots of humor and parenting support. To subscribe, write Customer Relations Manager, P.O. Box 53861, Boulder, CO 80322.

Needs: Networks

Child Care:

Child Care Action Campaign. Answers questions about child-care issues and publishes pamphlets on topics related to day care. Write: 330 Seventh Avenue, 17th Floor, New York, NY 10001.

Child Care Aware, a partnership for quality child care. Directs parents to their local child-care resource and referral agency. Call: (800)424-2246.

The Liedloff Continuum Network. A worldwide network of parents who want to bring the Continuum Concept into their family lives. For a membership list and newsletter, send SASE to: P.O. Box 1634, Sausalito, CA 94965 or call: (415)332-1570.

National Association of Child Care Resource and Referral Agencies. Directs parents to local child-care referral agencies. Write: 2116 Campus Drive, SE., Rochester, MN 55904 or call: (507)287-2220.

National Association for Family Day Care. Provides information about day care and names of local accredited providers. Write: 1331A Pennsylvania Avenue NW, Suite 348, Washington, DC 20004 or call: (800)359-3817.

Single Parents:

Parents Without Partners, a national, nonprofit educational organization for single parents. To receive their single-parent magazine and chapter newsletter, write: 8807 Colesville road, Silver Spring, MD 20910 or call: (800)637-7974.

Single Mothers by Choice, a national, nonprofit support network for mature women over 30. Write: P.O. Box 1642 Gracie Square Station, New York, NY 10028 or call: (212)988-0993.

Single Parent Resource Center, an international collection of single-parent self-help groups. Special groups for homeless single parents and mothers coming out of prison. Write: 141 West 28th Street, New York, NY 10001 or call: (212)947-0221.

Single Parents Society, a New Jersey-based organization for single parents. Call: (609)866-0766.

Work:

Businesses for Social Responsibility. Supports progressive work and family policies in the workplace. For more information, write: BSR, 1850 M Street NW, Suite 750, Washington, DC 20036 or call: (202)872-5206.

The Whole Work Catalog. Offers options for more rewarding work, including self-employment and home business opportunities. Write: The New Careers Center, P.O. Box 297, Boulder, CO 80306.

Inner Guidance System: Books

The Act of Will, by Roberto Assagioli, New York: Penguin Books, 1976. A transpersonal guide and training manual to the experience of "willing." Local new and used bookstores and libraries.

The Dance of Anger, by Harriet Goldhor Lerner, New York: Harper and Row, 1985. Offers insights about anger and the role it plays in the lives of women. Local bookstores.

Lifeways: Working with Family Questions, edited by Gudrun Davy and Bons Voors. Mentioned previously, but we cannot say enough about this wonderful book.

Solve Your Child's Sleep Problems, by Richard Ferber, New York: Simon and Schuster, 1985. Written by a medical doctor and somewhat technical, but the sound ideas to help your child fall asleep and stay asleep are worth the effort. Local bookstores.

Fences: Books

Children: The Challenge, by Rudolf Dreikurs, New York: E.P. Dutton, 1964. Helpful guide to finding the balance between letting children run wild and stifling them. Local bookstores and libraries.

How to Talk So Kids Will Listen and Listen So Kids Will Talk, by Adele Faber and Elaine Mazlish, New York: Avon Books, 1980. A classic on clear communication of limits and boundaries. Libraries and new and used bookstores.

Liberated Parents, Liberated Children, by Adele Faber and Elaine Mazlish, New York: Avon Books, 1974. Through real-life situations, demonstrates how the theories of Dr. Haim G. Ginott really work. Libraries and new and used bookstores.

Siblings Without Rivalry, by Adele Faber and Elaine Mazlish, New York: Avon Books, 1987. "How to help your children live together so you can live, too." Libraries and new and used bookstores.

When Your Child Drives You Crazy, by Eda LeShan, New York: St. Martin's Press, 1985. A wonderfully supportive book for parents, with practical suggestions on what to do during those difficult moments of childhood, by someone who's been there. Libraries and new and used bookstores.

You are Your Child's First Teacher, by Rahima Baldwin, Berkeley, CA: Celestial Arts, 1989. Can't say enough about this book! Bookstores can order it, if they don't have it in stock.

Sexuality: Books

The Art of Sexual Ecstasy, by Margo Anand, New York: Jeremy P. Tarcher, 1989. A loving, spiritual guide to sexual intimacy for couples. Bookstores, because you'll want your own copy of this one.

The Berenstain Bears Learn About Strangers, by Stan and Jan Berenstain, New York: Random House, 1985. Many parents find the Berenstains tiresome reading, but their books deal with important issues of growing up. Some sex-role stereotyping in the characters, so you may want to edit as you read aloud. Bookstores and libraries.

The Courage to Heal, by Ellen Bass and Laura Davis, New York: Harper & Row, 1988. This guide for women survivors of child sexual abuse has an extensive bibliography with suggestions for parenting couples, children, lesbians, single parents, sexual abuse survivors, and more. Bookstores and libraries.

Did the Sun Shine Before You Were Born? by Sol and Judith Gordon, New York: The Third Press, 1974. A beautifully illustrated children's book about sexuality. Presents families in all their various configurations. Check bookstores or ask the local Planned Parenthood chapter to order it for you.

For Yourself: The Fulfillment of Female Sexuality, by Lonnie Barbach, Garden City, NY.: Anchor Press, 1975. A sensitive, personal exploration of female sexuality. Bookstores.

Helping Your Child Recover from Sexual Abuse, by Adams and Fay, Seattle, WA: University of Washington Press, 1992. A sensitive aid for children of all ages. Local bookstores.

Male Sexuality, by Bernie Zilbergeld, New York: Bantam, 1988. A practical and human book that dispels myths about male sexuality. Bookstores and libraries.

Our Bodies, Ourselves, by The Boston Women's Health Book Collective, New York: Simon and Schuster, 1984. A perceptive, comprehensive guidebook for women. It's been updated and revised. Bookstores.

Raising a Child Conservatively in a Sexually Permissive World, by Sol and Judith Gordon, New York: Simon and Schuster, 1983. A clear, outspoken guide for talking to our children about sexual issues. Bookstores and libraries, or the local Planned Parenthood.

The Way of All Women, by M. Esther Harding, New York: Harper and Row, 1970. This book first appeared in 1933, and still accurately captures the truth of women's experiences. Libraries and bookstores.

Sexuality: Networks

Local Planned Parenthood chapters have written materials for parents and children of all ages on all aspects of sexuality. It is especially important for parents of daughters to be informed about the dangers of STDs, AIDS, and unplanned pregnancy, and how to avoid them.

Positive Intent: Books

How to Talk So Kids Will Listen and Listen So Kids Will Talk, by Adele Faber and Elaine Mazlish, New York: Avon Books, 1980. Still appropriate and helpful in the '90's! Libraries and bookstores.

Parenting Children in Unstable Times, by Ruth P. Arent, Golden, CO: Fulcrum, 1993. Provides insight and guidance we all could use for parenting in these difficult times. Local bookstores.

Endnotes

1. Lennart Nilsson, *A Child Is Born* (New York: Delacorte Press, 1977), 10.

2. *Free to Be You and Me*, conceived by Marlo Thomas, ed. Carole Hart, Letty Cottin Pogrebin, Mary Rodgers, and Marlo Thomas (New York: McGraw Hill, 1974), 26–27.

3. Irene P. Stiver, "Beyond the Oedipus Complex: Mothers and Daughters," in Women's Growth in *Connection*, Jordan, et al. (New York: The Guilford Press, 1991), 103.

4. Rudolf Steiner, *The Kingdom of Childhood* (London: Rudolf Steiner Press, 1971).

5. Kathleen Stassen Berger, *The Developing Person Through Childhood and Adolescence* (New York: Worth, 1986), 55.

6. Jean Baker Miller, "The Development of Women's Sense of Self," in *Women's Growth*, Jordan, et al., 13.

7. Ibid., 14–15.

8. Daniel Udo de Haes, *The Young Child: Creative Living with Two to Four Year Olds*, trans. Simon and Paulamaria Blaxland de Lange (Edinburgh: Floris Books, 1986), 80.

9. Ann Grassel, physical therapist and Aston Patterner, conversation with Jeanne Elium, Berkeley, CA, 29 Apr. 1993.

10. Rahima Baldwin, *You Are Your Child's First Teacher* (Berkeley, CA: Celestial Arts, 1989), 32.

11. Ibid., 37.

12. Jean Liedloff, *The Continuum Concept: Allowing Human Nature to Work Successfully* (Reading, MA: Addison-Wesley, 1985), 18.

13. Ibid.

14. Milton Moskowitz and Carol Townsend, "100 Best Companies for Working Mothers," *Working Mother*, Oct. 1993, 27–69.

15. Gayle Reaves, "U.S. Rated Dangerous for Young People," *San Francisco Examiner*, 26 Sept. 1993, sec. A4.

16. Kara Skruck, "Reliable After-School Care—For Free!" *Working Mother*, Oct. 1993, 6.

17. John Rosemond, "TV Inhibits Development," *The Peridot*, Spring/Sum. 1992, vol. 5, no. 1, 4.

18. Ibid.

19. Jane M. Healy, *Endangered Minds: Why Children Don't Think and What We Can Do About It* (New York: Touchstone, 1990), 202, 204.

20. David Gelman, "The Violence in Our Heads," *Newsweek*, 2 Aug. 1993, 48.

21. Frances Moore Lappé, *What To Do After You Turn Off the TV* (New York: Ballantine Books, 1985), 9–10.

22. Joan Anderson Wilkins, *Breaking the TV Habit* (New York: Charles Scribner's Sons, 1982), 10.

23. Gelman, "The Violence in Our Heads," 48.

24. Ibid.

25. Karen Rivers, "Human Values, Television, and Our Children," in *Models of Love: The Parent-Child Journey*, Joyce Vissell and Barry Vissell (Aptos, CA: Ramira, 1986), 210–216.

26. Percy Bysshe Shelley, "A Defense of Poetry," in *Bartlett's Familiar Quotations*, compiled by John Bartlett, ed. Justin Kaplan (Boston, MA: Little, Brown & Co., 1992), 409–410.

27. John Davy, "Living in Real Time," in *Lifeways: Working with Family Questions*, Gudrun Davy and Bons Voors (Stroud, Gloucester, UK: Hawthorn Press, 1983), 137.

28. Ibid., 140.

29. John Keats, "Endymion," in *The Norton Anthology of English Literature*, eds. M.H. Abrams, et al. (New York: W.W. Norton, 1968), 508–513.

30. Carl Sandburg, "Child Moon," *Chicago Poems* (New York: Holt, 1916).

31. According to Piaget, children between seven and eleven develop concrete operational thought, enabling them to reason about anything they can specifically perceive.

32. Kathleen Stassen Berger, *The Developing Person Through Childhood and Adolescence* (New York: Worth, 1986), 328–30.

33. Sol Gordon and Judith Gordon, *Raising a Child Conservatively in a Sexually Permissive World* (New York: Simon & Schuster, 1989), 27.

34. Ibid.

35. Penelope Leach, *Your Baby and Child: From Birth to Age Five* (New York: Alfred A. Knopf, 1985), 477.

36. Stiver, "Beyond the Oedipus Complex," *Women's Growth*, Jordan, et al., 105.

37. Ibid., 107.

38. Eda LeShan, *When Your Child Drives You Crazy* (New York: St. Martin's Press, 1985), 348.

39. Leach, *Your Baby and Child*, 305.

40. Stiver, "Beyond the Oedipus Complex," *Women's Growth*, Jordan, et al., 109.

❦ CHAPTER TEN ❦

THE "I CAN DO ANYTHING!" YEARS: EIGHT TO TWELVE

At nine, I can remember walking
on a fence, all around a park, thinking
I really liked being nine years old
and I wouldn't mind being nine forever.
I was finding out about the world....
I remember having a real sense
of joy, of confidence about negotiating
the world on my own....I felt secure
and self-contained. I had a sense that
I can get by in the world, even if it
means I am alone. There's a way for
me to negotiate it. I can do it.[1]

—Megan, middle twenties,

Emily Hancock, *The Girl Within*

The girl between eight and twelve stands at a threshold. She turns from her dreamy, family-centered world to discover what exciting adventures await just beyond the garden gate that once defined her horizons. Now her visions take in limitless possibilities. Like a young colt, she finds her long legs strong and untiring. She frisks far and wide, delighting in each new meadow. A favorite author Annie Dillard writes about this stage of childhood, "Children ten years old wake up, and find themselves here. . . . They wake like sleepwalkers, in full stride . . . equipped with a hundred skills. They know the neighborhood, they can read and write English, they are old hands at the commonplace mysteries, and yet they feel themselves to have just stepped off the boat, just converged with their bodies, just flown down from a trance, to lodge in an eerily familiar life already well under way."[2]

Developmental Tasks

Childhood growth can be likened to a tree; the core at birth is gradually covered by layer upon layer of increasingly complex behaviors and abilities. From birth to seven, a girl's growth is centered in the limbs and the will—developing the large muscles of the arms and legs and learning to exert her influence upon the objects and people in her world. She grows through imitating the tasks and behaviors she sees, naturally feeling part of everything around her.

During the years between eight and twelve, the focus of our daughters' development shifts to what Waldorf educator Rahima Baldwin calls the rhythmic system—the regular inhalation and exhalation of the lungs and the steady rhythm of the heartbeat.[3] The lungs and heart are associated with the emotions, and during the years from eight to twelve the feeling life blooms. In the section on the inner guidance system a little later in this chapter, we explore how parents nurture the developing soul of a girl during these years.

No longer do the objects in her world reveal their inner secrets, because the nine-year-old girl views them now from the outside. For the first time, she relates to the world around her as separate from herself, whereas before, she was incapable of feeling apart or alone. A new dawning that she is master of her own ship, that she can sail any sea she embarks upon now occurs. Every prospect excites her, and during these years, our daughter is touched by her destiny. Therapist and author, Emily Hancock, Ph.D., describes this girl as "the self-possessed child who serves as a touchstone for women's identity."[4] The tiny seeds that blossom into the gifts, talents, and resources that enable our daughters to serve the world as adults, whether through mothering children of their own, in community service, or by climbing the corporate ladder, touch fertile ground. Their joyous embracing of life at this time allows us glimpses of the competent women they may become.

The early years are often rewarding for parents, because of the young girl's unquestioning attachment and non-critical confidence in her parents' superior wisdom and authority. We may be quite shocked when our ten-year-old daughter no longer believes we are invincible and begins doubting our ideas and the worth of our opinions.

> ← JEANNE   I remember how fun it was to teach in the early childhood years, because these children eagerly looked forward to the lessons and still had confidence in what the teacher had to share. Not so, with those in third grade, who suddenly became skeptical and critical of everything, questioning the teacher's answers and even wondering whether I knew at all what I was talking about!

This is the age of Big Questions, and a cynicism creeps in if we are not careful to listen to and to treat a girl's wonderings with the respect they deserve.

> *I have questions that nobody even knows the answers to. Do you want to hear them? Why was the world made? Why are we here? Why did God even think about making us? And where did God come from? There!*
>
> *—Marilee, eight and a-half*

A girl of eight to twelve becomes concerned with the forces of good and evil. She questions us intently about where evil comes from and why it is allowed in the world. If we have protected her from the visual violence of television and video games, she will be free to meet evil on her own terms, hopefully in degrees which she is capable of handling, in the events and people she meets in her daily adventures at school and in her community. These ponderings and experiences contribute to her moral development, which in girls, according to extensive research by Harvard psychologist Carol Gilligan, Ph.D., involves the element of care;[5] she is concerned about how the people involved are affected by her decisions and actions, rather than simply with what is fair and just.

Girls in the middle years are better able to understand cause and effect relationships and the part they play in the outcome of events. They can now picture how their actions will influence another's feelings or alter situations, whereas before they reached the age of what child-development theorist Jean Piaget called "concrete operational thinking,"[6] they could not follow this complicated thread.

> *Mom, if I cook dinner two nights this week instead of one, can I go to Grandma's on Thursday? Aunt Jenny's taking Sarah then. It's only two days early, and if I cook an extra meal, it will make up for the one I miss making next week. Can I?*
>
> *—Janelle, eleven*

Girls this age go in and out of the mature thinking that Janelle revealed in the previous anecdote. One minute they seem so grown up that we wonder where the years went, then they surprise us by needing our help with something they long-ago mastered.

JEANNE | I remember my daughter at eleven being so self-assured. Her clarity about important values amazed me. We had these profound conversations about what she thought and felt. Then, in the same moment, she would turn around and need help opening a can of soup. I never could understand it.

The eight- to twelve-year-old leaves behind the secure world of imitation, fantasy play, and connection with everything. She turns toward an exciting new world beyond the garden gate that beckons with new adventure, Big Questions, and an unfamiliar sense of aloneness. Although she relishes the challenges, she also feels frightened and overwhelmed. This accounts for the wide swings in maturity she now exhibits. Our patience and understanding of her dilemmas provides a touchstone, a home base where she can check in when her explorations and exploits take her too far out of herself for comfort. When she asks for help with something seemingly easy for her, she is asking us to love her, to show our confidence in her new-found abilities to choose her own way on her life's journey.

Relationships become deeper and more complex during the middle years, and girls place more importance on their social friendships, especially with other girls their age. Negative aspects of the feminine nature may make their appearance in interactions where girls pair off into "best friends," rejecting a third friend, who feels left out and hostile.

> *My heart went out to my daughter every time she came home crying, because her best friend decided she liked someone else better. If I asked a few days later, she'd say, "Oh, I don't like her anymore either. Jane and I are best friends now." Three days later, it would have all changed again. I could never keep up, but I always felt her pain of being rejected.*
>
> —*Tanya, mother of Marta, twelve*

Needs

Harmony between parents is especially helpful. As the girl in the middle ages totters between a new, independent maturity and the more known, secure place she leaves behind, she often feels unbalanced within herself. Hermann Koepke, a well-known Swiss Waldorf teacher and author, emphasizes in his informative book, *Encountering the Self,* "The lack of balance in the child can be corrected by the harmony between father and mother. Children always experience this as a blessing, but especially so at this turning point...."[7] Parents provide a girl "surer-footing" when they openly communicate with each other about their daughter's needs at this time. Whether single, married, step, or divorced, we can make these transition years easier by setting aside time to consider the essentials of a healthy life, beyond nutritious food and drink, and talk about them with our daughters.

Parents are called to inner work. Bringing out the best and the worst, the job of parenting challenges us to confront our weaknesses and limitations. Philosopher Rudolf Steiner advised that children don't need perfect parents. What they need is to see their parents striving to be better.[8] We all have found that indulging our anger, for example, by hurling insults at our children only makes us feel better, if it does, temporarily. The guilt and bad feelings it causes is not worth our temper tantrums; out of necessity we seek other ways to express our anger.

As infants our daughters brought us the pressures of sleepless nights and constant demands. We called upon our inner resources to cope with this trying, yet blessed time. The ages between eight and twelve bring different challenges. Until now, our young daughter believed in our omniscience, our all-knowing authority about how the world works. She was free to grow, confident of our competence.

Now, she develops a clear-sightedness that allows her to see through the chinks of our carefully tended facade. She wonders whether we really know what we are talking about and questions our reasoning.

Rather than imitating our behavior, as she did when she was four, a girl now looks for motivations behind the things we do and say, and critically points out any disparities or discrepancies in our behaviors.

"Because I said so," and "Because that's how I've always done it," are not helpful responses to a girl of eight or twelve. We are forced to look inward to understand where we stand and why we stand there. Her Big Questions call us to again explore the meaning of our lives, our contributions, and whether we are modeling a life we want her to emulate.

Fathers make great allies now. Studies indicate that when fathers are actively present in their daughter's lives from their beginnings, girls develop close and lasting bonds with them.[9] Daughters especially need the support and involvement of their fathers in the middle years. In the traditional family where Father goes out into the world to work, he becomes associated with action and adventure. A daughter looks forward to his return in the evening, bringing news and excitement of happenings beyond her realm of house and school. Mothers who work in or out of the home can and do create fun and activity in their daughters' lives, but the masculine way of being in the world is especially appealing to the eight- to twelve-year-old girl.

Therapist and author, Emily Hancock, Ph.D. points out that during these years when girls are most particularly drawn to their fathers, the powerful influence of cultural limitations on what females can do and be is weakest. Girls in the middle years are given a hiatus from the prescribed roles of a gender-biased society. They are relatively free to be whomever they please; thoughts of themselves as strong, fast, skillful, funny, smart, and creative take precedent over being female.

If fathers were mystified before with the "girl things" their younger daughters delighted in, they may feel somewhat relieved to find their eight- to twelve-year-olds more adventurous and spunky. Egyptian Pharaohs were believed to have chosen nine-year-old girls as companions, because they were so interesting and lively, and historians of ancient Greece record that girls of nine left their mothers and were initiated into the service of the virgin huntress Artemis, known for her boyish wildness and strength.[10]

Girls in the middle years are alive with an energy and spontaneity that pushes them to explore and learn. Each girl flavors this impulse with her own particular temperament. Some flex their physical muscles, testing their strength in athletic pursuits, such as climbing trees, walking fences, and participating in team and individual sports with a relish that surprises many parents. Others pursue complex relationships, cultivating social interactions into a finely-honed art form. There are those girls who become quiet and dreamy, turning inward to the world of literature, inspired to future greatness through their storybook heroines. Still others become math and science wizards, aspiring engineers, doctors, and architects.

When fathers encourage their daughters to take risks and to follow where their souls are leading them, a healthy self-esteem blooms. Ideally, a father helps provide the tools a daughter in the middle years needs—and here we borrow a term from psychologist Robert Kegan, Ph.D.—"to go into business for herself;"[11] he provides the experiences that develop confidence and competence. If a girl wants to explore the stars, her father takes her to a planetarium, or gets her a telescope. If she aspires to compete at the Olympics, he finds her a coach, urges her on during practices, and attends her meets. If she gets lost in the world of books, he takes her to the library, shares his own boyhood reading experiences, or channels her toward the classics.

◁ JEANNE | When I was nine, my family moved to the country, where I loved to help my dad work outside, building fences, moving hay, feeding our 4-H livestock. He was proud of my willingness to work hard, my competitive love of playing softball, and my scholastic achievements. Living in the country suited my adventurous temperament perfectly, allowing me, with horse and dog, room to explore the world of nature I grew to love.

Girls deserve gender equity in education. Girls need us to take an active interest in their school experiences. Do they feel included in the school curriculum? Do their textbooks reflect the achievements of girls and women? Do teaching methods consider feminine learning styles? Do teachers encourage and reward girls to do challenging work? Are our daughters being taught in ways that support independence, assertiveness, analysis, curiosity, innovativeness, and creativity? Does their school provide ample staff and financial support for girls' sports programs?

Title IX of the Education Amendments of 1972, prohibits discrimination on the basis of sex in any educational program receiving federal funding. Every school or district should have a Title IX officer and a grievance procedure for hearing parental and student complaints. Each state has a Department of Education/Instruction and an Office of Civil Rights, when schools are not responsive to gender equity concerns. In the "Help!" section at the end of this chapter, we provide other resources to enhance and ensure quality and equal education for our daughters.

Girls in the middle years continue to need our protection. Although these years are filled with a new strength and zest for living, our daughters are vulnerable to the pressures of stress so common in this technological age. They are still susceptible to overload from the bombardment of mechanical devices and media assaults. Our daughters' classrooms and even our homes are abuzz with insistent stimuli we all must filter out—overhead lighting, traffic noises, radio, television, video games, video movies, computers, overhead projectors, plus what we encounter on the way to school, home, and work—traffic noises, neon signs, billboards, radios, and so on. Even the lure of "the mall" assaults the senses.

In addition to our environmental stressors, the burden of too much homework and pressures to perform put all children at risk. Girls at all ages need help in slowing down, spending time alone, pacing their activities, and shutting off the seductive barrage of modern electronics.

Learning healthful habits during the ages between eight and twelve eases the transition into adolescence.

Art and music nourish the feeling life and the spirit. With the middle years comes the capacity for quiet wonder. Encouraging the expression of her feelings and the longings of her spirit—the essence of who she is—via painting, for instance, nourishes a healthy progression through these transition years. Bringing her Big Questions into the form and substance of art provides a firm foundation from which to launch her queries. Home projects and school classrooms that provide the opportunity to paint are of great importance at this time.

Now that a girl's development centers in the heart and lungs, her growth is supported by movement and music. Singing and dancing bring air into the lungs and enrich the world of feelings, enlarging the capacity for anticipation, wonder, and reverence for life. Girls need more than ever to hear their parents sing, to share in a joyous round, to lift their voices in praise. Anthropologist, business consultant, and wise woman Angeles Arrien, Ph.D., advises us to "sing for our lives," because, as most ancient cultures knew, singing is a powerful source of healing. Dr. Arrien relates in her marvelous and insightful book, *The Four-Fold Way*, that Oceanic societies believe to learn how to tell the truth, we must begin to sing.[12]

> *I don't sing because I'm happy;*
> *I'm happy because I sing.*[13]
>
> —William James

Inner Guidance System

The active life of the eight- to twelve-year-old girl is most usually focused outward on activities and friends. She is interested in the relationships between people and things. For example, as a four-year-old she felt her doll as an extension of herself. By moving her doll through scenarios from her own life, the younger girl copes with the frustrations of living within a family. A nine-year-old, however, wonders how an office is managed or what a therapist does. She is concerned with how the wheels turn that make society run. She is skilled at organizing her own life, often a collector of miniature horses, stamps, bugs, or bird's nests. The great outdoors calls to her, and she is capable of rising with the sun, choosing her own clothes, getting her own breakfast, packing a lunch, riding her bicycle to a friend's house, and spending the day following her adventurous heart.

At the same time, much is happening in the inner life, and there are constant little reminders to pay attention to this sphere of her being, as well. Girls are more likely to experience nightmares and sleep interruptions during the ages from eight to twelve. Those emotions and traumas ignored during the day, while some fascinating venture captures her interest, make visual and vocal protest during the night. Our suggestions about how to deal with sleep disorders in Chapter Seven will help ease her night terrors and allow her inner guidance system room to mature.

Other signs that activity is going on beneath the surface of our daughter's outwardly-directed existence is the common occurrence of headaches, pains in the stomach, nausea, weakness, fevers, paleness, circles under the eyes, and general malaise. These symptoms rarely occur together and are usually short-lived. We must not dismiss their seriousness or discomfort, however, and if they persist we advise seeing a physician. The years between eight and twelve are generally the healthiest years of life,[14] and these symptoms are most often caused by external situations. Problems within the family, divorce, school pressures, and child abuse are common traumas of modern life that affect our vivacious adventurers.

To enhance a healthy inner guidance system, girls must trust their inner voices, their feeling/intuition and thinking functions. Dr. Emily Hancock, whose therapeutic work enables women to reach back to their childhoods and reclaim their eight- to twelve-year-old girl within, discovered that girls in the middle years "possess an uncommon clarity ... she has the ability to get outside herself. She has interests and abilities, likes and dislikes, and purposes of her own at home, at school, and in the neighborhood. Capable for the first time of self-reflection, she sees herself from an outer vantage point. She sizes things up, makes decisions about her self and her surroundings. More often than not, she takes a stance and develops the beginnings of a life theme. . . . Possessed of curiosity and keen insight, she...knows the truth."[15]

When we nurture and protect our daughters' keen insights—their wise inner voices—we help them develop the strength to thwart culture's attempts to limit their aliveness when they enter the adolescent years. Now they have few cultural limitations on what they can be and do. The more girls develop, the more our cultural restrictions drive their true voices underground. Friend and fellow therapist Liz Hannigan, M.A., who specializes in work with single parents, says of girls her ten-year-old daughter's age, "The more woman-looking they become, the more they need their parents' encouragement to take the initiative, to be inquisitive, to take risks.[16] The more they need our support to be themselves to and respect their inner-knowing.

Fences

...when we punish a child, we divert him from facing himself. There are people who say, "But if you don't punish him, you're letting him get away with murder." Just the opposite is true. When we punish a child, we make it too easy for him. He feels he's paid for his crime and served his sentence.

Now he's free to repeat his misbehavior. Actually, what do we want from a child who has transgressed? We want him to look into himself, experience some discomfort, do his emotional homework, begin to assume some responsibility for his own life.[17]

—Dr. Haim G. Ginott

Fences for the eight- to twelve-year-old girl consist of limits that will enhance the development of healthy personal boundaries, enabling her "to assume some responsibility for her own life." Because our daughters at this age are bent upon doing just that, our responsibility as

-283-

fence-setters involves hearing their feelings and restricting their actions when they are out-of-line with family rules. Remembering that girls seek connections in relationship above all else, we are better able to understand motivations behind their misbehaviors, rather than taking them as personal assaults.

Common complaints from parents of eight- to twelve-year-old girls include unwillingness to do their household chores—because they find it boring—and having to be on the go all the time—demanding parents drive them to lessons, friend's houses, the movies, and so on. This probably will not change until they can drive themselves. Other parents find whining, talking back, and extreme stubbornness difficult to deal with during the middle years of girlhood.

Nancy, age ten, vehemently denies her actions when confronted by her mother. "I feel so torn," says Nancy's mother, "She refuses to take responsibility about yanking her younger sister's toys away, throwing her clothes beside the hamper, rather than in it, or leaving her dirty dishes out on the counter." Although she can now assume more responsibility, a girl between eight and twelve is often torn between wanting to be grown up and remaining dependent upon Mom or Dad to do things for her. She grapples with being good and being bad. She needs gentle and persistent encouragement to begin to understand that making mistakes or needing guidance is part of growing and learning, and not an indictment of being bad. As she matures, a daughter can live more in the gray area of life, where choices and behaviors are not clear cut, not good or bad. But now she needs time, repetition, and tolerance to learn to become responsible for her own behavior.

To avoid the power struggles common to the middle years, make family rules and expectations clear. The nine-year-old girl is now capable of choosing chores and completing them with only occasional reminders. When our eleven-year-old fails to return from a friend's house at the agreed-upon time, our consequences must speak to her sense of justice and enable her to learn to follow through on her commitments. When she fails to honor our time agreement, she loses the privilege of visiting her friend for a designated time. She may complain, but she recognizes the fairness of the decision.

When we struggle with our daughter's misbehavior, it may be helpful to make a list of the behavior, what fence is needed, and possible consequences that meet the required sense of fairness, are age-appropriate, and teach inner control. We have provided an example to help you begin.

Problem/Task	Fence	Consequences
Fails to hang up clothes	Picket Fence	Clothes go into a "lost" box for a week

1.

2.

3.

4.

5.

Sexuality

Freudians call the middle years in a child's life the "latency years," meaning, not much is happening sexually. However, as parents all know, many girls between eight and twelve are interested in boys, their own bodies, and the "facts of life." On the average, girls mature sooner than boys do, but wide variations in development and degrees of curiosity occur among girls, and we are wise to follow their lead in readiness to discuss their sexual development.

> *I've always taken the middle path with Lucy. My menstruation was never a secret in our small house, and Lucy was always asking questions about this and that. Now at eleven, she's become shy about her body and sexual matters. I don't push her. She knows she can ask me anything, and I think it's best not to be in a hurry about these things. Let them unfold naturally, in their own timing.*
>
> —Noél, mother of Lucy, eleven

Ideally, a girl's sexuality naturally unfolds in it own timing, but little in life is ideal. Much too often girls in this culture are subjected to experiences that jolt them into premature sexual awakening. The high incidence of childhood incest and other sexual abuse, the earlier onset of menstruation, the sexual confusion some parents experience around their daughters' adolescence, parental and peer pressure to become sexually active, as well as parental pressure to abstain, the bombard-ment of explicit sexual material from television, movies, and magazines, the "you-must-be-sexy-to-be-liked" mentality, and the sexual harass-ment schoolgirls must endure in most of our nation's schools, are a few of the sexual issues facing girls as they grow into womanhood.

Childhood Incest and Other Sexual Abuse

A common form of childhood incest—sexual contact among family members—occurs between siblings. Researchers estimate that sisters and brothers in nine out of ten homes in the United States engage in casual sexual contact.[18] Most young children between two and four show a natural curiosity about bodies of the other gender, and their explorations and questions help them develop a sense of themselves as girls or boys. "Daddy has one, and brother Jeff has one. They are boys. Mommy doesn't have one, and I don't have one. We are girls," are observations most of us have probably heard from our young daugh-ters. "I'll show you mine, if you show me yours," is a common game between sister and brother. They are getting the "plumbing" straight in their minds.

Sexual exploration can continue into the middle years between siblings close in age, but according to clinical psychologists Miriam Ehrenberg, Ph.D., and Otto Ehrenberg, Ph.D., authors of the provo-cative book, *The Intimate Circle: The Sexual Dynamics of Family Life*, it usually stops short of intercourse, because of our culture's strong incestual taboo.[19] Children know it is wrong. Sexual contact between sister and brother becomes more problematic when the boy is older than the girl.

> *I came into therapy to deal with my feelings toward my boyfriend. I know he uses and manipulates me, but I really care about him. Lately I feel a huge rage rather*

than love for him. I can't throw it off like I've done in the past, and it's hurting our sexual relationship, too. In therapy I was shocked to realize I feel the same rage toward my older brother. Then I remembered things my brother made me do when I was little. Because he was the oldest by six years, my parents often left him as baby-sitter. I had forgotten how he used me sexually when my parents were gone and then threatened me if I told on him. The memories came flooding back in therapy. I feel so small and betrayed, and yes! ENRAGED!!

—Gloria, twenty-nine

Whenever a younger child is involved with an older one, coercion and the inability to say "No" become the concern. Early abuse from an older brother harmfully erodes the development of a girl's self-esteem, a healthy sexuality, and her feelings of power and self-confidence. Authors David Laskin and Kathleen O'Neill discovered while researching their informative book, *The Little Girl Book*, that women who are victims of brother-sister incest have difficulty with relationships and are less likely to marry.[20] We advise that older brothers, especially between the ages of eleven and seventeen, not become the family baby-sitter of a younger sister. The situation is too tempting when the hormones are running wild.

Authors and psychotherapists Miriam Ehrenberg, Ph.D., and Otto Ehrenberg, Ph.D., reveal that children are more likely to engage in sibling incest if their parents are distant, uninvolved, punitive, and judgmental.[21] When we take time for our children, letting them know we are genuinely there for them and willing to answer any of life's questions, their early sexual exploration with each other will be a natural phase into a healthy sexuality.

When sexual play between siblings becomes coercive, it has crossed over into sexual abuse. Although we find it difficult to talk about, sexual abuse is a serious threat to our daughters. In 1992 there were 2,936,000 reported cases of sexual abuse, 40 percent of which were validated.[22] The victim's median age was 9.2 years in 1986 and is decreasing yearly; by 1992, it was seven.[23] Another fact about sexual abuse difficult for parents to acknowledge is that it is a family affair. Rather than strangers, the perpetrators are most often siblings, parents, stepparents, grandparents, uncles, boyfriends, and family friends.

Because an abuser usually threatens a child not to tell, a victim rarely volunteers that she is being abused. She may give us hints that something is wrong. "I don't want to be with Uncle Joe." "I don't like the games Jake plays." "He makes me feel funny." "Please, don't make me go to Daddy's house ever again!" When we question our daughters, it is important to phrase our statements without blame, shock, or disgust. If they are being abused, they may feel ashamed, responsible for what is happening, and fearful we will not believe them. How our daughters react to sexual abuse varies with each girl. Where one will remember and deal with the trauma of a single incident the rest of her life, another will be able to work through the effects of prolonged abuse and put them behind her. When we respond to a daughter's disclosures with trust, care and compassion, she is better able to rely on our support to deal with her experiences.

Where there is sexual abuse, there are clues, if we are willing to see them. The following are signs that might indicate a girl is being sexually molested. Please consider them carefully.

Inappropriate questions. Many girls feel they are to blame for sexual molestation. They may ask, "Am I a bad girl?" or "Why do I do bad things?" Sexual questions that seem beyond a girl's years are important but tricky clues, because of the explicit sexual material children see these days. However, if a daughter asks about sexual acts or situations that seem unusual, or if she seems to take a leap in sexual knowledge, it is best to casually ask her for more information.

Reserved and remote behavior. The trauma of sexual abuse is difficult for girls in the middle years to deal with on their own. A change in their behavior from active and willing participants in family and school activities to quiet aloofness, excessive daydreaming, or physical reserve are clues to inquire about what's bothering them. This may be just the opening they need to pour out their troubles to us.

Nightmares and terrors. This clue alone may not be cause for concern about sexual abuse. Sleeping problems are common during the middle years, because of the shift from being centered in the body to a new focus in the emotions; there is a lot going on beneath the surface. If nightmares become a frequent and continuous problem, then we must consider their import in conjunction with other clues in this list. The "Inner Guidance System" section of this chapter offers more information on how to deal with repressed feelings and traumas.

Excessive mood swings. All girls are occasionally moody, and we become accustomed to them. Consistent and excessive variation from her patterns are important to watch.

Excessive behavioral swings. Severe withdrawal or exaggerated conflicting behaviors, such as explosions of anger, excessive pleasing, or deliberate displeasing are also signs to consider.

Strong self-hatred. Girls in sexual abuse situations will often turn their shame, rage, and hatred inward upon themselves. The greater the vulnerability when they were violated, the greater the rage girls feel. It often spews out through many of the above clues.

Extreme shyness or overfriendliness. Being uncomfortable around boys or men or becoming overly-affectionate with them may be a clue we want to investigate. Although fewer women sexually abuse girls, it does happen. Therefore, being excessively reticent or affectionate around older girls and women must also be cause for concern.

Inappropriate sexual play. When daughters seem preoccupied with sexual matters, have endless questions, appear overly curious about our bodies or sex lives, and we suspect they may be involved in sexual contact with other children, we must consider these signs with their overall behavior.

One of the behaviors from this list may not be enough to question our daughters about this delicate subject. Or it very well may be. The longer the abuse continues, the greater the emotional trauma.

A sexual abuse situation concerning our daughter smites our hearts. How do we approach her with all of the fear, shame, and guilt of our own sexuality all bunched up inside of us? How can we ask her what is going on without further hurting or traumatizing her? How do we deal with our own shame and disgust about what has happened to her, while giving her all the love and support she needs from us? We urge any reader who suspects that a girl they know is being abused to get help immediately. How we handle this emergency in our daughter's life can determine her growth into a healthy, happy adulthood. The "Help!" section at the end of this chapter includes resources and books for victims of sexual abuse and for parents needing information and support.

The best defense against sexual abuse is to teach our daughters good inner boundaries—the ability to know what she likes and wants and the courage to say "No" when the line is crossed. We recommend re-reading Chapter Nine's "Sexuality" section for information on the basics of saying "No." As girls mature, those basics broaden to include specific guidance on how to say "No" in sexual situations. How and when to teach this, is something we must all decide for ourselves. None of us want to unduly frighten our daughters or make them paranoid about every stranger and new situation. Our job might be easier if sexual abuse cases involved strangers and new situations. Unfortunately, abusers are almost always someone the girl knows well in situations she meets every day. Here are a few suggestions:

- From day one, be open to any questions she has about sexuality, so that she knows she can come to us with any problem.

- Answer questions carefully with as much factual information as she can hear, using accurate terms for body parts, such as breasts and vagina.

- Bring up sexual issues in regular family conversation, rather than scheduling "A Talk About Sex."

- Teach her that she is the owner of her body, that her body is private, and that she can say "No!" to touching that feels funny or uncomfortable to her.

- Follow her lead in privacy matters. Respect her need to have doors closed, have family members clothed, to bathe alone, and so on.

- Listen to her "No's." Telling us "No" when she is young is practice for future times when we hope she can say "No"—to drugs, to early sexual involvement, to smoking, to violence, to whatever temptations or injustices she will face in her life.

- Teach her the Family Rules. Here are some suggestions:

  Never go with or do anything with a stranger.

  Always have permission from us before you go with another family member, friend's parent, etc. after school.

  Go to school restrooms with a buddy.

  Friends don't make friends take off their clothes.

  Always stay with the class on a field trip, on the playground, and other school functions.

  Tell us about any uncomfortable or funny "games" a baby-sitter wants you to play.

  Tell us anything you want that made you feel odd, uncomfortable, or afraid.

- Hold family role-play sessions. Teach her what to say and do in dangerous situations and practice them together. Everyone can take turns thinking up tricky situations. "What would you do if a boy you know suggested you go over to his house when his parents were gone? What would you do if "Uncle Bud" wanted you to sit on his lap for a long time and wouldn't let you up? What would you do if the baby-sitter made you take off your clothes before it was time to go to bed? Authors and parents David Laskin and Kathleen O'Neill suggest three simple rules:

  Shout "No!"

  Run away.

  Tell an adult.[24]

- Use other opportunities that naturally come up to teach about sexual abuse. For example, incorporate information into what daughters share about their school's drug and alcohol abuse prevention program, or when a daughter brings up a situation she heard about from a friend, talk about what she would do if the same thing happened to her.

- Suggest that school authorities start a sexual abuse prevention. program.

Many of us find it difficult to communicate with our daughters about sexual matters. We wish the whole issue would just go away until they are safely grown, and then they discover how wonderful loving someone sexually is on their own. However, most of us find the thought of our daughters being hurt by sexual abuse much worse than talking to them about it, so we blunder on, hoping we say the right thing. If whatever we say is given in a gentle, casual, open, and light-hearted way, the content probably won't matter. Our underlying attitudes about our own sexuality communicate much louder than our words.

Culture's Sexual Messages

Even when we try our best to raise our daughters in an accepting and respectful atmosphere, culture's messages of sex, sexism, and sexiness filter through. What can we do?

Keep television viewing to a minimum. If television is one of our daughter's habits, we must take time to find out what this medium is teaching her. The explicit sexual material on MTV, regular programming, and in TV movies is often exploitive toward women. Girls learn to expect to be used sexually by men. Violence is often related to TV sex. Girls learn to associate violence and sex. Television stories portray women as good or lovable, if they are attractive and sexy. Girls learn they must be sexy to be accepted and liked. Relationships between TV women and men are often sexual or have obvious sexual overtones. Girls learn that relationships with males are sexual, rather than the many other satisfying forms relationships between genders can take.

Preview TV shows and movies a daughter sees on her own, and watch those we have not seen with her. Television programs and movies with sexual material offer opportunities to discuss our sexual values with our daughters. We must take time to watch with her, be open to her questions, and answer as candidly as we can. We advise that shows depicting violent sexual acts and sexual abuse be off limits until daughters are old enough to intellectually understand the potential emotional harm and physical injury involved in such behaviors.

TV and magazine ads subtly tell girls and women how to look. Actually, some ads are not so subtle! Young models in magazines for preteens are sexier than even five years ago and made up to appear more adult, giving the impression that girls must act and look older than they are to be "cool." The message that eight- to twelve-year-old girls must be seductive, rather than look their age, contributes to the increase in eating disorders, poor body image, and sexual precociousness of today's girls in the middle years.

> *I think most preteen magazines are horrible now. They present an image that's fake and focused on body image, instead of feeling good about individual differences.*
>
> *—Heidi, twenty-one*

We suggest having family discussions about the messages intended in the popular, slick preteen magazines, and/or finding alternatives for our daughters. One magazine we especially like is *New Moon: The Magazine for Girls and Their Dreams,* for girls eight to fourteen. A pamphlet about *New Moon* reads, "a new magazine created by girls and women for every girl who wants her voice heard and her dreams taken seriously." Departments include Body Language (about body image and health), Herstory (facts about girls and women in history), How Aggravating (In college why do you get a *bachelor's* degree?), She Did It! (Real life interviews of girls who excel), and Women's Work. Subscription information is included in the "Help!" section at the end of this chapter.

Listen to a daughter's music. Record companies, bowing to citizen pressure, now label albums containing explicit sexual or violent imagery with the phrase, "Parental Advisory: Explicit Lyrics." Despite being bombarded with sexual material, preteens are not particularly comfortable with it. Although the warning label is aimed at parents, we can help our daughters avoid embarrassment by informing them about the label.

Whether or not we try to limit their musical selections, musical lyrics provide another opportunity to talk about sex and the subject matter of today's music with our daughters. Keeping current can be difficult if we cannot appreciate their music, which happens between every generation. However, popular music reflects and some argue, creates, current styles, tastes, moral values, and life attitudes that our daughters will adopt. We influence our daughters only if we keep up on prevalent musical trends. Lately, it has become acceptable to appreciate the rhythm and blues, rock and roll, and jazz styles of the past. Introducing daughters to music from other eras widens their musical taste, as well as their selections.

Become aware of what we unconsciously teach our daughters about sexuality and body image. What we, a girl's parents, say and do teaches and reinforces culture's messages about sex and body image. Consider the following:

Do we stand in front of a mirror in our daughter's presence and complain about how fat we are?

Do we talk about how much better a person we know would look if she or he lost a few pounds?

Do we insist upon looking perfect, i.e. makeup on, hair just right, coordinating outfit, etc. before we can go out of the house?

Do we have to have the latest fashion in clothes, jewelry, make-up, shoes, and so on?

Do we hold a double standard for our daughters, insisting they be neat, well-dressed, and clean, while demanding less of our sons?

Do we criticize how our spouse looks or dresses in front of our daughters?

Are we uncomfortable using accurate terms for body parts?

Are we willing to discuss sexual matters when they arise?

We are *not* saying we must or must not do these things. Yet we encourage listening to what we say around our daughters and watching for ways we also buy into cultural beliefs about how we must look to be attractive, to be loved, to be decent human beings, that negatively affect our self-esteem or squeeze us into strict patterns of behavior. We suspect we can all add much more to the preceding list. Becoming aware of how we limit ourselves empowers us to raise daughters with wider vision and greater life choices.

Sexual Harassment

Most studies we found on sexual harassment involved high school students, where high percentages of the girls interviewed reported being grabbed, pinched, groped, badgered persistently for dates, and enduring suggestive comments at school.[25] We would not be at all surprised that girls in the middle years must also suffer sexual harassment; at least the values that sustain this behavior are learned during this time. Somewhere, somehow, girls learn they deserve this treatment, and boys learn it is okay to give it.

> *It's really embarrassing, and it happens anywhere! You might be walking down the hall to lunch with your class and pass another class waiting to go in. The boys all stare at you and say, "Hey, Fatty!" or "Look at those titties!" It's really disgusting, and they always say it low enough so the teacher never hears. There's really nothing you can do about it. All the girls hate it.*
>
> —*Mandy, ten*

Our point about sexual harassment in a chapter on girls from ages eight to twelve is that they do *not* deserve such violation at any age. Enduring such treatment day-after-day in a place they are required to be by law is humiliating. It erodes self-esteem, breeds fear, generates rage, and creates hopelessness in our daughters. They deserve something much better. They deserve our intervention. When our daughters encounter sexual harassment in their schools, immediately call the school's or district's Title IX officer. Among other duties, this person is responsible for hearing sexual harassment complaints.

Our daughter will not be the only one suffering abusive treatment at her school. If we have not already done so, now is the time to contact the parents of her friends for support and action. A group of *extremely concerned* parents descending upon the principal of their daughters' school carries great impact and negotiating power. Our daughters must constantly contend with the gender inequities of our current educational system; it is criminal to expect that they also endure sexual harassment.

The Early Onset of Menstruation

One hundred years ago the average age for beginning menstruation in the United States was sixteen.[26] Today it is 12.8 years of age, with a wide range from as early as 10 to as late as 16.[27] Researchers speculate about the reasons for this four-year drop in age of menarche. Many conclude that better nutrition contributes to this change in onset. Several years before a girl is ready to start her period, her body begins to store fat in preparation. Ninety-eight to 103 pounds seems to be the critical body weight for triggering the beginning of menstruation.[28] This causation seems to hold true when we consider girls who mature early. They tend to be heavier than their classmates, and they are more at risk to develop eating problems than average or late bloomers.[29]

We elaborate on the effects, experiences, and rituals surrounding menstruation in Chapter Eleven, dealing with girls from thirteen to seventeen, but it is helpful to prepare our eight- to twelve-year-old daughters for what is to come. Like other sexual matters, if we have been casual and open from the beginning, questions about menstruation will have already come up, and it will not carry the shock that it did for some of us when we were growing up.

Knowing she can go to her mother—most girls do prefer to talk about menstruation with their mother or another, older female—helps ease the way for a girl who gets her period before others in her age group. Being liked by their girl friends becomes more important to our eleven- and twelve-year-old daughters than being seen as competent or independent.[30] Early development gives a girl either greater status among her peers or sets her apart as the brunt of dirty jokes, crude remarks, and jealous ostracism. Some girls adjust to their early physical maturity with amazing aplomb, while other feel depressed, isolated, and shameful.

What can be a lonely time for some girls is eased by an open, loving, and understanding relationship with their mothers. Fathers can help, too, by respecting their daughters' need for privacy, avoiding teasing about sexual matters or growing up, continuing to show genuine interest in their concerns, and being the loving, fun father their daughters cherished before they went through this remarkable change. Single mothers will need to continue to provide opportunities for their daughters to be involved with men they respect and trust, and single fathers will find helpful the assistance of women who can give the loving and understanding support a young girl needs during this momentous passage.

The Positive Intent

Great things happen for girls during the "I Can Do Anything!" years. They test their competence, challenge their parents, approach life with confidence, and often master the many things they try. If our daughters have always been active, rowdy, and a handful to manage, we can expect more of the same. If they were quiet and demure as six-year-olds, we may be surprised to suddenly have a rambunctious eight-year-old on our hands. Where did this outspoken, confident, and boisterous creature come from?

Mothers may be challenged during the middle years by what sometimes appears to be their daughter's turning away from them. Fathers may be particularly challenged by their daughter's new interest or passion for their attention and time. When daughters experience their mothers as competent and in equal relationship to their fathers, this natural turning is simply a shift in perspective or priority arising from the development stages of the middle years. Although daughters seek out their fathers at this time and enjoy doing things with them, they almost always remain in close contact with their mothers. When daughters view their mothers as weak, dependent, or giving in to their fathers, the turning can be more permanent, with a daughter's feelings of anger and betrayal toward her mother extending into adulthood.

Learning to listen for the positive intent underlying our daughters' behaviors provides an opening for better understanding and communication between us. Knowing they will not be judged, ridiculed, or punished for their behaviors or for confiding their feelings to us, empowers girls to preserve the all-important connection with their inner wisdom. This is especially important for girls in the middle years as they approach adolescence and the age of conforming to culture's female stereotypes by taking their true selves underground. Having courage—the ability to speak one's truth with all one's heart—is probably the greatest gift a girl can develop. Respecting her Voice, her inner truth, allows a daughter the freedom of the full expression of being human. Hearing what she really means strengthens a daughter's courage. The following are examples of behaviors and statements we may encounter from girls eight to twelve.

Statement: That's stupid.

Positive Intent: *You wish you didn't have to deal with this.*

Statement: Nobody likes me.

Positive Intent: *You need help with your friends.*

Statement: It's not my fault.

Positive Intent: *You try so hard to be good.*

Behavior: Ignoring Mom's requests to do chores, and responding to Dad's.

Positive Intent: *You like working with Dad right now.*

Behavior: Our daughter hurts a friend by excluding her from play at school. When confronted, she says, "I don't want to play with Jill, because she's telling bad stories about me."

Positive Intent: *Your best friend just turned against you, and you just don't know what to do about it.*

Statement: You're always picking on me.

Positive Intent: *Am I pushing you too hard?*

Each girl has her own unique expression of her aliveness. Therefore, we provide the following exercises to allow you to examine your daughter's statements and behaviors for the positive intent. Remember that what drives us nuts now may be the very talents or resources that enables a girl to follow her destiny. No matter what the behavior, girls try to solve their problems in a positive way to survive and to belong.

Statement:

Positive Intent:

Statement:

Positive Intent:

Statement:

Positive Intent:

Behavior:

Positive Intent:

Behavior:

Positive Intent:

Behavior:

Positive Intent:

Taking Action

The eight- to twelve-year-old girl develops on all levels. Biologically, her limbs lengthen, and she grows taller; around ten her body begins to prepare for the onset of menstruation by storing body fat in her breasts, hips, and thighs. Psychologically, she develops a closer relationship with her father, while deepening her connection with her mother; her girl friends become more important; and she deals with the issues of being special and belonging through competitive "who's in, who's out" interactions. The eight, nine, and ten-year-old is not particularly limited by gender stereotypes, feeling free to investigate the world and aspire to wherever her heart leads her. The girl of eleven and twelve becomes more vulnerable to cultural messages concerning body image, what it takes to be popular, and how girls should think and behave. A girl in the middle years also becomes more centered in her soul life, the feelings of her heart, and she needs our guidance to learn to express her uniqueness, those small seeds that will someday sprout into gifts, talents, and resources.

Music is good for the soul. Learning to play a wooden, pentatonic flute or a recorder is especially helpful for the deep breathing needed to develop the lungs and offers a soulful means of expression. This is a great time to begin music lessons, because our daughter's ability to concentrate is more developed, and she thrives with the structure and accomplishment practice brings to her often chaotic energies.

Art, storytelling, and poetry are especially meaningful now. Girls of all ages are touched by carefully-chosen stories, lively poetry, and self-expression through artwork. Using these activities in the middle years enhances our daughter's development into adolescence. They provide a down-to-earth way to bring her feeling/intuition into tangible form. Letting her emotions flow onto paper, for example, in lively reds and yellows brings satisfaction and feelings of accomplishment. She learns to channel her feelings into creative expression, rather than turning them inward upon herself.

Sadly, many of our schools have eliminated regular art classes and often do not even incorporate it into daily classroom routine. These art forms are important enough in all our lives to make them part of our family time together. Here are a few resources to get you started. If you have not already, be sure to check Chapter Nine about girls from birth to seven for more ideas.

Face Painting, by the editors of Klutz Press, Palo Alto, CA: Klutz Press, 1990. Includes great ideas for faces and paint, too! Find at local toy outlets and children's bookstores.

The Harvest Craft Book, by Thomas Berger, Edinburgh, U.K.: Floris Books, 1992. A delightful collection of crafts made from nature's bounty in the Fall. Available from the Anthroposophic Press, RR 4, Box 94 A-1, Hudson, NY 12534 or call: (518) 851-2054.

Check the *HearthSong* catalog for wonderful art supplies, craft ideas, and kits. Call Customer Service at (707)585-9776 or write: 6519 N. Galena Road, P.O. Box 1773, Peoria, IL 61656-1773.

The Natural Way to Draw, by Kimon Nicolaides, Boston, MA: Houghton Mifflin, 1969. A great guide to freedom from the fear of drawing. Local bookstores.

Nature Crafts for Kids, by Gwen Diehn and Terry Kratwurst, New York: Sterling Publishing, 1992. The cover promises, "50 Fantastic things to make with Mother Nature's help." Local bookstores.

Painting With Children, by Brunhild Muller, Edinburgh, U.K.: Floris Books, 1987. Available from the Anthroposophic Press (previously listed, p. 258).

Watercolor for the Artistically Undiscovered, by Thacher Hurd and John Cassidy, Palo Alto, CA: Klutz Press, 1992. Even the most timid among us will be encouraged to try their hand at painting. Available from *HearthSong* (previously listed, p. 257).

Housebuilding is good for girls, too. Between eight and twelve, the personality of a girl—her unique self—is developing and becoming strong. During these years, she explores the world outside the home, learning what interests her, how things work, and what runs them. In the midst of their adventurous explorations, whether through story-books or actual roaming, girls also need quiet, secret places where they can dream, be alone, or whisper with a friend. Building these protective spaces provides a sense of competence and accomplishment for the eight- to twelve-year-old girl. A wonderful guide available through local bookstores is: *Housebuilding for Children*, by Lester Walker, Woodstock, NY: The Overlook Press, 1977.

Include math and science in daily life. Although many girls in the middle years are not intimidated by math and science, the wheels of unequal education for girls are in place in the middle grades and influence them. We help our daughters by incorporating math and science into their everyday lives as we do reading and the arts.

Cooking is a fun and delicious way to learn about following directions, chemical combinations, fractions, and measurements. Having her own savings account offers a girl the chance to learn about the value of money, saving, and accurate record-keeping. Letting a daughter figure the tip when the family eats out, weigh the produce, pay for groceries, and check the change builds math skills she will need all her life. Teach her the art of score keeping when watching or playing games like softball, baseball, basketball, football, and soccer. Help her figure her batting average for the season. Take up stargazing as a family and learn the configurations of the heavens.

Give her a clothing allowance—go through her closet with her each season to assess what she needs; go on a pricing trip to find out how much the items she wants cost; then allow her to purchase her choices, based on her allowance. If there is an item she wants beyond her budget, suggest ways she might earn the extra money. This teaches girls how to live within a budget and make sensible choices about how to spend money.

Put a daughter in charge of plotting the family vacation, marking the route on a map and figuring the mileage; even trips to the grocery store are fun and good practice at map reading and math. Family gardening teaches her about the growing seasons, germination times, natural laws, and patience. When girls breed, raise, and care for pets they learn about gestation, birth, death, the habits and needs of other members of the animal kingdom, responsibility, and love. The following resources will give you more ideas:

Celestial Delights, by Francis Reddy and Greg Walz-Chojnacki, Berkeley CA: Celestial Arts, 1992. Describes the best astronomical events through the year 2001. Local bookstores.

Math Matters, activity pamphlets from the National PTA. Send SASE to The National PTA, 700 North Rush Street, Chicago, IL 60611-2571 or call: (312) 787-0977.

Money Doesn't Grow on Trees: A Parent's Guide to Raising Financially Responsible Children, by Neale S. Godfrey, New York: Simon and Schuster, 1994. Explores values and money, allowances, money management, and lots more with children from ages two through adult. Local bookstores.

Science Wizardry for Kids, by Margaret Kenda and Phyllis S. Williams, Hauppauge, NY: Barron's Educational Series, 1992. Full of interesting and fun experiments, using materials we have around the house. Local bookstores.

Wonder Science, a magazine with physical science activities for family fun. Subscriptions are $7.50 per year. Write: The American Chemical Society/The American Institute of Physics, 1155 16th. Street NW, Washington, DC 20036 or call: (202)452-2113.

Don't let girls "off the hook" for their behaviors. "My parents always let my sister off easy," says Fred, a father of two girls. "And I don't want my daughters to rely on their feminine charm to manipulate their way out of having to be responsible for their behavior. I'm not against charm; we all need it sometimes to get along in the world. But, there's a way we as fathers, especially, fail to hold girls accountable for their mistakes, because they're so cute."

Support a girl's femininity. Many girls between eight and twelve are the proverbial tomboys. They are often crazy for horses, tree-climbers, and Dad's shadow during these years. We applaud the more equal opportunity both girls and boys have these days to be themselves, and girls in the middle years thrive on the opportunity to engage in team sports and other activities formerly considered "boy stuff." They also blossom when encouraged to develop "girl stuff," too. Tea parties, knitting, setting a proper table, social etiquette, dancing, and all the fine graces we associate with femininity are fun and enhance the development of a well-educated, modern woman. *The American Girl's Handybook*, by Lina Beard and Amelia B. Beard is a delightful place to start (See "Help!" section, p. 303).

Parents unite! Support your daughters! Gender equity and sexual harassment are only two issues facing our daughters as they grow toward womanhood. As their locus of attention and activity moves away from home out into school and community, they meet the many challenges and injustices of a society that permits racism, sexism, ageism, and so on.

By forming community and communication with parents of our daughters' friends, we can begin to struggle with the inequities we all face. Speaking out when our schools fail to provide safety and protection from sexual harassment teaches our daughters that we all have a right to defend ourselves against injustices. A lone voice among many may not be heard, or may be considered simply a pest or "busybody" by those in charge. The collective voices of a community of concerned parents, however, carries clout, and can effect change.

Both girls and boys were getting harassed at Bett's middle school. The day she came home with the front of her blouse ripped from some boy jerking her around, did it for me. I called every parent I knew, a lot I didn't know, and told them to be at the school the next day. And to plan to stay. Ten parents showed up, and we just hung around the halls. The kids were pretty rowdy, and there were a few smart remarks, but Bett came home that day intact. That Friday night those parents all got together for a potluck dinner to plan strategies, organize committees, and elect committee chairs. We signed up for shifts to monitor the halls and decided who would meet with school authorities. Folks even arranged to get time off from their jobs to take a shift. It was that important to all of us that our kids go to school in peace. It worked.

—Julian, father of Bett, eleven

Help! Is Out There—Where to Find It

Be sure to check Chapter Nine for additional resources.

Developmental Tasks: Books

Encountering the Self, by Hermann Koepke, Jesse Darrell, trans. Hudson, NY.: Anthroposophic Press, 1989. A sensitive and insightful focus on the ninth year of development in the Waldorf educational philosophy. From the Anthroposophic Press (previously listed, p. 258).

In a Different Voice, by Carol Gilligan, Cambridge, MA: Harvard University Press, 1982. A psychological study of the development of girls and women. Local bookstores.

On the Threshold of Adolescence: The Struggle for Independence in the Twelfth Year, by Hermann Koepke, Catherine Creeger, trans., Hudson, NY: Anthroposophic Press, 1992. This engaging book chronicles the changes teachers, parents, and families go through as their children enter adolescence. Available from the Anthroposophic Press (previously listed, p. 258).

Raising Black Children, by James P. Comer and Alvin F. Poussaint, New York: Penguin Books, 1992 (previously listed, p. 259).

Women's Growth in Connection, by Judith V. Jordan, Alexandra G. Kaplan, Jean Baker Miller, Irene P. Stiver, and Janet L. Surrey, New York: The Guilford Press, 1991. A collection of writings on the idea of a relational psychology from researchers and therapists at the Stone Center, Wellesley College. Local bookstores and university libraries.

Needs: Books

A Guide to Non-sexist Children's Books, vol. II, by Denise Wilns, Chicago: Chicago Academy Press, 1987. A resource for finding nonsexist books for girls and boys. Local bookstores.

The American Girl's Handy Book, by Lina Beard and Adelia B. Beard, Boston: David R. Godine, 1987. A delicious assortment of everything imaginable of interest to girls. Available from *HearthSong* (previously listed, p. 257).

Ariadne's Awakening, by Margli Matthews, Signe Schaefer, and Betty Staley, Stroud, Gloucester, UK: Hawthorn Press, 1986. Written from a New Feminine perspective, this thoughtful book traces the history of relationships between men and women and what we must do today to confront the grave issues we face to ensure the continuation of life on earth. Available from the Rudolf Steiner College Press and Bookstore, 9200 Fair Oaks Blvd., Fair Oaks, CA 95628 or call: (916) 961-8729.

Awakening the Hidden Storyteller, by Robin Moore, Boston, MA: Shambala, 1991. How to build a storytelling tradition in your family. Local bookstores.

The Book of a Thousand Poems, New York: Peter Bedrick Books, 1983. Poems of childhood on every subject. Available from *HearthSong* (previously listed, p. 257).

Books for Today's Young Readers, by Jeanne Bracken and Sharon Wigutoff, New York: City University of New York, Feminist Press, 1981. A guide to fiction for ten- to fourteen-year-old readers. Local bookstores.

Children Without Childhood, by Marie Winn, New York: Penguin Books, 1984. An intimate look at why our children are growing up too fast in the world of sex and drugs. Local bookstores and libraries.

Earth Child: Games, Stories, Activities, Experiments, and Ideas About Living Lightly on Planet Earth, by Kathryn Sheehan and Mary Waidner, Tulsa, OK: Council Oak Books, 1991. A wonderfully inviting book to interest anyone in science. Local bookstores.

Endangered Minds: Why Children Don't Think and What We Can Do About It, by Jane M. Healy, New York: Simon and Schuster, 1990. Is our use of technology actually changing our children's brains? Local bookstores.

The Girl Within, by Emily Hancock, New York: Fawcett Columbine, 1989. A therapist's intriguing account of her clients' recovery through rediscovery of the nine-year-old girl within. Local bookstores.

Girls Are People, Too, by Joan Newman, Metuchen, NJ: Scarecrow Press, 1982. A helpful resource on choosing positive image books for girls. Local bookstores.

Inner Work, by Robert Johnson, San Francisco: Harper and Row, 1986. A practical guide to using dreams and active imagination for personal growth. Local bookstores.

Men and Just Desserts, by Sonya Friedman, New York: Warner Books, 1983. An insightful guide to teaching competence in girls and women. Local bookstores.

Questions Kids Wish They Could Ask Their Parents, by Zoe Stern and Ellen Sue Stern, Berkeley, CA: Celestial Arts, 1993. An insightful dialogue between a mother and her eleven-year-old daughter. Local bookstores.

Steiner Education in Theory and Practice, by Gilbert Childs, Edinburgh, U.K.: Floris Books, 1991. A comprehensive overview of the Waldorf philosophy of education based on the theories of Rudolf Steiner. From the Anthroposophic Press (previously listed, p. 258).

Tell Me a Story, by Chase Collins, Boston: Houghton Mifflin, 1992. A creative guide to learning the art of storytelling. Local bookstores.

Watercolor for the Artistically Undiscovered, by Thacher Hurd and John Cassidy, Palo Alto, Calif.: Klutz Press, 1992. A user-friendly book with brush and paints included. Simple instructions to invite even the most timid artist. Order from *HearthSong* catalog (previously listed, p. 257).

What to Do After You Turn Off the TV, by Frances Moore Lappé, New York: Ballantine Books, 1985. Full of wonderful ideas for the entire family to enjoy together. Local bookstores.

The Wounded Woman, by Linda Leonard, Athens, OH: Swallow Press, 1982. Personal insights into healing the father-daughter relationship. Local bookstores.

365 TV-Free Activities You Can Do With Your Child, by Steve Bennett and Ruth Bennett, Holbrook, Mass.: Bob Adams, 1991. Games and activities for all ages with materials from around the house. To order, call: 1(800)677-7760.

Needs: Magazines, Booklets, Catalogs, and Newsletters

The AAUW Report: How Schools Shortchange Girls, a shocking look at how girls are treated from preschool through grade twelve. 1992. Order from: AAUW Sales Office, P.O. Box 251, Annapolis Junction, MD 20701-0251 or call: 1(800)225-9998, ext. 91.

The Company of Women, a merchandise catalog to benefit victims of domestic violence and rape. Full of T-shirts, posters, and hard-to-find books about and for women and girls. Order from: The Company of Women, 102 Main Street, P.O. Box 742, Nyack, NY 10960-0742 or call: 1(800)937-1193.

New Moon, a magazine for girls eight to fourteen. Subscribe from: New Moon Publishing, P.O. Box 3587, Duluth, MN 55803-3587 or call: (218)728-5507, and ask your local library to carry it.

New Moon Parenting, a newsletter for adults who care about girls. Subscribe from: New Moon Publishing (see above).

Parental Discretion: Movie Previews for Responsibile Parents, a triweekly publication with ratings and concise reviews of current films, with no overriding agenda. Objectionable elements and viewing recommendations for all ages. Write: High Text Corporation, P.O. Box 758, Colluvial, TX 76034 or call: (817)428-2001.

Needs: Networks

The National Coalition for Sex Equity in Education. Contact for information about local and state programs to improve gender equity in your daughter's school. Also ask for their positive image book lists for girls and boys. Call: (908)735-5045.

National Coalition on Television Violence. Monitors the violence level in television programs and movies and provides research and education about the harmful effects on our children. Write: NCTV, P.O. BOX 2157, Champaign, IL 61825 or call: (217)384-1920 for articles and their latest statistics.

Phi Delta Kappa, provides research and support for programs in gender equity in education. Write: 8th and Union Streets, P.O. Box 789, Bloomington, IN 47402-0789.

TV Busters, a national program started by a fifth-grade teacher to help kids discover how rich life can be with little or no television. Can involve teachers, classes, schools, entire communities. For information, write Pat Marker, Box 600, Excelsior, MN 55331.

Inner Guidance System: Books

Are You There God? It's Me Margaret, by Judy Blume, New York: Dell Publishing, 1970. Delightfully covers all the questions of a young girl nearing adolescence. Local bookstores and libraries.

Nightmare Help, by Anne Sayre Wiseman, Berkeley, CA: Ten Speed Press,1989 Uses the actual dreams of children with sleep problems in a straightforward and useful guide to helping children confront their fears. Local bookstores.

Inner Guidance System: Newsletters

K.I.D.S. Express, a newsletter to help children adjust to divorce. Subscribe by writing: P.O. Box 782, Littleton, CO 80160-0782.

Fences: Books

Back in Control: How to Get Your Children to Behave, by Gregory Bodenhamer, New York: Prentice-Hall Press, 1983. Helpful in dealing with preteens and teens. Local bookstores.

Liberated Parents Liberated Children, by Adele Faber and Elaine Mazlish, New York: Avon Books, 1975. Includes positive suggestions for setting limits, giving feedback, and understanding our children. Local bookstores.

Positive Discipline for Single Parents, by Jane Nelsen, Cheryl Erwin, and Carol Delzer, Rocklin, CA: Prima Publishing, 1994. A practical guide to coping with the responsibilities of a single parent. Local bookstores.

Siblings Without Rivalry, by Adele Faber and Elaine Mazlish, New York: Avon Books, 1987. Subtitled: "How to Help Your Children Live Together So You Can Live Too." Local bookstores.

When Your Child Drives You Crazy, by Eda LeShan, New York: St. Martin's Press, 1985. Delightful reading, supportive of parents, and very wise. Local bookstores.

Sexuality: Books

Helping Your Child Recover from Sexual Abuse, by Adams and Fay, Seattle, WA: University of Washington Press, 1992. Helpful for any age. Local bookstores.

The Intimate Circle: The Sexual Dynamics of Family Life, by Miriam Ehrenberg and Otto Ehrenberg, New York: Simon and Schuster, 1988. Includes sex education for parents, interviews with American family members, and an informative discussion of sexual issues. Local bookstores.

Positive Intent: Books

How to Talk So Kids Will Listen and Listen So Kids Will Talk, by Adele Faber and Elaine Mazlish, New York: Avon Books, 1980. A simple, supportive, and effective guide on how to stop misunderstanding your children. Local bookstores.

Making Peace in Your StepFamily, by Harold H. Bloomfield, New York: Hyperion, 1993. Written with warmth and humor with lots of helpful exercises. Local bookstores.

Men Are from Mars, Women Are from Venus, by John Gray, New York: HarperCollins, 1992. A practical guide for improving communication and getting what you want in relationship. Local bookstores.

You Just Don't Understand: Women and Men in Conversation, by Deborah Tannen, New York: William Morrow and Co., 1990. A fascinating study of the differences in how and why women and men communicate. Local bookstores.

Endnotes

1. Emily Hancock, *The Girl Within* (New York: Fawcett Columbine, 1989), 6.

2. Annie Dillard, *An American Childhood* (New York: Harper & Row, 1987).

3. Rahima Baldwin, *You Are Your Child's First Teacher* (Berkeley, CA: Celestial Arts, 1989), 12.

4. Hancock, *The Girl Within*, 3.

5. Carol Gilligan, *In a Different Voice* (Cambridge, MA: Harvard University Press, 1982), 19.

6. Baldwin, *First Teacher*, 10.

7. Hermann Koepke, *Encountering the Self: Transformation and Destiny in the Ninth Year*, trans. Jesse Darrell (Hudson, NY: Anthroposophic Press, 1989), 15.

8. Baldwin, *First Teacher*, 16.

9. Irene P. Stiver, "Beyond the Oedipus Complex: Mothers and Daughters," in *Women's Growth in Connection*, Jordan, et al. (New York: The Guilford Press, 1991), 109.

10. Hancock, *The Girl Within*, 25.

11. Robert Kegan, *The Evolving Self: Problems and Process in Human Development* (Cambridge, MA: Harvard University Press, 1982).

12. Angeles Arrien, *The Four-Fold Way: Walking the Paths of the Warrior, Teacher, Healer, and Visionary* (San Francisco: Harper San Francisco, 1993), 85.

13. Glenn Van Ekeren, *The Speaker's Sourcebook: Quotes, Stories, and Anecdotes for Every Occasion* (Inglewood Cliffs, NJ: Prentice Hall, 1988).

14. Koepke, *Encountering the Self*, 92.

15. Hancock, *The Girl Within*, 16–17.

16. Liz Hannigan, M.A., family therapist, conversation with Jeanne Elium, Walnut Creek, CA, 17 Nov. 1993.

17. Dr. Haim G. Ginott, as quoted in *Liberated Parents Liberated Children*, Adele Faber and Elaine Mazlish (New York: Avon Books, 1974), 203.

18. Miriam Ehrenberg and Otto Ehrenberg, *The Intimate Circle: The Sexual Dynamics of Family Life* (New York: Simon & Schuster, 1988), 193.

19. Ibid., 198.

20. David Laskin and Kathleen O'Neill, *The Little Girl Book* (New York: Ballantine Books, 1992), 193.

21. Ehrenberg and Ehrenberg, *Intimate Circle*, 198.

22. Statistics compiled by The American Humane Association, given in a telephone conversation with Laura Kennedy, authors' technical assistant, Denver, CO, 25 Feb. 1994.

23. Ibid.

24. Laskin and O'Neill, *Little Girl Book*, 193.

25. Tammy Hyun Joo Kresta, "Top High School Students Say Cheating, Violence Rampant," *San Francisco Examiner*, 20 Oct. 1993, sec. A7.

26. Marie Winn, *Children Without Childhood* (New York: Penguin Books, 1984), 162.

27. *The AAUW Report: How Schools Shortchange Girls*, commissioned by the American Association of University Women Educational Foundation and researched by the Wellesley College Center for Research on Women, 1992, 11.

28. Winn, *Children Without Childhood*, 162–163.

29. AAUW, *How Schools Shortchange Girls*, 11.

30. Ibid.

CHAPTER ELEVEN

THE "YOU JUST DON'T UNDERSTAND ME" YEARS: THIRTEEN TO SEVENTEEN

Question: How can I recognize an adolescent?
Answer: You can tell the adolescent not so much
by the way she looks as by the way she slams
the door in your face after you have said
something offensive, such as "hello."[1]

—Lewis Burdi Frumkes, *The KGB Diet*

I n broad strokes, the teenage years have been painted as trying times for parents, as well as girls. Judging from the number of parental complaints, jokes, teenage suicides, and our own memories of growing up, we know life can be rough for many families with teenagers. Not all parents dread these years, however, and many girls weather quite well the storms of change that accompany the transformation from small buds into full blooms. Whether our daughters' teenage years are full of blue skies or dark storm clouds, parents are continually challenged to listen with open minds, avoid judgment, make time for family relationships, let our daughters know how they affect us by expressing our feelings, set clear, firm fences and consequences, ask ourselves hard questions, and evaluate our priorities.

Developmental Tasks

Intellectual Changes

One focus of growth during the teenage years is the intellect. Our daughter has evolved from the eight-year-old who pictorially understands her world into the fourteen-year-old, now capable of abstract thinking and reasoning. She no longer accepts things at face value but begins to form her own opinions based on what she experiences. She is flooded with new concepts, new understandings of the human experience, high ideals, and more complex questions. Child development theorist, Jean Piaget described adolescence as "the time of life when a child develops the ability to imagine herself as someone else."[2] She tries on new personae, feels her emotions more deeply, and fervently argues her new points-of-view—often with little substance or experience to support them. This does not keep her from pontificating on her next theory, but she needs our uncritical support to discuss her ideas.

> *My dad gets really stupid during dinner table discussions. He always brings up some story he read about in the paper and acts like an authority. When I give my opinion, he tells me I'm too young to know what I'm talking about. I resent his insulting remarks. Don't I have a right to an idea? Sometimes I just want to disappear, I feel so embarrassed.*
>
> *—Anita, fifteen*

The adolescent girl longs to make sense of the world. Her search leads her to critically question those around her, especially parents and other family members. She is particularly sensitive to the contradictions in our behaviors; for example, telling Grandma we cannot come to dinner on Sunday, because we have plans when we have none, or warning her not to drink alcohol when we do. Being treated unfairly provokes her sense of justice, as when we set earlier curfews for her than we do for her little brother.

> *Teachers are so unfair! They tell us we can choose any topic we want for a class project, and then they have to*

give their okay, before we can go ahead with it. It's totally communistic!

—Jannie, sixteen

Changes in the Feeling Life

The discrepancies our daughters discover between the beauty, honor, and justice they expect and the ugliness, corruption, and deceit they find brings them to the depths of despair. This critical inner eye turns most harshly upon themselves, where they imagine only imperfection. Unless their awareness and energies are channeled into positive relationship and action, they risk being caught in the net of depression, a common condition affecting adolescent girls that can lead to multiple problem behaviors, such as drug use, shoplifting, promiscuity, and teenage pregnancy.

I've had a lot of trouble with Lavona, ever since she turned fourteen. As a single parent, my salary barely covers rent and food, so our clothing budget is small. She's been very depressed this year of high school, because the girls tease her about not having the latest styles. I realized something was really wrong when I found new lingerie under her usual underwear. When I questioned her, she was sullen and sassy. That's when I knew we needed help with her depression and shoplifting before she got into real trouble.

—Grace, mother of Lavona, sixteen

Teenage girls are known for their wide mood swings, because they are quite deeply connected to their feeling life; despair quickly turns to euphoria when things go their way, when their best friend appreciates them, when they discover a new underdog to defend. Parents often feel as though they are on an emotional roller coaster, ready to deal with one mood as it changes into another. Many times we are hard pressed to understand at all what our daughters are trying to tell us. The development of the intellect, however, enables adolescent girls to use thinking to work on their emotions when they have moved into the Clear

Thinking Zone. As we model for them how to express our feelings without blame or judgment, their emotional expression matures into the ability to listen to another's point of view, conciliation, compromise, or an agreement to disagree and still remain in-relationship.

Physical Changes

Another developmental shift occurring during adolescence is the onset of menstruation and all the bodily changes that accompany it. The natural weight gain necessary for menarche is cause for concern to many teenage girls. Without a confident body image, girls may develop eating disorders and an obsession with their weight, appearance, and the "in" behavior. Parents become an embarrassment, are inadvertently at fault for our daughters' troubles, and mysteriously develop an inability to understand anything.

The ebb and flow of estrogen and progesterone, as these female hormones shift to find a proper balance in our daughters' developing menstrual cycles, contribute to their unpredictable emotional upheavals. Keeping our cool and remembering we are not to blame for everything, enables us to weather their range of feelings with respect, humor, and patience.

Development of a Self

Based primarily on studies of boys, many traditional, psychological theories describe human development as an ever-increasing movement towards independence, separation, and autonomy. The teenage years are supposedly filled with various crises, rendering children more and more separated from parental values, guidance, and direction, until the culture deems them autonomous adults. Because most girls and women are consistently judged more dependent, less separated, and less autonomous than boys and men, we wonder what they do during the teen years. The new research and ensuing theories about the psychological development of girls and women were discussed previously in Chapter Two. The findings indicate that girls in adolescence face extremely complex and difficult challenges, often forced to battle for their place in relationship, their voices, their very lives.

Rather than striving for separation and independence, teenage girls attempt to deepen and make their relationships more intimate and more authentic; that is, they struggle to tell the truth about what they see and experience. They strive to bring their whole beings into their relationships—their dreams, their fears, their moods, their sexuality, their newly-formed opinions. Being in-relationship fosters an adolescent girl's sense of self, enabling her to give care to others while caring for herself, which we believe is a true sign of adulthood.

Needs

Once upon a time in Norway, there lived the tussefolket, or fairy folk. It was common knowledge that they could spell themselves to look like someone human, someone we know, a friend or family member. During this time there lived Else, a dairy maid, and Lars, a young man of the village. They liked each other very much and in token of their friendship, they exchanged gold bracelets with their names engraved upon them. One summer day Else was to take the cows to a high meadow, where several dairy maids before her had disappeared. Her family and Lars cautioned her to be careful. Their fears were well-grounded, because upon reaching the meadow, Else saw Lars before her, beckoning her to follow him into the woods. But this couldn't be Lars; she had just left him that morning in the village! Realizing it was a tusse spelled to resemble Lars, she took off her bracelet, attached it around the neck of her faithful dog, and urged

*him home to her parents. Else lingered in the
meadow as long as she could, but the handsome
tusse was very charming. Just as she was lured
into the woods, her family and Lars rushed into
the meadow, calling, "Else, you are Else, you are
not a fairy! You are Else!" As soon as her name
was called, the spell was broken, and Else rushed
into the waiting arms of her family.*[3]

—The Dairy Maid (Norway) An Adaptation

Adolescent girls need their parents to "call their names."
Folklorist Lise Lunge-Larsen believes that old stories describe the
dangers that face girls and women in life transitions.[4] Teenage girls are
in transition between childhood and womanhood. In this state of in-
betweenness, they risk being drawn into situations where they feel
afraid and uncertain about what to do and how to say "No!". They can
easily lose themselves in the outside clamor to be popular by taking
drugs, engaging in early sex, cheating on tests, shoplifting, and so on.
They need us to remind them of their true identities, to "call their
names," to say, "You are Else, not a fairy." When our daughters are in
between and in danger of losing themselves by conforming to behavior
we dislike or fear, we must hang on to our vision of their seeds, those
budding gifts, talents, and resources we know they have within them,
waiting to burst forth into bloom.

**Crushes play an important role in our teenage daughter's
development.** The search for an inner identity during the early teen
years becomes focused outwardly onto a person whom a girl admires
and desires to be like. The object of these early "crushes" may be
someone in her immediate life, such as a teacher, minister, camp
counselor, or older classmate, or may be someone cherished from a
distance, such as a rock star or teenage movie idol. A crush serves to
assuage a young girl's longing for beauty and perfection. Admiring
from afar, she attempts to fulfill her heart's desire for the close
connection with the spiritual life she experienced as a child. Her

passion for the adored person may embarrass or cause us concern, because we fear our daughter may be taken advantage of and hurt, if her feelings are misunderstood or not returned.

Jenny worried us for a time when she was fourteen. She got a crush on a girlfriend's brother, a guy in junior college. I guess he was around a lot when Jenny visited her girlfriend's house. Anyway, he was everything we hoped Jenny would never be interested in—slovenly, slick, drove fast cars, probably into pot, charming in a demeaning sort of way. She, of course, couldn't see any of this, and we got into some real heated matches. I learned it's best to keep the family rules clear, say nothing against the guy—because all she sees is perfection—be patient, but firm about the boundaries, and she'll eventually get over it. This guy kind of led her on, giving her lots of attention and teasing her about liking him. Then she saw him come out of a bar one night after a school football game so drunk he couldn't stand up on his own. She cried and spent a lot of time by herself in her room for weeks afterwards, but she was cured of him. I'm just thankful, it was her feelings that were hurt.

—Bud, father of Jenny, fourteen

Our daughter's crushes are a natural part of growing up, the memory of hurt or disillusionment, poignant reminders of her girlhood innocence. Our patience and understanding, free of judgment and ridicule, will empower her to distinguish between wishing and reality and to endure disappointment and hurt.

Girls need a best friend. Sometimes a best friend fills the adolescent girl's need to find perfection in the world. They may become so close they do everything together. They dress alike, participate in the same school activities, share confidences, and support each other through trials from parents, teachers, boys, other girls, and their developing bodies. Like her first love, girls carry the memories of her best friendships and the interpersonal skills she learned from them throughout her life.

Teenage girls must develop balance in their lives. Pressures to conform, to be popular, to belong, to be attractive, to get good grades for college, to excel, and to live up to parental standards and expectations weigh heavily on the adolescent girl of the technological age. Culture's push toward materialistic success devalues and leaves little time for the less visible, inner work that goes on during this time, as well as the development of interpersonal and intellectual skills.

Waldorf educator and author Betty Staley reminds us, in her wonderful book about the teenage years, *Between Form and Freedom*, that teens must develop a middle between thinking and acting. This middle is the soul life, the world of feelings from which develops the highest of human aspirations—love, charity, and artistic inspiration. Betty Staley suggests that our western way of living in the will is out-of-balance without the eastern way of living in thought. Our adapted list of the adolescent's need for balance follows:

Western Willing	Eastern Thinking
physical activity	stillness
intensity	routine
to affect the world	to move inward
to belong	separateness[5]

As we guide our daughters to be physically active, we must also encourage time for silence; time to ponder life's inner questions that loom large before them without interference from loud, electronic music, the chatter of friends, or household hustle and bustle. While teenage girls relish the intensity of school activities, social events, and jobs, and they need the routine of regular family mealtimes, daily chores, and challenging homework. Perhaps as much as girls from birth to seven, girls in the teen years need parents to provide a comforting routine and a listening ear.

I wasn't sure how we would survive financially on only one income, but it seemed very important that I be home during Megan's teenage years. She's a Senior now, and looking back I'm glad I could provide the stability, routine, and support she needed to get

through band practices and performances, rigorous
study and assignments, and all the other extra-
curricular activities she had, not to mention social
times with friends! It wasn't always easy—we had our
battles—but Megan managed those years more
gracefully than I did!

—*Kelly, mother of Megan, seventeen*

During the adolescent years, girls are called outwardly into school and community activities. They want to make a difference, influence how things go, feel they make an imprint upon the world. At the same time, their souls draw them inward to consider the Big Questions about who they are, where they are going, how they want to live their lives, what living a good life entails.

The conflict between the need to belong to a group and the need to be seen as unique and individual is the dominant struggle of adolescence. The human need to belong, to know one's place in a group, is possibly greatest during adolescence, when a girl struggles to stay in relationship while developing a self, separate from her parents. "I watched as my daughter's individuality was swallowed up by her peer group," remembers single mother, Liz Hannigan. "Finally, I said to her, 'I know you want to fit in with your group. How can you belong in a way that is your own? If you're going to flip you hair up in the front like your friends do, how can you change it in other ways so that your style comes out, and you still fit in?' We talked about other ways she wanted to be like her friends and how her own taste and sense of style could shine through. She liked having a taste of her own power to belong and be different at the same time."[6]

Girls need to know they are important, useful, and valuable people. Minding the bubbling stew of a girl's hormonal impulses, exciting ideas, peer group temptations, academic challenges, family expectations, and soul longings is a tremendous task. She doubts she can handle it all. Self-esteem lags just when a girl needs it the most. One way to support our daughters during these confusing times is to acknowledge their ideas. We can let them know their opinions count without having to agree with them. "You have given that idea lots of thought," we can say; or "Have you considered this? It supports your point." Showing real interest in their theories encourages the development of critical and strategic thinking. It also makes for lively dinner conversations.

Another way to bolster girls' fragile self-esteem is to encourage participation in family activities, holidays, traditions, and rituals. At some point in our daughter's growing up we realize this is probably the last family vacation we will take together, or the last time she will be willing to perform that cute, holiday puppet show, and so on. Daughters do grow up to form their own families and lead their own lives.

However, the premature leaving of the family during the teen years, so common in our fast-paced, isolated life-styles, contributes to a girl's feelings of confusion, aloneness, and low self-worth. She fights to stay home from the family vacation, balks at taking part in the family's traditional holiday rituals, and complains she spends no time with her friends. We can empathize with her wish to be with friends, while acknowledging her important place as a family member. The family should be the group a girl can count on amidst the fickle membership of a peer group. Although she may be reluctant to admit it, she looks to family to sustain her during the difficult times when she feels she does not belong anywhere.

The roles she played when she was younger need to be changed or enlarged to confirm her new maturity and, therefore, responsibility within the family. She deserves a more adult status. Perhaps she will write a new puppet show for others to perform; will plan the holiday menu, make the guest list, choose table decorations; or will decide where the family goes on vacation this year, make reservations, and find someone to feed the dog. Knowing we need their ideas, talents, and efforts offers our daughters incentive to remain active family members.

Girls need to learn goal-setting.

⊰ JEANNE | Something I notice over and over again about the women I work with, women friends, and women I went to school with is that few of us have goals. We don't have long-term, lifetime goals with clear steps to realize them. Many of us have vague ideas about how we want our lives to be, or what we want to be doing, but we haven't defined them in clear, manageable terms. I knew that at some point in my life I wanted to write, but I hadn't visualized the steps needed to bring this about.

My husband and other men I know have clear two-year or five-year plans, sometimes even longer, about how they will achieve what they want in life.

Perhaps culture's limited view of what woman could or should achieve discouraged the setting of long-range goals, or perhaps most women have not realized the importance of having goals and achieving them. Whatever the reasons, the inability to set goals and determine the steps necessary to achieving them hinders girls and women.

Whether a goal involves breaking a destructive habit, acquiring a new possession, or reaching a higher level of job performance, the steps required to meet it provide direction, incentive, guidance, reward, and a sense of accomplishment and completion. Girls as young as ten benefit from the structure of goal-setting, and older teens understand its importance as a tool for achieving competence. Teaching our daughters the art of goal-setting to fulfill their wants empowers them toward independent action in their future lives.

Opportunities to teach girls how to set and realize goals are common during adolescence. When we think twenty-five dollars is enough for a pair of jeans, but our daughter begs for a fifty-dollar pair that all her friends are wearing, we can help her plan how to earn the extra twenty-five. Goals are best realized when written down in "black and white." Help her define her goal clearly, and carefully plan the steps necessary to fulfill it. Be sure to include a time commitment. Here is an example:

Goal: To buy a pair of (her brand) jeans by July 31st.

What I have: $25.00 from Mom and Dad

What I need: $25.00 more

Steps:

1. Check my savings account to see if I can afford to use $25.00.

2. Call Elaine Jones to see if she needs baby-sitting.

3. Raise baby-sitting rates from $1.50 an hour to $2.00 an hour.

4. Put up an ad about pet-watching for vacationers at club pool.

5. Check ads for sales on jeans.

6. Do price comparisons to find the best deal.

It will not take long for a daughter to see the usefulness of goal-setting in her daily life. How to complete a term paper, how to stop biting her fingernails, how to get up the courage to talk to the cute boy in chemistry lab cease to be such obstacles. Almost anything can become more easily managed when the goal is clear and the steps are laid out on paper before her. She may even teach us a lesson or two about realizing our lifetime goals.

Girls need mentors.

In twelve years of school,
I never studied anything about myself.[7]

—Twelfth-grade African American girl,
The AAUW Report: How Schools Shortchange Girls

Until recently women and girls were rarely pictured in school texts, in the media, in the arts, in the community, or in the world as anything but someone working behind the scenes, as assistants to great men. Those few females who made names for themselves come easily to mind—Joan of Arc, Madame Curie, Queen Elizabeth, Emily Dickinson, Eleanor Roosevelt, Rosa Parks. Reading about these great women's courage helps somewhat, but most adolescent girls need flesh-and-blood models of feminine strength, power, and wisdom.

Providing opportunities to meet distinguished women in the career field a girl is contemplating encourages her to follow her dreams. Older girls who remain outspoken and self-assured give younger girls permission to voice their opinions, speak out in school classes, and formulate their own world-views. A friend who loves making home a sacred, peaceful place to nurture her family, an aunt who heads her own company, a neighbor down the street who writes children's books, a beloved physics teacher, a former baby-sitter who studies native ways of healing in Peru are all rich learning resources for our daughters.

Mothers, whether they make a career at home, outside the home, or both, often become their daughters' mentors. Girls are assured a healthier womanhood, when they see their mothers striving to live a good life, balancing their care for others with care for themselves, being competent in and loving their chosen work, and standing firm in their beliefs and commitments. Our daughters will perhaps guide us as our culture and individual members re-envision The Feminine, bringing its energy into a more balanced relationship with masculine powers. We empower them in this healing process by seeking strong female mentors as their teachers.

Inner Guidance System

Girls of nine and ten exhibit what Harvard researcher and therapist Annie G. Rogers, Ph.D., calls "ordinary courage," the ability "to speak one's mind by telling all one's heart."[8] By early adolescence—twelve to thirteen—girls begin to lose this courage to speak the truth about their experiences and to push underground what they really think and feel. They begin to give up all resistance to the cultural conventions of what Annie Rogers terms "feminine goodness."[9] They learn to close off any bad thoughts or feelings, try always to be kind and nice, and work out difficulties behind the scenes to avoid causing unpleasant situations.

Girls in early adolescence lose connection with their inner guidance systems. This loss of inner knowing sets girls adrift in a sea of confusion. While boys are most at risk to develop psychological problems during early childhood, girls are most at risk to suffer during adolescence. This risk goes across racial and socio-economic lines, and often strikes those girls who are the most vital, the most psychologically alive.[10] We discover one day that the tussefolket have stolen our bright, confident, lively daughter away and left a sullen, dreamy, reluctant imitation in her place. Indeed, therapist Emily Hancock, Ph.D., found in her work with women that around adolescence, girls develop a "contrived self,"[11] which steals or takes the place of the authentic self. That part of a girl who was outspoken, fun-loving, and radical, and who delighted in creating a scene, loved to be shocking, and demanded center stage goes underground. There this authentic self waits, dormant, until she is rediscovered years later, when the woman discovers that something essential is missing.

Loss of connection with her inner guidance system results in a dramatic decline of a girl's self-esteem. Before puberty, she had what Harvard researcher Carol Gilligan, Ph.D., describes as "an insistence on knowing what one knows and a willingness to be outspoken."[12] In early adolescence a girl begins to doubt her own perceptions and feelings and turns to "a reluctance to know what one knows and a fear that one's experience, if spoken, will endanger relationships and threaten survival."[13]

Because her self-esteem is based on her feelings of being in relationship and in taking care of those relationships, a girl becomes cautious of what she says for fear of "turning others off." She begins to communicate her ideas as "just my opinion," "You may not agree with this," "This may not seem right, but ... ," or "I don't know." She is slower to raise her hand in classes at school and more reluctant to express her opinions if they go against the *status quo*. Studies of 3,000 children, commissioned by the American Association of University Women in 1990, confirm these changes. Sixty percent of the elementary girls agreed to the standard indicator of self-esteem, "I'm happy the way I am." In middle school, 37 percent of the same girls agreed to the statement. By the time they reached high school, only 29 percent of these girls felt they were happy the way they were. Other studies show that girls in early adolescence are much more likely than boys to suffer from depression, hold negative body images, develop eating disorders, criticize their intellectual capabilities, and fall off in academic performance.[14]

How can we help our daughters weather the storms of early adolescence, keeping their self-esteem intact? How do we encourage them to keep their voices, to remain in touch with their inner guidance systems?

At all ages, encourage interdependence. Mutually empathetic relationships, where each person cares for the other's well-being allow the development of a self-in-relation. This self-in-relation is at the root of our daughter's self-esteem. When we do not hear or respond to our daughter's feelings and thoughts, she begins to feel that she is a problem, that the problems that develop between us are really within herself. She begins to believe that she is bad, unworthy of our love and attention, that her thoughts carry no value. She begins to disconnect, and her feelings of isolation cause a sense of helplessness. When girls are threatened with isolation, they take any opportunity to make connection. They may attempt to become very, very good, or act out their feelings of fear, anxiety, and anger in problematic ways.

When we return a daughter's first baby smile, she happily kicks her feet, her impact upon our relationship acknowledged. As a toddler, she watches us closely as she walks unsteadily toward the open gate, knowing what our response will be, and we do not fail her as we rush to grab her hand and lead her back to safety of fence and yard. The daughter in the middle years challenges the integrity our relationship by criticizing the inconsistencies in our behaviors. Her confidence in herself and in our relationship is strengthened as we listen to her opinions, examine our motivations, and strive to do better. Our teenage daughter grows in self-esteem and confidence, as we faithfully "call her name," constantly remembering for her, who she truly is.

At all ages, encourage independence. Our daughters crave independence within relationship; to think their own thoughts and be respected, to choose their own friends and have our confidence, to organize their own activities, rooms, and clothes and receive our approval.

At all ages, and especially at early adolescence, encourage their expression of feelings and thoughts. Hearing the truth about girls' experiences, negative and positive, allows them to nurture the essential voice within that connects girls and women to their souls. When we are open to whatever our daughters have to say, they are more able to keep their entire beings in relationship. They have no need to hide the thoughts and feelings they fear will drive others away and lead them into isolation and loneliness. They do not have to send parts of themselves underground to survive within their families.

Therapist Annie G. Rogers, Ph.D., admits that allowing adolescent girls their say can be "profoundly disturbing and disruptive." She relates an incident she observed involving the girls she worked with through the Harvard Project on the Psychology of Women and the Development of Girls. "... I've watched girls exclude and cruelly scapegoat a single girl. Furious with them, I wanted to stop this behavior. It would be so simple to impose my authority rather than to stay with the girls, wanting to know what they knew in their own terms."[15] As Annie

Rogers listened and observed, she learned why they had excluded the girl, who was caught in her own deceit and manipulation. When given the opportunity, the girls were able to voice their disgust and confront the traitor in their midst.

When allowed their say, our daughters may speak aloud what had previously been unmentionable family secrets. They notice that Uncle Charley drinks too much at dinner. They wonder why the bathroom smells like smoke after Grandma Bea has been in there. They ask what their father was doing downtown with an unknown woman. They speak out against the injustices they see in their families, their schools, their communities, and in the world at large. They defend the underdog, challenge our prejudices, and question our values.

At all ages, applaud girls' achievements. Our daughter's firsts are easy to cheer—first full night's sleep, first steps, first words. Her first attempts at independence are not so easy—first "No!", first grabbing away toys, first toddle out the front gate. Perhaps we do not recognize a girl's misbehaviors as steps toward becoming her own person, but the more we can applaud her attempts to develop a self without judging her wrong or bad, opinionated or headstrong, moody or bitchy, the stronger her self-esteem will be as she enters adolescence.

It is vitally important to applaud our daughters for their *achievements*, rather than for their appearances. Too often girls grow up in our consumer-oriented culture recognized for buying into the stereotypes of feminine goodness—sweet, pretty, slender, compliant, helpful. Our daughters may be these things, and we can be glad for it. We also need to allow a voice to the other side of the feminine—moody, full-bodied, passionate, strong, assertive—or our daughters will grow up as caricatures of healthy women, with something essential missing.

Unintentionally, fathers can undermine their daughters' self-esteem by thwarting their ability to achieve. Some experts believe that more fathers are concerned their daughters follow the dictates of culture's sex-roles and enforce this belief by allowing their sons freedom to roam, get dirty, and make mistakes, while restricting their daughters to home, doing household chores, being nice and pretty, and making good grades.[16]

Mothers who know how hard it is to achieve in a gender-biased society, often make the mistake of pushing their daughters too hard, of expecting perfection in all they attempt. This can be as damaging as expecting too little or limiting girls' choices by restricting them to what is proper for girls to do. Setting unrealistic goals undermines self-esteem by discouraging girls from trying at all.

Teachers who expect high performance from girls because they are girls, contribute to low self-esteem when they fail to recognize female students for their achievements. Myra Sadker, Ed.D., and David Sadker, Ed.D., well-known researchers in education, reveal that at all grade levels, teachers give girls less praise, criticism, and help than they give boys. When a girl has difficulty with a problem, teachers are more likely to do it for her, than to work with her until she understands and can complete it on her own.[17]

At all ages, girls need their parents behind them, cheering their ideas, opinions, mistakes, risk-takings, heroic deeds, successes, and near misses. Our daughters' achievements bolster their self-esteem and competence. Just as important as reaching the goal, however, is recognizing the effort, initiative, thoughtful planning, and knowledge gained from their attempts. By sharing our own teenage stories, we remind them that what they see as a failure now, may be looked back upon as an important growing experience. It is truly a self-assured person who can say, "I learned a lot from that disappointment."

My daughter worked night and day as a friend's campaign manager for class president. They both had great ideas on how to improve school conditions, such as violence and sexual harassment. Jill's good at speech-writing and slogans and a good leader, too. When her friend lost after all their hard work, Jill was devastated. After the shock and disappointment wore off some, I pointed out what Jill got from all her efforts—skills at organizing people, how to delegate tasks, practice at public-speaking, admiration of school staff, and closer bonds with new and old friends, important skills that last a lifetime.

—Jeff, father of Jill, fifteen

Fences

Adolescent girls may outwardly struggle against family rules, traditions, and values, but inwardly they still expect—and need—us to hold the limits firmly and choose fair and redemptive consequences. By the time they are teenagers, our daughters count on our guidance, understanding, applause, advice, and insistence on acceptable behavior within the family.

We have to acknowledge to ourselves, if not to our daughters, that we cannot, at this point in their growing up, really control them. Time spent under our supervision has decreased proportionately with their increase in years. They are ultimately in charge of their own decisions and choices, and we have little control over what they do on their own time. The only real power we have is in the strength of the relationship between us and the model of how we live our lives.

Family conflict is valuable. Few of us relish the stress, possible hurt feelings, and just plain muck that disharmony within the family brings. We would rather ignore thorny problems, hoping they will disappear on their own. However, researchers at the Stone Center, Wellesley College, found that girls who grow up in families that allow conflict have higher self-esteem and a greater capacity for deep, fulfilling relationships with others.[18] When we abandon our daughters during tough times by pretending nothing is wrong or denying the importance of the issues, they feel isolated and estranged from the one source of support on which they should be able to rely. Ongoing patterns of conflict avoidance within the family contribute to adolescent girls' loss in self-esteem and general lack of well-being. Learning to manage disagreements, air grievances, confront unfairness, solve conflicts, and handle anger—their own and others—prepares our daughters to meet life's challenges unafraid, with confidence and competence.

Frequently re-evaluate fences. A common cause of discord during middle adolescence is the failure to recognize our daughter's new maturity. Limits that kept her safe and comfortable when she was eleven probably feel constricting and offensive at sixteen. Modifying fences when she demonstrates the readiness for it confirms a girl's sense of mastery over her behaviors.

With all my girls, I always insisted on a regular time for homework—after dinner around the kitchen table. That way they could finish their work before bedtime, and I was there to help if they wanted it. Now that Margie's in high school, I've had to relax that family rule a little. She does a lot of her studying during a free period and at her after-school baby-sitting job. The younger girls still have the after-dinner routine, but if Margie is already finished, we agreed she can use that time to talk on the phone with friends. She seems pleased that I have confidence in her, and she hasn't abused the privilege so far.

—*Marie, mother of Margie, fifteen,
Amy and Jo, nine*

Take time to talk and negotiate. Choosing appropriate fences and consequences during the teen years requires great flexibility on the part of parents as well as daughters. Trying to control through guilt, threats, bribes, lectures, and punishment is futile and leads to power struggles and disengagement. Focusing on the relationship between us and our daughters and what it needs in order to flourish goes to the heart of what is important in the lives of girls. Daughters are much more willing to see our sides of things—why we believe a certain fence is necessary—when we try to understand their feelings and needs. Being able to have their say and to negotiate for what they want empowers girls to know their own minds, stand their ground, and take action without waiting for someone else to do it for them.

Go for the big stuff. The struggle to become more responsible and adult is a hard one for many adolescent girls. Nagging them about trivial issues only heightens the conflicts between us. Hair styles and colors, nose rings, and peer group speech patterns may be irritating and even ugly to us, but focusing on these habits misses the point and widens the distance between us. The point is that our daughters behave so outrageously to discover what they really like, to develop their own aesthetics and style. Most of all, they experiment to test our relationship; will we continue to love and respect them no matter how they look?

Fence-setting in the adolescent years involves seeing beyond the purple hair and blood-red fingernails to the essence of who our daughter is now and who she is becoming. Focusing on the big stuff of relationship allows room to grow and forgives her temporary lapses in what we term sensible behavior. We can let her all-black ensemble go out the door without comment, but we must confront her with our feelings when she says something nasty. Her messy room can be handled by closing the door, but together we must deal with her breaking curfew on Friday night. We can forgive her occasional failure to fill the car with gas, but she must assume responsibility for damage done when she borrowed Mom's new dress. Remembering that how we work things out between us is often more important than what we decide must happen, keeps us focused on what behaviors are crucial to nurturing family relationships.

Let girls do it their way. Self-reliance, responsibility, and competence are developed through doing. When we insist our daughters do things the way we think they should be done, they miss valuable lessons in thinking for themselves, risk-taking to see if their ideas work, making mistakes, learning what went wrong, and discovering how to fix it.

> *My brother always had these bright ideas. If he didn't want to wash the car, he'd hire a friend to do it. Then he got upset when he didn't have the cash to go to a movie. That didn't stop him from finding new ways to do things, though, and my parents kind of encouraged him. It was a different story when I wanted to try something bizarre. Dad would always say, "Oh, I don't think that's such a good idea. You'd better stick to the sure thing." I encourage my own daughter to experiment with her ideas. Otherwise, how will she know what she is capable of doing?*
>
> —*Joan, mother of Veronica, fourteen*

Discuss fences and consequences in private. "Saving face" is important to teenage girls, especially when siblings or friends are around. Discussing limits and boundaries in private shows respect for our daughter's feelings and recognizes her maturity. That difficult time when adolescents find no use for adults and are embarrassed to be seen with us will be short-lived if we matter-of-factly discuss difficult issues in private.

Sexuality

Girls growing up today seem much more open about sexual matters than just a generation ago, but we question whether their frankness comes from a sense of ease and confidence in their sexuality, or from a bravado born from the early familiarity provided by the explicit sexual content of movies, television, books, and peer interactions. Cultural messages to be sexually active and sophisticated place burdensome pressures on adolescent girls. In 1985, the Alan Guttmacher Institute reported that more teen pregnancies, abortions, and childbirths occur in the United States than in any other industrialized nation in the world. Alarmingly, the U.S. is the only developed nation where teen pregnancies are on the rise.[19]

We might ask, "What is going on here?", when we consider the opportunities for education and birth control available to our nation's youngsters. Close examination of our daughters' lives in a society that sexualizes everything from mouthwash to cars, shows us how they are led into participating in adult behavior before they are emotionally ready. Let us consider the sexual issues our daughters face during adolescence:

Power and sex, sex and power. Various theories abound concerning the development of our current balance of power between the sexes. Some experts believe ancient woman recognized that when she gave sexual favors to the strong man of her tribal group, he returned the gesture by furnishing her and her offspring with a steady supply of meat. This powerful, sexual contract ensured their survival and possibly led to our modern version of smart-woman-behind-the-scenes-manipulating-a-strong-man. This arrangement seemed to work well for premodern humans. It is unfortunate the whole thing got out of hand, however, with men taking on a disproportionate power over women's sexuality.

More girls and women in our culture are raped by men; more girls are sexually abused, and more men are the abusers; more girls endure sexual harassment from boys at school; more women than men report they have had negative sexual encounters; more men make the laws concerning women's sexual and reproductive rights; and so on.

Faedra Lazar Weiss, Research Assistant at the Girls Incorporated National Resource Center, explains the problem well. "Adults need to acknowledge the fact that sexual relationships are relationships of power that young people need to learn to manage."[20] Adolescent girls must feel self-confident enough to say "No!" to sexual relationships when the person is not right, when the time is not right, when they are not ready. The hard facts are that most teens no longer question *whether* they will be sexually active; the question today is *when*, and too often the *when* is blurred when girls feel pressured and are afraid to say "No," because they feel powerless to do so. The self-confidence to say "No!" and to set firm and clear boundaries develops from high self-esteem and the feeling that girls have power over their lives. Providing opportunities for girls to develop the personal inner boundaries we discussed in Chapter Six assists them towards a healthy womanhood.

Girls get mixed messages. How clear and comfortable are we about our own sexuality? As so many of us uncover the painful memories of childhood sexual abuse, and we deal with the mixed sexual messages of our culture, we wonder how any of us achieve sexual happiness. Our daughters are confused, because we are confused. Parents, insecure about our own sexuality, give daughters mixed messages. We may fear our daughter's sexual involvement, while pushing her toward it, because we want her to be popular, or we have a vicarious involvement with her sexuality that becomes too personal and intrusive. A mother whose sexual development was arrested in adolescence has unfinished business that prevents her from separating her own sexual boundaries from her daughter's dating life.

> *My mom wanted to be my confidante about everything. She was always prodding me to tell her about my dates—what was the boy like, what did we do, did he kiss me on the first date, did I like him, were we going out again, and on and on. She tried to*

*be like my closest friend, you know? Dressed like I did,
hung around whenever my friends came over, took
part in our conversations. Some of my friends thought
she was such a great mom, because she was so up on
everything, you know? But I thought it was an
intrusion. Like, what did she really want me to do?
Have sex on my dates and tell her all about it? I don't
know, and she would never talk straight with me. I'm
just glad I never got pregnant or anything.*

—*Maryanne, twenty-one*

Another mixed message girls receive concerns the use of contraceptives. When we take daughters to get birth control but warn them not to have sex or deny the connection between using "the pill" and having sex, we are only kidding ourselves. It is important our girls are protected against pregnancy, but along with the birth control, we must also engage in conversation—lots of conversation—about responsible sex, safe sex, use of the contraceptive, alternatives to intercourse, getting regular check-ups, love, personal sexual satisfaction, pleasing one's partner, and what it takes to have a fulfilling relationship. Many parents shy away from discussing such adult matters, but our teenagers are engaging in adult behaviors without the emotional understanding or guidance to protect them from the dangers and burdens of early sexual involvement. Our daughters can no longer afford our mixed messages of denial or feigning ignorance.

Fathers sometimes confuse seeing their daughters as sexual persons with treating them as sexual objects. Adolescence can be an alarming time for fathers who find they are aroused by their daughters' awakening sexuality. When these feelings arise, many fathers draw back and separate themselves from their daughters, disgusted and afraid they may behave inappropriately. Where a father was once warm and receptive to his daughter's affections, supportive of her every endeavor—her greatest fan—he becomes aloof, withdrawn, too busy for the fun and exciting adventures they shared. Certainly, any overt sexual come-on is confusing and harmful, but the withdrawal of a girl's father is painful and perplexing for both of them.

Especially if the relationship between father and daughter is a close one, a girl wonders what happened and what she did to cause this loss. She first looks outside for explanations, and then comes to herself, thinking that perhaps if she is pretty enough, or smart enough, or outrageous enough, surely she can mend this rift between them.

> *Doing things with my daddy is what I remember most about my childhood years between eight and twelve. He was an avid hiker, and he'd take me on long weekend outings into the hills behind our house. He taught my best science lessons—to identify birdcalls, native plants, and land formations. We collected pretty rocks, our pockets bulging as we came down out of those hills, to add to the rock garden we built together. My daddy seemed to like those times as much as I did, our mutual admiration for each other shining through in our talk and laughter. I turned thirteen one summer, the summer I got my period, and that was the end of our glorious courtship. Daddy seemed embarrassed to be around me, unsure of what to talk about, and we no longer explored those hills alone. I've never quite gotten over that loss, and it took me a long time to figure out what I might have done. I guess I've tried to recapture our early connection in every one of my relationships since then.*
>
> *—Jean, forty-one*

Fathers must make the distinction between appreciating a daughter's natural sexual development and seeing her as a sexual object. At each stage of development, as fathers choose what behaviors they are comfortable with around their daughters, they set the pattern of relationship between them. Some decide that taking showers together or even sharing the bathroom should stop before a girl enters the middle years, between eight and twelve. Some will end these natural family rituals earlier; some later. Family habits of nudity and privacy vary, depending upon the parents' own childhood taboos and allowances governing sexual behavior. Most girls become shy about their bodies around seven or eight, and fathers can follow their lead in their desire for privacy.

Some daughters do not make it easy for their fathers. This first man in their life is a hero, the one whose affections and attentions they crave. They sometimes go to great lengths to win his love and approval. Unless a father is clear about his own sexual boundaries, it will be difficult for him to stay in appropriate connection with his teenage daughter. And most of all, a girl needs close connection with her father. Many studies conclude that the quality of the father/daughter relationship crucially affects a woman's capacity to have a mutually loving and sexually fulfilling attachment.[21]

Researcher and author Victoria Secunda writes in her insightful book, *Women and Their Fathers*, that unless fathers are able to be emotionally available while their daughters are growing up, these adult women will have difficulties in developing and keeping satisfying relationships.[22] Studies also find that fathers involved in their daughters' care from the beginning are less likely to be confused by their own erotic response to their daughters' sexual appeal.[23]

Purdue University researcher Phame Camerena, Ph.D., advises fathers to shift from their role as disciplinarian in their daughters' lives to confidant.[24] When fathers understand their daughters want to make their own decisions, they can provide the emotional support girls need to develop more adult-like behavior. Knowing that Dad is there for reassurance, advice, and applause gives girls confidence to assume more responsibility for their behaviors. This leads to high self-esteem and competence.

Key to a father's close and loving connection with his daughters is a healthy and sexually fulfilling relationship of his own with his life mate. Here he can explore any feelings that arise as his daughters mature; here he can give and receive affection and sexual intimacy; here he can re-clarify when he feels "off track" with his daughters; here he can get support for the great job of fathering he does.

In this culture, menstruation is a taboo subject. In Chapter Four we discussed our culture's taboos surrounding menstruation. The fact that such a powerful force affects half the population every month and goes relatively unnoticed—or is supposed to be—is worth mentioning again. In the very least, girls are confused about the beginning of this biological miracle, to bleed each month and not to die.

When boys reached puberty in ancient cultures, they were physically taken away from the tribe to begin the rigorous training that would make them into men. Ancient rites-of-passage for girls, however, were ceremonies of waiting, waiting for their womanhood to awaken. Modern parents are at a loss about how to mark this monumental passage in their daughters' lives. Too often we let institutions tell our daughters about the "facts of life." Schools show the proverbial movie; birth-control clinics hold sex-education classes; church youth groups discuss gender relationships. Our daughters say, "Don't tell Dad!" And they undergo the one experience that probably has the greatest impact upon their lives in secret and silence. Mother almost always knows, and close friends usually know, but a girl's deepest feelings about this change within her usually go unspoken.

(A school bell rings...four girls run On-stage from different corners of the space. They twitter and coo and dance around each other giggling. They ask each other with great interest and secrecy, almost at once.)

FOUR GIRLS. Have you? No. Have you? No. *(They...scurry offstage... The school bell sounds again. The four enter again, only Nan has changed in some small way. She walks instead of running or she affects a womanly posture. All meet again at C, and repeat the questioning as before. After all the girls have answered "No.")*

NAN. Yes. *(The others shriek in horror and run Offstage, leaving Nan alone. She comes D., and kneels. Praying.)* Dear God, why has this happened to me? They teach us that you're good and loving and forgiving and only punish bad people and sinners. I don't remember doing anything to deserve this. Mama calls it the "curse" and says that all girls get it and have it till they're old. Why would you want to put a curse on all the girls? Lord, it hurts so much sometimes in my stomach and my back, I think there's something wrong inside of me. I'm so afraid, too, that people will see, that it'll show through. It's bad enough that is comes from there, but God, why did you have to make it red? And Lord, if it happens to every girl, why did you choose me to be first? All the other girls think I'm...awful or somethin'.

Please, Lord, what I'm asking of you is, please, make it go away. I ask this in Jesus' name. A-men. *(The school bell sounds again. The three other girls enter as before, and meet at C.)*

THREE OTHER GIRLS. Have you? No. Have you? No. Have you?

GIRL TWO. Yes. *(All shriek and run Offstage. Nan and Girl Two together, embracing. The school bell sounds again. They all enter. Girl Three waddles in.)*

ALL. (To Becky.) Have you?

BECKY. No.

ALL. (To Girl Three.) Have you?

GIRL THREE. Yes. *(They shriek in acceptance. Nan, Two and Three go off together. Becky tries to follow. They snub her.)*

BECKY. (Kneels D.) Lord? Why is this happening to me? Is there something wrong with me? Mother says my time will come, just like all the other girls, but I'm afraid I'm some sort of mistake. I mean, just look at me. *(Indicating her chest.)* I see everyone staring at me, wondering what's the matter with me. Grandma says it's a gift from you. Well, if you can give it to all the other girls, why can't you give it to me? Lord, I'm askin' this one thing and I'll never ask anything again. Please make it come. In the name of the Father, Son and Holy Ghost. A-men. *(School bell rings. She exits....)* [25]

—Excerpted from *Quilters*,
A play by Molly Newman and Barbara Damashek

We must recognize the importance of our daughters' first menstruation as a rite-of-passage, as a leaving behind the sheltered life of childhood and entering into the rights, privileges, and responsibilities of womanhood. Each of our daughters feels differently about how this important event is honored. Some are embarrassed by any observance at all; others welcome the special attention given to them at this time. There are fathers who take their daughters to dinner, present them with memorable gifts, or write a poem to express their feelings about their daughters' new status. There are mothers who hold celebration teas for their daughters and their friends, with fine china, silver tea service, white dresses, and dainty cakes. Others invite their women friends for a gathering to honor their daughters, telling their own initiation stories, offering soothing massages, and teaching other time-proven remedies for cramps, backache, and fatigue.

Therapist and single mother Linda Riley, M.A., relates how she taught her daughter, Melanie, to honor and listen to her body during her menstruation. "A day or so before she expected her period, I encouraged Melanie to slow down her activities, go within, be quiet. Girls respond differently, I know, but she always needed quiet time, to shut out the world. Her first day was usually a rough one, so I allowed her to stay home from school, if she wanted to, and we agreed she need not do her chores around the house that day. She often spent the day in her room, curtains closed, listening to quiet music or reading. She never abused the privilege, and she seems to have a better understanding and connection with her cycles and her body than I ever did." [26]

Current attitudes imply there is something wrong when a girl or a woman slows down or curtails activities during her period. Advertisements proclaim that their product allows females to continue their lives as usual during menstruation; they can swim, play tennis, climb a mountain, and they'll barely notice their period. This is just the trouble—females are taught to barely notice their bodies, to ignore this creative, healing, renewing mystery.

Let us take time to celebrate with our daughters their entry into what the ancients called "the blood mysteries." By listening and talking with them, we will know what rituals will touch their souls, what invitation they need from us to enter into the feminine realms with confidence, a lightness of heart, and a pride in their approaching womanhood.

The Positive Intent

Before our eyes, our daughters grow overnight from tiny seedlings into sturdy beings, whose buds hold the promise of glorious blossoms to come. They are starting to bloom, or as one father we know puts it, "to boom!" The immense changes in their active brains and bodies sometimes overshadow their emerging uniqueness. We wonder how to deal with our daughters' moods, passions, crushes, and demands.

I see Sammie more clearly than ever. She's so good with small children, in bringing out the best in them. In fact, she brings out the best in whomever she's around. But, her moods! I think she's so overwhelmed by the changes in her body, other people's expectations of her, and her expanded ability to think rationally, she gets lost. Her unique gifts are hidden in all the drama, until she baby-sits or works as a counselor at summer camp. There she's really in her element, and she shines.

—Jane, mother of Sammie, fourteen

A girl in the teen years wavers back and forth between clarity and confusion, looking to us to keep an even keel, to provide a place of calm in the midst of great turmoil. When, in the darkness, we call her name, in a flash her soul shines through.

When I was a young teen, my biggest dream was to be driven in a limo to go shopping at the mall. I can't believe where my head was at! Now, I'm twenty-one, in college, and studying women's health issues. My focus is helping women who can't help themselves. I think all girls in this culture have to go through the "mall phase of life." It was fun in one way, but thankfully I came out of it. Some of my old high school friends are still there. That's scary!

—Madra, twenty-one

"I want to do it my way," is the underlying positive intent of our teenager's behavior. Glaring contradictions abound. "I want to dress like everyone else, so I can be unique and fit in with my friends." "I want to go where I want to go, in spite of my friends and my parents!" Teenage girls are pulled first one way and then another by the mixed messages of their families, friends, the media, other cultural institutions, and the yearnings of their own hearts. Being self-directed while staying in contact with family, friends, and others often puts girls in inevitable double binds, where they feel no one can understand them.

⟨𝔢 JEANNE | When my daughter was fourteen, I had difficulty finding the words to let her know I understood what she was going through. During a particularly hard moment, she expressed her frustration with something, and I responded from my psychological training, "You really feel badly about this." My daughter looked at me, as though I was from another planet. "Oh, great! You want me to feel bad, too!!!" I was shocked at her outburst, because I thought I had named how she was feeling and that she would feel better knowing I understood. Now, she tells me, looking back, that all she really needed was for me to be on her side. The positive intent of her response was, "Just be on my side and listen. It's hard to face this alone."

So much of our teenage daughters' behaviors carry this contradiction: "I don't want to face this alone. Help me, but don't tell me what to do, because you don't understand." Waldorf educator Betty Staley explains this teenage dilemma well. "Parents need to simply accept that teenagers want the impossible from their parents. They want parents to guide them without forcing them, they want advice without commandment, limitations without punishment, and understanding without responsibility. They want adults around when they need them—but only as helpers, not as authorities."[27]

What is a parent to do? The following examples came to us from our own experiences and from those of our clients. We hope they offer insight into your teenage daughters' underlying messages:

Statement: That curfew is unfair; I can't possibly explain it to my friends. You don't understand, so butt out!!!

Positive Intent: I need you to trust me more.

Statement: Mom, would you not talk to my boyfriend for thirty minutes when he calls to talk to me?

Positive Intent: You be the Mom and let me be the girl.

Statement: I don't see why I can't go to an R movie. You treat me like a baby!!!

Positive Intent: *I don't like the rules.*

    Statement: You are being sexist. My brother not only drove at sixteen alone, you gave him a car. I am seventeen. I cart my little sister everywhere in that old, beat-up van. The least you can do is let me take the van to the beach Saturday, so all my friends can go together. That's a lot safer than having us all drive cars over those twisty roads. You wouldn't hesitate to let my brother do it!!!

Positive Intent: *I need to renegotiate some boundaries.*

Our daughters have their own unique ways of describing feelings, complaining, whining, and making their points. Fill in the statements you hear regularly from your daughters, and listen for the positive intent beneath their words.

Statement:

Positive Intent:

Statement:

Positive Intent:

Statement:

Positive Intent:

Taking Action

Throughout our daughters' lives they look to us for understanding, support, advice, and sometimes, action. The time and energy we invested while they were little, pays off during the teen years when their biological and soul urges pull them in often contradictory directions, requiring us to be flexible, patient, and kind. We find it helpful to remember that many girls breeze merrily through adolescence with grace and confidence, enjoying school, their friends, social events, and even their families with the best good humor. Parents weather the few stormy crossings, because they took time to be active participants in their daughters' lives. Following are helpful ways to be supportive allies for our girls. Chapters Nine and Ten includes suggestions also appropriate for the teen years.

Do things together as a family, father and daughter, and mother and daughter. A notorious rumor about teenagers is they hate to spend time with their families, preferring the company of their peers, whom they feel understand them better. This is true, *and* they need the security of their families, where they can be themselves without fear of judgment and rejection. Family is the center of a girl's tapestry of relationship, and our efforts to keep her involved, if only occasionally, provide a safe harbor in times of difficulty.

Each parent benefits at least as much as daughters do from spending time alone with them. We suggest parents choose activities that they enjoy doing. Fathers who continue to be involved in their teenage daughters' lives, who invite them to the movies, dinner, or a football game, and who spend time really listening and truly trying to understand their newly developing opinions, give their daughters the precious gift of being valued for who they are. Mothers available for intimate talks on any subject, skiing trips for females only, or shopping forays into a big city with dinner and the theater, teach their daughters the valuable lesson that women need each other as friends and allies.

Become involved in a daughter's school and social activities. Many parents become uneasy when a daughter begins to date. Who is this strange male she spends so much time with? Is he caring, trustworthy, and kind? And what about those other kids we see hanging around when we pick her up from school? The best way to stay informed about our daughters' friends and activities is to become involved ourselves. Volunteer as chaperone for school functions and trips. Host parties in your home for your daughter and her friends. Suggest she invite a friend or two along on a family outing or vacation. Invite her boyfriend over for a night of popcorn and video-watching. Our daughters may be horrified when we take such an active part and insist we know her friends, but it is our responsibility. Calmly inform her of the family rules, tell her it is our job to know who she goes out with, and be open to her suggestions about how to meet her friends. With her new maturity comes more say in how meetings are arranged.

Sponsor and/or coach a team sport. A good way for a father to share his passion for baseball or soccer with his daughter is to volunteer as coach for a local team. Community sports not only provide opportunities for parents and daughters to join together. They also rally the much-needed public support of sports programs for girls.

Fight for girls' rights to gender-equity in education. Does your daughter's high school invest as much money, effort, and time in team and individual sports for girls? Is she being taught higher mathematics and science as fairly as possible? Do teachers and school guidance counselors support her to pursue any subject she shows interest in, whether it is physics, shop, or literature? Our daughters deserve better educational opportunities than most are getting in our nation's schools. If you are concerned after observing in her classes and talking with her teachers about their teaching practices and what they think boys and girls need, contact the Title IX officer of your district, the State Office of Civil Rights, or the State Office of Education/Instruction for information about what parents can do to improve educational opportunities for girls.

Celebrate "Take a Daughter to Work" Day. Created by the *Ms.* Foundation for Women, "Take a Daughter to Work" Day is an annual event to inspire self-esteem in girls. By sampling a few of the numerous career opportunities open for women, girls develop more realistic and concrete ideas about their future job possibilities. Because experts predict that females will hold two out of every three new jobs by the year 2,000,[28] "Take a Daughter to Work" Day seems a good investment for all our futures. For more information, write the *Ms.* Foundation for Women, Dept. P, 141 Fifth Avenue, Suite 6S, New York, NY 10010.

Help teens get involved in social service. Girls between thirteen and seventeen develop a keen sense of fairness and justice. Where they are reluctant to help out with household chores, they can be tireless dynamos when others need help. Doing errands for shut-ins, reading and writing letters for people in nursing homes, volunteering in day-care centers, tutoring younger students, serving food in shelters for the homeless, all provide needed services, build character, and foster an awareness of cultural, ethnic, socio-economic, and religious differences.

Most cities have youth programs, such as the East Oakland Fighting Back Project in Oakland, California, where a successful toy-gun exchange program yielded over 300 make-believe weapons. Volunteers there hope that giving kids non-firearm toys will help reduce family and street violence in their communities.[31] Helping projects such as this one empowers teens to actively work for safe and healthy schools and communities.

Take any complaint of sexual harassment seriously. Our daughters, at one time or another during their school careers, will be subjected to the following behaviors, identified by The American Association of University Women:

> Sexual comments, jokes, gestures, or looks
>
> Shown or left sexual pictures or notes
>
> Graffiti about them written on bathroom walls
>
> Sexual rumors about them
>
> Rumors that they are lesbian
>
> Spied upon as they dress or shower
>
> Flashed or mooned
>
> Touched, grabbed, or pinched in a sexual way
>
> Clothing pulled in a sexual way
>
> Brushed against in a sexual way
>
> Blocked or cornered in a sexual way
>
> Forced to kiss against their will
>
> Forced to perform some other sexual act
>
> Clothing pulled down or off[29]

As we have said before, we consider it a great injustice that girls must endure this treatment in their schools. As parents we must find solutions to this shocking situation. Get to know other parents; meet with school officials; develop a plan for making our daughters' schools safe and interesting places to be.

Be alert for signs of sexual abuse. Therapist Joan Stern, M.A., Director of the Contra Costa Suicide Crisis Line, explains, "It's hard for parents to see symptoms of sexual abuse in their teenage daughters, because no one wants it to be true. This is complicated by a girl's natural need for privacy in her teen years. Withdrawal and depression are normal adolescent reactions to breaking up with a boyfriend, or to getting a bad grade in a crucial class at school. The need for privacy should be considered in conjunction with the following other symptoms."[30]

1) Severe misjudgments regarding risk-taking. Abused girls take lots of risks. They feel the worst has already happened to them, therefore, they can do whatever they want, because it can't get worse. These girls find themselves in all sorts of hazardous situations, unsure how they got there, such as walking through a dangerous park alone at night without considering the risks involved. They just do not see it coming. Because they are young and inexperienced, these girls often repeat being hurt, raped, or victimized, thinking their situations cannot get any worse. They often injure themselves repeatedly, feeling their lives have hit bottom; therefore nothing else matters.

2) Trouble with authority. Top-down directives do not work with abused girls. The adults they counted on failed to protect them, therefore, they learned that adults cannot be trusted to do what is best. Judgments and lectures are not effective ways to win their trust. We must find alternative communications that let them know they can count on us to help them.

3) Poor negotiation skills. Depending upon the kind and length of abuse, girls feel unable to work things out, because their survival depended upon indirectly relating to their abusers and hiding

the abuse from others. They often confuse seduction with negotiation. They need to be gently and patiently taught how to work things out without assuming a seductive, victim stance.

4) Affection confused with love. One client put it very clearly, "I didn't love him when I married him. I was only eighteen, and he was the first man to be nice to me." Abused girls tend to jump early and quickly toward men who offer gentleness and kindness. They often end up in a marriage with children, tied down to family life at an early age. Many of these marriages fail, and the victims find themselves hurt again. Knowing the difference between affection, compatibility, love, and the commitment required for lasting relationships comes with maturity.

5) Failure to plan for the future. Because, in their experience the worst has happened, abused girls tend to generalize their abuse trauma into broad areas of their lives. They settle for much less than they need; they get so entangled they cannot get out without help; they assume they will lose before they engage; or they are impulsively aggressive toward men. One young woman remembers, "I'd march into a bar and pull any man in sight right off his stool, just to be the one in control!"

Be aware of suicide danger signals. Although boys are more successful, because they choose more lethal means, adolescent girls are four to five times more likely to attempt suicide.[32] If life's upheavals seem to be getting our daughter down, be alert for the following changes in her behavior:

- Decreased appetite
- Change in sleep patterns
- Withdrawal from friends and social activities
- Angry outbursts, fearfulness, and touchiness
- Major personality changes
- Frequent physical complaints or tiredness
- Self-destructive behavior

- Preoccupation with death

- Obsessive fear of violence

- Irrational, bizarre behavior

- Overwhelming guilt or shame

- Feelings of hopelessness, sadness, or despair

- Giving away belongings

Our daughters often feel overwhelmed just trying to cope with the confusing biological, psychological, cultural, and spiritual influences they meet in adolescence. When other traumas occur, such as divorce, death of a friend or family member, loss of a valued relationship, drug usage, sexual abuse, molestation, or harassment, they can feel pushed beyond their limits. One of the previously mentioned symptoms may not be enough to indicate suicidal tendencies, but if our daughter is going through a hard time, for reassurance we suggest seeking professional guidance.

Parents must work on their parenting partnership. Our daughters are especially perceptive of personal interactions during adolescence. Married parents provide a daily model for a loving, sharing relationship. Any inequities, disagreements, or inconsistencies are brought to light by our daughters' critical eyes, and we are held accountable for our behaviors. Divorced parents are challenged to put our differences aside to focus on clear ways of helping our daughters healthfully through their teen years. Those of us in stepfamilies may find teenage girls especially rebellious or particularly withdrawn, while they sort out their special place in the new family and make sure of their natural parent's alliance.

Those of us in couples, no matter the configuration, owe it to ourselves and our daughters to continually strive to improve our relationships. Families whose heads show genuine respect for and affection to each other create the loving, nurturing havens adolescent daughters need to awaken to a healthy womanhood.

Talk to our sons. Ask boys whether their lives would be different if they were a girl. How do they think girls should act? Are they aware of the sexual harassment girls endure at school? What can they do about it? We must enlighten our sons as well as our daughters to the cultural injustices and stereotypic attitudes perpetuated by the media, schools, and the work world. None of us can be free to fulfill our dreams until we all are.

Help! Is Out There—Where to Find It

Remember there are helpful resources in the "Help!" sections of Chapters Nine and Ten that may also be applicable to the teen years. Some of those listed here are specifically helpful during our daughters' adolescence.

Developmental Tasks: Books

All Grown Up and No Place to Go, by David Elkind, Reading, MA: Addison-Wesley Publishing, 1984. Deals with teens in crisis. Local bookstores.

Between Form and Freedom: A Practical Guide to the Teenage Years, by Betty Staley, Stroud, Gloucester, U.K.: Hawthorn Press, 1988. A practical guide to the teenage years with valuable and sensitive insights into the hearts and minds of teens. Topics include teenagers and the family, teenagers and friends, teenagers and school, pregnancy and the teenager, teenagers and drugs, teenagers and food. Order from the Anthroposophic Press, R.R. 4 Box 94A1, Hudson, NY 12534 or call: (518) 851-2054.

Beyond Sugar and Spice, by Rivers, Barnett, and Baruch (previously listed, p. 258).

How to Father a Successful Daughter, by Nicky Marone, New York: Fawcett Books, 1988. Practical and straight advice for fathers to help their daughters become happy, confident women. Local bookstores.

Mother Daughter Revolution: From Betrayal to Power, by Elizabeth Debold, Marie Wilson, and Idelisse Malavé, New York: Addison-Wesley, 1993. Support for mothers to ease tensions between themselves and their daughters. Frees girls of stereotyped images. Local bookstores.

Thirteen to Nineteen: Discovering the Light, by Julian Sleigh, Edinburgh, UK: Floris Books, 1982. Through conversations with parents, this insightful book helps us gain understanding of our own process through adolescence to allow more clarity with our teenagers. Available from Anthroposophic Press (previously listed, p. 258).

Women and Their Fathers: The Sexual and Romantic Impact of the First Man in Your Life, by Victoria Secunda, New York: Dell Publishing, 1992. In-depth description of how the father/ daughter relationship sets the tone for future relationships in a woman's life. Local bookstores.

Women's Growth in Connection: Writings From the Stone Center, by Jordan, et. al., New York: The Guilford Press, 1991 (previously listed, p. 259).

Needs: Books

Dare to Live, by Michael Miller, Hillsboro, OR: Beyond Words Publishing, 1989. Explores the prevention of teenage depression and suicide. Local bookstores.

Family Traditions, by Elizabeth Berg, Pleasantville, NY: Readers Digest, 1992. A multi-cultural collection of family traditions and celebrations. Local bookstores.

Free Spirit Publishing, "Self-Help for Kids," a catalog of books, posters, games, cards, and much more to enrich the lives of children and teens. Write: 400 First Avenue North, Suite 616, Minneapolis, MN 55401-1730 or call: 1(800) 735-7323.

GirlTalk: All the Stuff Your Sister Never Told You, by Carol Weston, New York: HarperPerennial, 1992. Covers everything in the life of an adolescent girl. Chapters include education, sex, friendship, body, love, and family. Local bookstores.

Go Ask Alice, by Anonymous, New York: Avon Books, 1971. Actual diary of the experiences of a teenage drug addict. Fascinating reading for parents and teens. Local bookstores.

The 7 Habits of Highly Effective People, Stephen R. Covey, New York: Simon & Schuster, 1989. Dare we call this a gender-balanced approach to achieving personal success? Local bookstores.

Needs: Organizations

Girls, Inc., formerly Girls Clubs of America. Write for their informative study: *Past the Pink and Blue Predicament: Freeing the Next Generation from Sex Stereotypes.* Write: Girls Inc. National Resource Center, 441 W. Michigan Street, Indianapolis, IN 46202 or call: (317)634-7546.

National Clearinghouse for Alcohol and Drug Information, for comprehensive materials and a recommended booklet: *Growing Up Drug Free*, write P.O. Box 2345, Rockville, MD 20852. The booklet suggests educational activities by grade level and numerous resources for kids and parents.

Inner Guidance System: Books

All That She Can Be, by Eagle and Colman, New York: Simon & Schuster, 1993. Helpful and supportive ways to maintain self-esteem throughout the teen years. Local bookstores.

Failing at Fairness: How America's Schools Cheat Girls, by Myra Sadker and David Sadker, New York: Charles Scribner's Sons, 1993. Offers startling insight into what happens for girls in classroom and how parents and teachers can help. Local bookstores.

The Girl Within, by Emily Hancock, New York: Fawcett Columbine, 1989 (previously listed, p. 304).

The Hungry Self: Women, Eating & Identity, by Kim Chernin, New York: Harper & Row, 1985. Highly recommended for an understanding of women's relationship to food and body image. Local bookstores.

Meeting At the Crossroads: Women's Psychology and Girls' Development, by L.M. Brown and Carol Gilligan, Cambridge, MA: Harvard University Press, 1992. Chronicles research conducted by the Harvard Project on Women's Psychology and Girls' Development and the resulting theories on women's psychological growth. Local bookstores.

Raising Black Children, by James P. Comer and Alvin F. Poussaint, New York: Penguin Books, 1992 (previously listed, p. 259).

Reinventing Eve, by Kim Chernin, New York: Times Books, 1987. A readable, spiritually aware, and personal account of a modern woman in search of herself, including new theories of women's psychological development. Local bookstores.

Values Clarification, by Sidney Simon, Leland Howe, and Howard Kirschenbaum, New York: Dodd Mead, 1985. Offers questions and situations that require moral and value judgments. A great place for parents to begin to explore with their teens the important questions and dilemmas of life. Local bookstores.

Women's Ways of Knowing: The Development of Self, Voice, and Mind, by Mary Field Belenky, Blythe McVicker Clinchy, Nancy Rule Goldberger, and Jill Mattuck Tarule, New York: Basic Books, 1986. The 1987 winner of the Distinguished Publication Award and based on in-depth interviews of 135 women, this book explores why women still feel silenced in their families, work, and schools. Local bookstores.

Fences: Books

Parenting Teenagers, by Don Dinkmeyer and Gary D. McKay, Circle Pines, MN: America Guidance Service, 1990. A supportive guide to the STEP program—the Systematic Training for Effective Parenting of Teens. Local bookstores.

Parent/Teen Breakthrough: The Relationship Approach, by Mira Kirshenbaum and Charles Foster, New York: Penguin, 1991. Suggestions on how to become our teen's ally, so we can talk, listen, and negotiate, without alienating her. Local bookstores.

Raising Self-Reliant Children in a Self-Indulgent World, by H. Steven Glenn, New York: St. Martin's Press, 1988. One of the best books in print for teaching responsibility and self-motivation to children. Local bookstores.

Setting Limits, by Robert J. MacKenzie, Rocklin, CA: Prima Publishing, 1993. Good, practical advice, especially applicable for the years between eight and seventeen. Local bookstores.

Sexuality: Books

Circle of Stones: Woman's Journey to Herself, by Judith Duerk, San Diego, CA: LuraMeida, 1989. A short but powerful poetic journey through time. Chronicles what women's menstrual cycles might have been and how they could be reincorporated into their lives today. Local bookstores.

The Intimate Circle: The Sexual Dynamics of Family Life, by, Miriam Ehrenberg and Otto Ehrenberg (previously listed, p. 308).

Raising Child Conservatively in a Sexually Permissive World, by Sol Gordon and Judith Gordon (previously listed, p. 267).

The Wise Wound: Myths, Realities, and Meanings of Menstruation, by Penelope Shuttle and Peter Redgrove, New York: Bantam Books, 1986. A fascinating account of the ancient blood mysteries and menstrual taboos. Local bookstores.

Sexuality: Organizations

Federation of Parents and Friends
    of Lesbians and Gays
Family and Chapter Support Office
P.O. Box 20308
Denver, CO 80220

National Gay and Lesbian Task Force
1734 14th Street NW
Washington, DC 20009-4309
(202)332-6483

Sexuality: Hotlines

National AIDS Hotline: 800-342-AIDS

STD Hotline: 800-227-8922

Teens TAP (Teaching AIDS Prevention)
800-234-TEEN

The Positive Intent: Books

A Good Enough Parent, by Bruno Bettelheim, New York: Vintage Books, 1987. A thoughtful book that reaffirms the joys of parenting. Local bookstores.

Love Is Letting Go of Fear, by Gerald Jampolsky, New York: Bantam Books, 1980. Helps readers understand the positive motivations behind behavior. Local bookstores.

Parenting Children in Unstable Times, by Ruth P. Arent, Golden, CO: Fulcrum Publishing, 1993 (previously listed, p. 267).

Endnotes

1. Rebecca Sinclair, "Surviving the Teenage Years," *Progressive Woman*, June 1992, 5.

2. Caryl Rivers, Rosalind Barnett, and Grace Baruch, *Beyond Sugar and Spice: How Women Grow, Learn, and Thrive* (New York: Ballantine Books, 1979), 138.

3. Lise Lunge-Larsen, "The Dairy Maid," *New Moon: The Magazine for Girls and Their Dreams*, Spring 1993, 16–17.

4. Joe Kelly, "Calling Our Daughter's Name," *New Moon Parenting*, June/Jul. 1993, 13.

5. Betty Staley, *Between Form and Freedom: A Practical Guide to the Teenage Years* (Stroud, Gloucester, UK: Hawthorn Press, 1988), 93.

6. Liz Hannigan, M.A., family counselor, a conversation with Don Elium, Touchstone Counseling Services, Pleasant Hill, CA, 18 Nov. 1993.

7. *The AAUW Report: How Schools Shortchange Girls*, commissioned by the American Association of University Women Educational Foundation and researched by the Wellesley College Center for Research on Women, 1992, 61.

8. Annie G. Rogers, "Voice, Play, and a Practice of Ordinary Courage in Girls' and Women's Lives," *New Moon Parenting*, June/Jul. 1993, 11–12.

9. Ibid., 11.

10. Carol Gilligan, "Joining the Resistance: Moments of Resilience in Women's Psychological Development," an address to the Spring Foundation for Research on Women in Contemporary Society conference, "The Resilient Woman: Struggle in the Face of Adversity," Stanford University, Palo Alto, CA, 25 Jan. 1992.

11. Emily Hancock, *The Girl Within* (New York: Fawcett Columbine, 1989), 4.

12. Gilligan, "Joining the Resistance."

13. Ibid.

14. Gini Kopecky, "The Age of Self-Doubt," *Working Mother*, Jul. 1992, 47.

15. Rogers, "Voice, Play, and a Practice," *New Moon*, 12.

16. Kopecky, "Self Doubt," *Working Mother*, 47.

17. Ibid.

18. Alexandra G. Kaplan, Nancy Gleason, and Rona Klein, "Women's Self Development in Late Adolescence," in *Women's Growth in Connection*, Jordan, et al. (New York: The Guilford Press, 1991), 127.

19. Staley, *Between Form and Freedom*, 206.

20. Faedra Lazar Weiss, *Past the Pink and Blue Predicament: Freeing the Next Generation from Sex Stereotypes*, a paper sponsored by Girls Incorporated, formerly Girls Clubs of America, Aug. 1992, 14.

21. Victoria Secunda, *Women and Their Fathers* (New York: Dell, 1992), xvi.

22. Ibid.

23. Kopecky, "Self Doubt," *Working Mother*, 48.

24. Hilary Cosell, "Dads Make a Difference," *Working Mother*, Aug. 1993, 85.

25. Molly Newman and Barbara Damashek, "Quilters," 1986. A play based on the book, *The Quilters: Women and Domestic Art*, Patricia Cooper Baker and Norma Buferd, 1977.

26. Linda Riley, M.A., M.F.C.C., interview with Jeanne Elium, Walnut Creek, CA, 21 May, 1993.

27. Staley, *Between Form and Freedom*, 105.

28. Letty Cottin Pogrebin, "The Stolen Spotlight Syndrome," *Ms*, Nov./Dec. 1993, 96.

29. Sally Shannon, "Why Girls Don't Want to Go to School," *Working Mother*, Nov. 1993, 60.

30. Joan Stern, M.A., family counselor, conversation with Don Elium, Touchstone Counseling Services, Pleasant Hill, CA, 15 Dec. 1993.

31. Examiner Staff Report, "Experts Tell Kids They, Too, Can Help Make Cities Safer," *San Francisco Examiner*, 9 Dec. 1993, sec. A36.

32. AAUW, *How Schools Shortchange Girls*, 79.

Chapter Twelve

The "I'm Trying To Find Myself" Years: Eighteen to Twenty-Nine

College Career Counselor:
*What is your focus now that you
are an adult young woman?*

Kelly, twenty-two:
*Who am I? What are my talents?
How do I develop them? How do
I apply them?*

*The only limit to our realization of tomorrow
will be our doubts of today. Let us move
forward with strong and active faith.*[1]

—Franklin Delano Roosevelt

Developmental Tasks

Our daughters have grown from the tiny buds we cradled in our arms into the young saplings who stand tall and sure before us. The little nubs of passion, obsession, or habit that may have worried us when they were four, now bloom into the gifts, talents, and resources that move them into their futures.

When Lisa was four, she took in any ailing creature she found. Now she is finishing her medical internship and is applying for work with the international disaster medical aid.

—Ana, mother of Lisa, twenty-six

When she was five, we built her doll house, much to her design. Everything had to be just so. Today, she is one of the first women to join a local architecture firm in our town.

—Jason, father of Marion, twenty-eight

Pamela was the baby-sitter for the entire block, constantly taking care of little kids. I wanted her to be a lawyer, doctor, or even a dentist, because she has the aptitude for it. But, no, she majored in child development in junior college, met her husband there, and has two kids, one of each. Now that her kids are older, she's gone back to school and has a home day care of her own. She tells me she wants to teach. She followed her own mind and seems happy about it.

—Joel, father of Pamela, twenty-seven

The developmental tasks for girls during the "I'm Trying To Find Myself" years involve just that—trying to find where they fit in their lives, with others and in the world at large. The difficult challenge facing daughters in contemporary times is to avoid what writer and therapist Emily Hancock, Ph.D. calls the "ready-made roles" that culture prescribes for women "in lieu of defining themselves and directing their own choices."[2] These ready-made "patterns of womanhood"[3] offer young women an escape from having to choose the course of their lives for themselves.

JEANNE | When I entered college, I considered a social work curriculum, because I wanted to work with disadvantaged children. It was a tough program, and I confided to my dad my doubts about doing well there. He advised me to take up a teaching field, because I would always have a job if something ever prevented my husband from working. Although I was not married at the time and had no immediate plans of marriage, I took his advice and graduated in elementary education. I retired after two years of teaching, disillusioned, disappointed, and burned out. It just wasn't for me. I do not blame my dad for advising me to follow a career he thought would offer me financial security no matter what. I know he had my best interests at heart. I opted for an easy way out, however, choosing security over following my heart. After twenty-five years of searching, I now have work I love.

Young women are freer than ever before to choose their own destinies in their own timing. Many choose their lives first, then mate or career, or both. They are free to know their own voices, to speak out, rather than remain silent and behind-the-scenes. They have the power to *decide* whether to marry and when, whether to have children and when. We encourage them to take the *lead*, rather than follow; to *earn* their own way, rather than depend totally upon someone else; and to *take* their own paths, rather than to escape into culturally-prescribed roles for women.

This is not an easy task that lies before our daughters. They are expected to think, feel, and act in creating their many roles in the world. They need courage to choose, know, apply, decide, lead, and take action in their lives. Rarely have these masculine verbs been applied to the lives of women. They have done them, of course, but covertly, quietly, and usually without recognition. Now we expect it of them. What do they need to send them on their way?

Needs

Daughters need patience, support, room, and understanding.
Daughters in the young-woman years often experience mad starts and devastating stops. While some of us know our own minds, make

choices, and get on with our lives with no trouble, getting started for many of us is hard. Others have no difficulty beginning a project, but lack follow-through. Some of us get sidetracked along the way, having marvelous adventures, but it takes some effort to get us back on course. Although some may know from the beginning, for many young women these early-adult years are times of testing, sampling, and experimenting to understand the flavor of their heart's desires.

The teen years for boys are known as times of trial and error, and parents may wonder why their daughters did not try out some of these side roads when they were younger and less was at stake. Some girls do. The cultural constrictions and parental restrictions many girls face while teenagers, however, delay their self-determination to get their lives underway.

What is the hurry? It may be that parents want to get on with our own lives and out from under the financial burdens of adult children. This is quite natural and as it should be. Understanding the enormity of the task before our daughters enables parents to provide the guidance, support, and understanding helpful for making life-decisions.

Find mentors. Developing peer support systems and finding mentors who model healthy, successful, and fulfilling life-styles provide lifelines for fledgling adult daughters. When daughters choose marriage and children as a career, other mothers—new and experienced—are vital support in learning the skills of motherhood and hearth-tending. College professors, counselors, friends, friends-of-friends, coworkers, bosses, other professionals, and even parents, are potential guides on the path to discovering a career direction. Other parents, who together have successfully integrated career and family life, are important resources for alternative work solutions.

Letting Go. One of the hardest things for many parents, especially parents of daughters, is to allow them to make their own life choices. We can offer our concern or advice about marrying young, quitting college, or choosing a career, but inevitably their decisions must be their own. We empower our daughters when we show our trust in their inner wisdom to choose for themselves without our discouraging words, "I told you so's," rescue attempts, or threats of doom. Daughters of all ages measure their self-worth in terms of the quality of their relationships. Knowing they have their parents' support, interest, and acknowledgment, rather than their judgments and criticism provides stability and reassurance to continue on their way.

Inner Guidance System

From birth to seven a daughter's arms and legs led the way in her expression of self. Her task was to develop her will to explore the world through her senses, to soak in information by touching, climbing, seeing, smelling, running, reaching, tasting. She and the world around her were closely connected. Between eight and twelve, she took in the world through her breath and heart, expanding and deepening her feeling life, the life of her soul. During her teen years, the development of her mind sent her in search of intellectual truths about the world, and she stretched to comprehend it all. Throughout our daughter's years of growth wound the complex threads of an ever-growing tapestry of relationships, strengthening her ability to care for, love, empathize with, and empower the development of herself and others.

The interweaving of the will, the feeling life, and the intellect with the capacity for care create a whole, healthy woman, who during the years between eighteen and twenty-nine, sets out on the journey toward her future. Her inner guidance system guides her toward her life's purpose through her dreams, fantasies, thoughts, hunches, and feelings. How well we have been able to protect a daughter from the clutches of gender stereotypes and other cultural messages that say "Girls can't do that!" affects her confidence in her inner wisdom. From this inner place, she finds her next step, she knows her limits and boundaries, and she recognizes her strengths, talents, and resources. From this inner place, she knows when to say "No" to the unwanted or unnecessary and how to say "Yes!" to her heart's desires.

When daughters lose touch with their inner guidance systems, they may feel unsure, lost, stuck, or bored during the young-adult years. They wander aimlessly from one experience to the next for years. Parents often have a particularly difficult time supporting their confused pilgrims, but the soul unfolds according to its own inner rhythm. If by age twenty-eight, a daughter has not found her way, life usually provides the experiences to nudge her out of the nest or cocoon she has tried to hide in. Marriage, early divorce, the demands of motherhood, an unsatisfying job, financial worries, an accident, death of a loved one, serious illness, an important promotion, and so on bring her into the vales of self-reflection and soul-making.

Continuing to support our daughters by listening, respecting their thoughts and opinions, and staying in contact by dealing with conflict between us enhance their confidence in their inner wisdom. The more they engage their feeling/intuition, thinking, and willing, the more competent they can be in their chosen lives.

Fences

Throughout our daughters' childhoods, we struggled to guide them by setting fences and choosing natural outcomes for their behaviors. This parental responsibility is far from easy, but vital for the development of healthy inner boundaries. The passing of the fence-setting responsibility from parents to daughters is usually a gradual transition, occurring in the late teens into the early twenties. From our guidance they became self-motivated, flexible, dependable, and responsible, or "response-able." To be *able to respond* to their own inner guidance, to another's pain, to the needs of their families, communities, and the larger world, is the true mark of a healthy woman. Fence-setting then comes full circle as our daughters struggle to guide their own children in the development of healthy inner boundaries.

Sexuality

During the young-adult years, most daughters leave their childhood homes to go to college, to live with friends, to get married, or to create a home on their own. Because of this separation from parental supervision, a daughter's sexual life has room to blossom. Although she may have been sexually active while still living at home, we do not often openly acknowledge our teenager's sexual activities. We make sure she knows about birth control and safe sex, but we do not really want to know about the details. All parents and daughters are different in this regard, of course, but living away from home may bring the reality of a daughter's sexuality into the parent/daughter relationship for the first time.

Situations and questions never before confronted may have to be dealt with now. How do we handle the sleeping arrangements the first time she brings a young man home from college? What if she decides to live with a group of young women *and* men? How do we feel about her moving in with a lover? Would we want to try to prevent such an arrangement? How does her sexual life affect younger siblings, or our own sexual relationships? Hopefully, we have considered our positions before our daughter informs us of her plans. At this point, we cannot control how she chooses to live her life. We do have a right to express our feelings about how her sexual life interfaces with our family life. This may be a time to be flexible, understanding, firm, open to alternatives, and kind. Telling her clearly and honestly how we feel allows her room to find ways to be true to her own relationships and needs and to be considerate of ours.

Mothers and young-adult daughters often find a new freedom to share about sexual feelings, experiences, concerns, and questions. A daughter's more mature sexuality allows a transition from a mother/daughter connection to a shared friendship of commonality and solidarity.

Despite the new sexual equality, a young woman's sexuality differs from a young man's. Most women still seek relationships with a sexual component, rather than sexual encounters. They want deep connections that embrace sexual intimacy as well as commitment to relationship, shared goals, fun, lively conversation, quiet moments, and alone time. A woman's sexuality is wider in scope than a man's. Her sexuality matures within the ever-increasing complexity of her relationships, as she bears children, births new ideas, or brings forth her accomplishments into the circles of community and work. Although men's goals and roles are changing regarding family and children, their ancient, primary, instinctual sexuality drives them to plant the seed, lay the foundation, or build the structure, and then move on to another conquest. Women's instinctual natures connect them to the fruits of their sexuality for a lifetime.

The Positive Intent

At all ages of our daughters' lives, we hold the image of their essential wholeness in our hearts. From the beginning, we saw their tiny efforts to put forth shoots of green into the light, and we imagined them years from then, tall, straight, in full, glorious bloom. We were the diligent gardeners, feeding, shielding, fence-building, weeding, staking, and pruning. We had to remember that each new habit, trait, or behavior our daughters tried out had, although it might have been very difficult to acknowledge at the time, the positive intention of helping them find their true selves. We recognized for them their unique natures. They used us, sometimes painfully so, to define their boundaries—where we ended and they began. They pushed, and prodded, and provoked, and criticized to test our world views. Our patient—and not-so-patient—endurance empowered them to form their own paradigms. We constantly called their names to remind them of who they truly are.

Although they continue to seek our support and connection, now we must step back and let our daughters find their way. Whether they plunge self-confidently toward their futures, or plod surely along, whether they toddle hesitantly forward, or make fitful starts and stops, whether they hover stubbornly in the wings, or get stuck in the mire, whether they veer off onto adventurous side roads, or follow the straight and narrow, whether they strike off alone, or take up with a companion, they are continually awakened toward their destiny of a healthy womanhood.

> *All fuses now, falls into place*
>
> *From wish to action, word to silence,*
>
> *My work, my love, my time, my face*
>
> *Gathered into one intense*
>
> *Gesture of growing like a plant.*[4]
>
> —*May Sarton*

Resources

A Room of One's Own, by Virginia Woolf, New York: Harcourt Brace Jovanovich, 1929. A classic collection of thoughts about women by one of our best writers. Local bookstores.

A Way in the World: Family Life as Spiritual Discipline, by Ernest Boyer, Jr., San Francisco: Harper & Row, 1984. An inspiring guide to developing a spiritual life within the family. Local bookstores.

Ariadne's Awakening, by Margli Matthews, Signe Schaefer, and Betty Staley, Stroud, Gloucester, UK: Hawthorn Press, 1986. A penetrating look into "feminine" and "masculine" through the lens of Rudolf Steiner's anthroposophy that calls us all to a New Feminine. Available by writing the Rudolf Steiner College Press and Bookstore, 9200 Fair Oaks Blvd., Fair Oaks, CA 95628 or call: (916) 961-8729.

The Chalice and the Blade: Our History, Our Future, by Riane Eisler, San Francisco: Harper & Row, 1988. Insight into where we have been and our potential future. Local bookstores.

The Courage to Heal: A Guide for Women Survivors of Child Sexual Abuse, by Ellen Bass and Laura Davis, New York: Perennial Library/Harper & Row, 1988. Offers valuable insight and a personal workbook. Local bookstores.

The Dance of Anger, by Harriet Goldhor Lerner, New York: Harper & Row, 1985. A woman's guide to understanding anger within relationship. Local bookstores.

The Feminine Face of God: The Unfolding of the Sacred in Women, by Sherry Ruth Anderson and Patricia Hopkins, New York: Bantam Books, 1991. A personal account of finding a feminine spirituality. Local bookstores.

Getting the Love You Want: A Guide for Couples, by Harville Hendrix, New York: Harper & Row, 1988. A practical guide to intimacy and personal growth in relationship. Local bookstores.

The Girl Within, by Emily Hancock, New York: Fawcett Columbine, 1989. Offers a sensitive, insightful approach to recovering the parts of a woman that went underground while growing up in a gender-biased culture. Local bookstores.

Goddesses In Everywoman, by Jean Shinoda Bolen, New York: Harper & Row, 1984. Presents a mythological perspective to understanding the many qualities of women. Local bookstores.

Lifeways: Working with Family Questions, edited by Gudrun Davy and Bons Voors, Gloucestershire, UK: Hawthorn Press, 1983. A collection of wonderfully insightful essays by parents about family questions. Available from the Anthroposophic Press (previously listed, p. 258).

The Mismeasure of Woman, by Carol Tavris, New York: Simon & Schuster, 1992. A biting but fascinating account of "why women are not the better sex, the inferior sex, or the opposite sex." Local bookstores.

Mother Daughter Revolution: From Betrayal to Power, by Elizabeth Debold, Marie Wilson, and Idelisse Malave, Reading, Mass: Addison-Wesley Publishing, 1993. Important information for women and everyone who knows a woman. Local bookstores.

Of Woman Born: Motherhood as Experience and Institution, by Adrienne Rich, New York: Bantam Books, 1986. By one of the best feminist writers of our times. Local bookstores.

Raising a Son: Parents and the Making of a Healthy Man, by Don Elium and Jeanne Elium, Hillsboro, OR: Beyond Words Publishing, 1992. A practical parenting guide to what sons need to become healthy men. Local bookstores.

Revolution from Within: A Book of Self-Esteem, by Gloria Steinem, Boston: Little, Brown and Company, 1992. A revealing personal account of one woman's search for self. Local bookstores.

The Road Less Traveled, by M. Scott Peck, New York: Simon & Schuster, 1978. Illuminates the spiritual perspective of relationship. How to become a more sensitive parent; how to become one's own person; how to confront and resolve problems in a loving way. Local bookstores.

The Second Shift, by Arlie Hochschild, New York: Avon Books, 1989. Provides alternative ideas for two-career couples. Local bookstores.

The 7 Habits of Highly Effective People: Powerful Lessons in Personal Change, by Stephen R. Covey, New York: Simon & Schuster, 1989. A holistic approach to solving personal and professional problems. Local bookstores.

Toward a New Psychology of Women, by Jean Baker Miller, Boston: Beacon Press, 1976. A monumental work that revolutionizes the way we look at women's development. Local bookstores.

Why Can't a Woman Be More Like a Man? by Celia Halas, New York: Macmillan, 1981. After thirteen years, still offers insightful information about women's experiences. Local bookstores.

Women Who Run With the Wolves: Myths and Stories of the Wild Woman Archetype, by Clarissa Pinkola Estés, New York: Ballantine Books, 1992. In the tradition of a true storyteller, Clarissa Pinkola Estés weaves the tale of modern woman. Highly recommended. Local bookstores.

You Just Don't Understand: Women and Men in Conversation, by Deborah Tannen, New York: William Morrow and Company, 1990. A fascinating study of the different conversation styles and motivations between men and women.

Endnotes

1. Franklin Delano Roosevelt, his last speech that was never given, as printed in *Respectfully Quoted* (Washington, DC: Library of Congress, 1989).

2. Emily Hancock, *The Girl Within* (New York: Fawcett Columbine, 1989), 107.

3. Ibid.

4. May Sarton, "Now I Become Myself," *Collected Poems: 1930–1993* (New York: W.W. Norton, 1978), 191.

Jeanne Elium is a full-time author and mother of both a son and a daughter. She is a former university instructor, women's counselor, and elementary schoolteacher. Jeanne currently leads seminars for parents with her husband, Don, on Raising A Son and Raising A Daughter.

Don Elium is a father and marriage, family, and child counselor in private practice, as well as a professional author and speaker. He works extensively with men and women in recovery from the post-traumatic stress of childhood abuse with a special interest in healing the wounds of father/daughter relationships.